SPRINGBOARD FOR A LEAP BACK INTO HISTORY

THE CHICAGO

THE · DISCOVERERS

THE RIVERS OF AMERICA

Edited by
HERVEY ALLEN and **CARL CARMER**

As Planned and Started by
CONSTANCE LINDSAY SKINNER

Associate Editor
JEAN CRAWFORD

Art Editor
FAITH BALL

THE CHICAGO

by HARRY HANSEN

Illustrated by HARRY L. TIMMINS

RINEHART & COMPANY, INC.

New York   *Toronto*

*The drawings on the title pages are
from the sculptures by J. E. Fraser
on the pylons of the Michigan
Avenue Bridge*

To
ELEANORE AND MARIAN
NATIVES OF CHICAGO

Contents

ix

PART ONE

Gateway to the Prairie

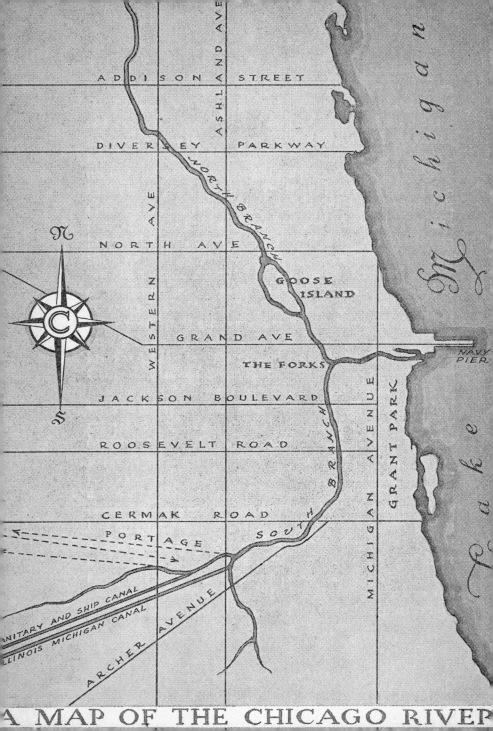

A MAP OF THE CHICAGO RIVER

I

Baffling, Erratic, Reversible River

ONE June day, not long ago, when the sun had routed the gray mists of the morning, I walked up Michigan Avenue in Chicago to take a good look at the Chicago River. The friend who went with me thought I wanted to see the bridge, with its huge sculptured figures, and Wacker Drive, which has replaced the old South Water Street produce market with a sweeping esplanade. No, I explained; primarily I wanted to see the river, for it had acquired historic significance for me. "But you've seen it a thousand times," protested my friend, "and, besides, what is it but a creek that doesn't know which way to go? Sometimes it flows south, and sometimes it flows north; on some days it has to be regulated by pumps and on others it stagnates and gets covered with a scum of bottle green. The city could have filled it up long ago and made a fine parkway out of it, and everybody would have been better served."

I was tempted to tell him the story of the alderman from the First Ward, who, when the Chicago was mentioned in the Council Chamber, never failed to remind his colleagues, in oratorical tones, that the city owed its very existence to the river. I saw that the work I had undertaken—to trace the far-reaching influence of this circumscribed and supposedly insignificant body of water on human affairs—had made me counsel for the defense. I gladly accepted the task. For I knew how often the river had been called names—from the earliest times until today, it had been called a channel, a canal, a bayou, a creek, an outlet for a marsh, a ditch and even a sewer. Yet it was the most useful and productive of all the big-city rivers of the continent. The Chicago not only determined the site of this vast, sprawling city of three million energetic people; it opened a route to the commercial wealth of the middle empire, the breadbasket of America. In the one hundred years of its greatest usefulness, the years that coincided with Chicago's first century, it had moved huge cargoes of grain and manufactured goods and made possible a terminal that brought most of the great railroads of the country to its banks. Its main channel was never navigable for more than five or six miles, but those miles were the key to the lock that opened the treasure of a continent. Without any effort I could become more oratorical than the First Ward alderman, more boastful than the Association of Commerce.

I thought of that when I reached the spot where the plaza of the Michigan Avenue bridge joins Wacker Drive. The bridge had just signaled, by red lights and clanging bells, that it was about to open to let a ship pass, and I walked up to the massive stone wall of the embankment to watch it approach. This is something men like to do the world over; the strange thing is that the silent progress of a vessel seems to impose silence on the beholder and creates a moment of meditation, a brief recess from our hectic rush through life's thoroughfares. When the bars of the bridge went down four long lines of motor cars, which had been hurrying toward it like black beetles on the run, came to a stop, with purring engines. And then, with a rasping crunch of steel on steel, the huge double-decked bridge parted in the middle and two leaves rose upward, shutting out the light, until they stood against the sky like gigantic ski jumps.

The ship was a long and narrow freighter, a hulk of black steel that lay deep in the water. Its white superstructure, built high on the bow, came forward like the muzzle of a sea monster, nosing out its path. This was the chartroom and the bridge. Then it dropped down to a flat deck, level with the top of the hull, a great floor of steel plates covering compartments filled with freight. There were twenty-two of them, and on their hatches rested a huge crane. Above the final quarter of the ship rose another white superstructure, containing quarters for the crew, with the engine room below, and a white-banded funnel rising above it. The two slim masts, supporting the radio antennae, hardly reached the height of the leaves of the bridge.

This was an inelastic monster, built not for beauty but for use. Inside its hulk it carried cargoes of great value. It moved down the channel as carefully as through a canal, with propeller blades slowly slapping the water and a white plume of steam idling above the funnel. A 30-foot speedboat shot past the hulk, leaving a wake of white foam; its waves played a merry dance between the sides of the freighter and the walls of the embankment, but had no effect on the motion of the heavy ship, which moved on through the farther bridges. One by one their gates came down, their leaves rose and stood like black barriers against the sky.

This river is the Chicago, and the spot on which we stood was a springboard for a leap into history. The presence of this water determined the route of French traders and missionaries two hundred and fifty years ago. It made a fort on this spot a necessity for the safety of the young republic. Because it led into the heart of Illinois it caused the state to place its boundary farther north in order to include it. Its importance as a channel of communication dictated the extension of its waters in the canal that united the Mississippi with the Great Lakes. It made inevitable the rise of a trading and shipping post along its banks, and thus provided the reason for the location of a world metropolis, which took its name and made it famous throughout the earth.

Yet it was a baffling and cantankerous river from the first.

The French called it a channel, a river and a bayou. Though it counted a length of over thirty miles along its branches and forks, the bateaux of the pioneers moved scarcely five miles upstream before they grounded on the sticky mud of the divide. With great hardships they pulled out their barges and dragged them five to seven miles over the bogs to the Des Plaines.

Nature made a freak of the Chicago River. By failing to erect a barrier high enough to keep forever separate the waters that fell into Lake Michigan from the waters that drained into the Illinois and thence into the Mississippi, it gave the Chicago the dilemma of both coming and going. When the ice broke in the spring, the swollen river, in flood, swept everything before it as it raced to the lake; then, subsiding like a spent torrent, it piled up its sand in bars and idled slowly to the sea.

It was both the gate to the middle prairie and the obstacle that kept men from entering it. So they cut the divide with a canal and ended the difficult portage. Then, needing water, they reversed the river and took its water from the lake, sending the current upstream.

Burdened with sewage and debris, carrying on its back the heavy loads of commerce, the intractable stream fought men's devices. Again and again, in time of heavy rain and melting snows, the river god turned back to his first love, the lake; thwarted by steel locks, he thundered at the gates and spread pollution as a sign of his wrath.

It is a river of contradictions.

It flows past great modern buildings and ugly makeshift structures. It sees the opulence of Chicago's market place and the filth of its back yards. Moving in haphazard fashion where man is in a hurry to complete his work, the Chicago has challenged his resourcefulness and ingenuity. To overcome the river's handicap man has built over fifty bridges: some of them ugly contrivances of steel and concrete; some, like the eight-track railroad bridge, wonders of modern engineering; others, like the double-deck Michigan Avenue bridge, useful and decorative. Goaded by obstacles, men fell upon the river, removed the playful meanders of its

youth, widened its banks, deepened its channel, chained
it to become a bearer of burdens. Charlton Lawrence
Edholm voiced its lot in poetry:

> They have bound me with bridges,
> With tunnels burrowed under me.
> Incessant, unresting,
> All day and all night
> Traffic roars over me,
> And my outlook to the blessed sky
> Is barred with girders, cables, stacks;
> My banks, with docks close-hedged,
> Inexorably hem me in.
> Vacantly,
> Through smoke and floating smudge,
> The sun looks down upon me
> Like the bleared eye of an old, old man. . . .

Within sight of the river have occurred the major
triumphs and catastrophes of Chicago. The vital element in its growth—transportation of raw and finished
materials—has thrived along its banks. All but a few
of the major railroads that cross the continent thunder
over its bridges. Around its banks has arisen the largest
concentration of population, the greatest urban wealth,
between the eastern and western seaboards. Within hailing distance occurred Chicago's worst disasters: the
Indian massacre, the great fire, the burning of the Iroquois Theatre, the sinking of the *Eastland*. Within sight
of the river disembarked the thousands that thronged
to its two world's fairs.

The freighter moves on, the leaves of the bridge
fall back to normal level, the barriers rise, and the restless motor traffic once more throbs like the beat of the

city's heart. The turmoil of the water subsides. Soon all ripples have vanished and the surface lies motionless. A slight, greenish scum appears. A bottle, half submerged, teeters unsteadily but does not change its place. There is no perceptible current. The Chicago has become the river that does not move.

2

Personal Appearance

MY FIRST glimpse of the Chicago River came
with my first look at the crowded streets, the huge box-
like buildings and the crude iron bridges of Chicago.
Fresh from Iowa, I left the old Union Station and
crossed the Adams Street bridge. There below me was
the river, black as an inky flood, with tugs hooting
and churning the waters and barges moving past.

Such a river was more like a creek to me. I had
been born on the banks of the Mississippi; it was so
wide that one could not discern the movement of human
beings on the other bank. As a boy I had taken part in
Sunday-school picnics on white-painted wooden steamboats. Lying in bed at night I had heard the eerie whoo-
hoo of steamboat whistles. That was truly a river, with a
current strong enough to tear acres from the land and
lose them forever in the flood.

Though still in my teens and far from voting
age, I had come to Chicago to attend the Republican National Convention for my newspaper, the
Davenport *Republican*. The newspaper had been stand-
pat for years, but I was an insurgent, a follower of

Albert B. Cummins's doctrine of tariff modification for the benefit of the farmer, and an enthusiastic supporter of Theodore Roosevelt, who had shouldered Mark Hanna out of the picture and was running the convention with wires leading direct into the White House. The morning it opened I picked up the Chicago *Tribune* and saw John T. McCutcheon's cartoon of the political situation: T. R. on a horse, dashing around the race track without a competitor. The cartoon had a double significance, for a few days before Chicago had attended the derby at the Washington Park Race Track, the last to be run in Chicago for many years. To political observers the nomination of T.R. seemed a sure thing, but as a responsible editor I took my duties seriously. Just to be safe I had prepared two front pages to run on the nominating day—one with T.R. the certain nominee, the other with the top line blank and room for a special wire about the lucky candidate.

I didn't imagine, in those days of wonder and new experiences, how often I was to cross the Chicago River in my future career. It didn't occur to me that daily, for years, I would be gazing at those waters, while exasperated at the icy blast from the northwest as I headed for the commuters' train to Winnetka or faced the hot rays of the summer sun on my way to the *Daily News* office on Wells Street. Those were the days when an unsightly loading platform for the city's refuse occupied the spot where the handsome Daily News Plaza now stands.

The Union Railroad Station, on the banks of the river between Monroe and Adams, had stood there since the great fire of 1871; it was provincial in its proportions, a narrow building of pressed brick with a mansard roof and curious corner dormers, with much yellow tiling on the inside walls and the pungent smell of disinfectant in its rooms. Below, on the riverbank, ran the tracks of the Milwaukee, the Burlington, the Alton, and the Pennsylvania, pouring their thousands into this congested square. On the cobbled streets outside, back up against the porch and allowing hardly any room for pedestrians, stood dozens of buses and express wagons. Across Adams street were the railroad quarters for immigrants and there Fred Buehler, an energetic, little man in blue uniform and cap, had charge of the arriving immigrants. There I used to go to see Poles and Lithuanians arrive with their outlandish togs, bundles and children; there Fred would talk to me about his boy and his poems. For both were his hobbies.

In my days on the *Daily News,* which came after college had given me further experience of Chicago life, we published many protests against the old station, many appeals for a really modern station such as New York had, and for a big post office on ground near it. Today Chicago has, on that site, a union station as big as the Baths of Caracalla, and beyond it an enormous post-office building, "the largest in the world." The noisy buses have yielded to spick-and-span taxicabs; there are channeled drives in and out and proper runways leading to the trains. But when I use the station now I wander about in it, seeking the warm and homely life of the old, unable to recapture the feeling that life is exciting, that the seconds and minutes must be caught and harvested, that riding on a train is a breath-taking event. And I doubt that the change is wholly in me.

3
Main Stream

Below Wacker Drive at the Michigan Avenue bridge a large motor cruiser, with seats for thirty, lay moored, awaiting customers. A sign announced the price of a ride as fifty cents. I descended the wide stone steps and asked a few questions. "How about a trip along the river?" I asked.

"It's all my life is worth, mister," said the captain. "See that water? It's full of snags. Besides, they're building the new subway under the river and obstructing the channel. The other night two men asked me to take them to the North Western Station and I did. They paid me $2 for the trip. On the way I fouled a piece of timber and broke a propeller blade. It cost me $18 for repairs."

I looked out over the river and observed the motionless bottle. "What's the reason?" I asked.

"No current," he replied. "The government lets us have just so much water out of the Lake. They measure it with a teacup. Just now it's shut off. After a while, when the river gets too gummy, they let in a little water and flush it out.

"Why do you want to ride on the river?" he continued. "There's nothing to see. Take an hour's ride on the lake and see the sky line. We get lots of couples, large parties too. They enjoy the ride on hot nights. We have cocktails and soft drinks for those that like them."

I thanked him and said I had other plans. There was the main stream to inspect, the bridge to visit. I

FORT DEARBORN

walked back up the stone stairs and recalled that this was the site of Fort Dearborn. About where I stood, just west of the south end of the bridge, the northwest blockhouse had jutted out on land now obliterated by the river. For some distance east there had been a fence, a brick powder magazine and barracks. The main part of the fort had stood south of this line, and a second blockhouse had jutted out on the southeast corner. There had been a tunnel in the hill of the fort, leading down to the water's edge. It must have been located within fifty feet of where I stood.

This reminded me that the fort had stood on a sandy hill eight feet high, but the pavement under my feet was easily twice as far from the river. For Michigan Avenue rests on an artificial elevation of steel and concrete, with stairways leading to the ground level, where motor cars are parked and a road leads to the lower floor of the bridge. Man has not been content to leave the landscape as the winds and waters shaped it through many centuries.

The river had curved around this hill and the lake had sent its breakers against a sand bar, less than one hundred yards away. Now the lake seemed half a mile away. The land had been extended, piers and breakwaters had been built. Today the river begins with the locks directly beside the great Outer Drive bridge and it is one and a half miles from this point, its source— government permitting—to the Forks, where the North Branch has joined the main stream from time immemorial. Likewise it is now a little over six miles to the head of navigation of the old river.

Every foot of ground facing the main stream has been associated with the changing fortunes of Chicago. The south bank, from Michigan Avenue east, has become a great freight terminal, begun when the Illinois Central Railroad first delivered its grain to the big elevators that served the lake vessels. The Nickel Plate still displays its signboard over a freight house that shows its age by its construction. The switch engines still shunt cars back and forth in Chicago's front yard.

To overcome its unsightly character Chicago built its park and the Field Drive beyond the yards.

Opposite, the north bank saw the start of a great Chicago industry. In pioneer times this was a sandy spit. Today it is crowded with large warehouses that stretch all the way to the Outer Drive bridge. Here stands a long, low building that holds the rolls of paper that come to the Chicago *Tribune* from the northern mills. Still discernible is the fading paint of a large sign that declares the *Tribune* is "undominated." It recalls the newspaper's opposition to the policies of Franklin D. Roosevelt and was placed there when the president came to Chicago, October 5, 1937, to dedicate the Outer Drive bridge.

Here, too, one of the pivotal industries of America, the manufacture of harvesting machinery, had its beginning. The man from Virginia, Cyrus Hall McCormick, was already thirty-eight when he determined to locate his factory on the banks of the Chicago, within six-hundred yards of the site of Fort Dearborn. He came in 1847 with $100 in his pockets and confidence in his reaper, of which samples had been built for him in Brockport, New York. It was an improvement on a machine originally planned by his father in Rockbridge County, Virginia. Cyrus had made the essential invention, a lateral instead of a vertical cutter, and perfected it. Here McCormick saw the logical site for his factory —close by the crowded shipping of the lake, on the river that, within one year, would connect with the new canal and take his reapers direct into the interior of the farming country. In 1847 he erected his sheds on the north bank and the next year, joined by his brothers Leander and William, he built seven hundred reapers. The factory whistle had come to Chicago.

The Michigan Avenue bridge has been recognized as a focal point in Chicago's life. Just as London Bridge of the Middle Ages was the place where public announcements were made and heads of criminals were exposed, so Michigan Avenue bridge carries more memorials of the past than any other public monument.

The four pylons of the bridge have been embellished with heroic representations of men and events symbolical of the city's history. Just as the figures are more than life-size, so the description of their activities is spiced with vainglory and boastfulness. Yet monuments are not documents. The east pylon at the north end of the bridge celebrates the Discoverers—Jolliet, Marquette, La Salle and Tonty, who "typify the spirit of brave adventure" in the white man's development of the Middle West. The west pylon commemorates the Pioneers and specifically mentions John Kinzie, fur trader, who settled near this spot and was "one of a band of courageous pioneers who, with their lives at stake, struggled through the wilderness, breaking soil for the seeds of a future civilization." The west pylon at the south end of the bridge is called Defense and commemorates the Fort Dearborn massacre of 1812. Those who fell "will be cherished as martyrs in our early history." On the east pylon stands Regeneration, commemorating the great fire of October, 1871, which devastated the city, whereupon the citizens rebuilt a new and greater city, "imbued with the indomitable spirit and energy by which they have ever been guided." Besides these four groups of statues a number of bronze tablets, either on the bridge or near by, direct attention to the historic importance of this site. The old road that led from Green Bay and Fort Howard to Fort Dearborn ended on the north bank; there is a marker at the head of the stone steps leading to the water. On the opposite side of the street, in the embankment wall, a marker identifies the house of John Kinzie, here designated as the "mansion," the name used in the records. On the rail of the bridge near the Discoverers a bronze bas-relief commemorates Louis Jolliet and Père Jacques Marquette, the first white men to pass through the Chicago River, in September, 1673. On the opposite railing, near Defense, is a bronze bas-relief for René Robert Cavelier, Sieur de la Salle and Henry de Tonty (here spelled Tonti) who passed through the river on their way to the Mississippi in December, 1681.

The original traders, who built their cabins within hailing distance of the spot where this bridge crosses the Chicago, saw the river as a sluggish stream meandering between hillocks of sand, which were separated by marshy depressions called sloughs. There were so many on the south bank that it was easier to reach the Forks in a rowboat than to walk or ride over the sand. This was one reason why pioneers preferred the level north bank for cabins, taverns and farms. On the south bank, between the present Michigan and Wabash avenues, the government, about the year 1831, erected the first lighthouse. This, with the blockhouses of the fort, produced Chicago's first sky line. One day an unusual crash brought the settlers to their doors. The sky line was no more. The lighthouse had fallen into a heap of rubble.

Today the main stream is practically straight to the Forks, where the current turns south. The change that has come over the river would startle not merely the pioneers; it would astonish as well the Chicago leaders of fifty years ago, who knew the south bank as the site of crowded markets and produce commission houses, which backed up to the water's edge. Today the double-decked Wacker Drive, named after Charles H. Wacker, long chairman of the Chicago Plan Commission, provides a magnificent esplanade where once stood ramshackle brick buildings. The eye sees large, impressive bridges span the river at the principal streets, with a new one being built at State Street. Great office buildings rise on each side, including the massive Merchandise Mart, with 93 acres of floor space, the wholesale house of Marshall Field & Company.

On the southwest corner of La Salle Street and Wacker Drive stands the Builders Building. Here, since 1932, has hung a tablet commemorating the mission of the "Guardian Angel of the Miamis at Chicagoua," established by Father Pierre François Pinet, S.J., in 1696. No one knows exactly where Father Pinet built his cabin, but presumably it stood somewhere along the main stream, although misleading directions in old documents have led historians to place it as far away as Grosse Pointe, far up on the North Branch. Also visible from the river today is the corner of Lake Street and Wacker Drive (formerly Market Street), where the building of the Hood Rubber Company bears tablets identifying the spot as the site of Mark Beaubien's Sauganash Tavern, where on August 10, 1833, the first town trustees of Chicago were elected, and where, in 1860, the Republicans erected the Wigwam and nominated Abraham Lincoln for the presidency. The main river, having been joined by the North Branch at the Forks, has now turned south, and close at hand appear the massive buildings of the Chicago Civic Opera Association, the pride of the late Samuel Insull, and the Chicago *Daily News,* rising opposite each other, the first on the east bank and the second on the west bank of the river at Madison Street. The latter building, the first to make use of air rights over the tracks of the Milwaukee railroad, also houses Marshall Field's Chicago *Sun.*

Despite the imposing architecture of Wacker Drive, there are reminders near by of the earlier days. Noisy elevated trains and cumbersome trolley cars still pound over the double-decked bridges at Wells Street and at Lake Street. The land northeast of the intersection of the main stream and the North Branch is full of weeds, cinders and rubbish and appears much as it did when the settlers first staked out their claims on this site. On the south bank, near Wells, the barges of Herman's Fisheries advertise fresh and smoked fish, and from curious little shacks that resemble the smokehouses of farms rise wisps of blue wood smoke.

Whence came these names—Chicago, Illinois, Lake Michigan, Mississippi—the key names of the West?

Father Allouez is one of the first of the French missionaries to discuss the name of the great fresh-water lake that adjoins the Lake of the Hurons. In the *Jesuit Relations* of 1666 he speaks of the Lake Ill-i-ni-oues, as yet unexplored, and says the Fox Indians called it Match-i-hi-gan-ing. Thus, in the earliest records, the two familiar names take form. Hennepin, writing in

1679, is more specific; the lake, says he, is called by the Indians, Ill-i-nouck; by the French, Illinois; by the Miamis, Misch-i-gon-ong, that is, Great-lake-place-of. Actually, the last word is an Algonquin compound of Michi, or Missi, great, and say-ay-igan, lake. In a few years the confusion is cleared up. Father Marest, writing an oft-quoted letter from Kaskaskia, November 9, 1712, drops the ong (place-of) and for the first time calls the lake Michigan, saying it is wrong to call it Illinois, because the Illini do not live there. Thus, Michigan, the Great Lake, is named, taking its title from the same root as Mississippi, the word that means not Father of Waters, but the great river.

Does Chicago mean skunk or garlic? By turns amused and chagrined that a world metropolis should be named after such malodorous objects, Chicago writers have debated the meaning of the word. The evidence seems to prove that Chicago means the place of the powerful wild onion.

The sounds that we transcribe as Chicago were applied to this region long before the white man came. The French heard the Indians say it and reproduced it as Checagou. In varying forms it was applied to the portage, the river, the wild onion and the skunk. Henri Joutel, historian of La Salle's expedition of 1684-1687, says specifically that the place was called Checagou because of the species of wild onion growing there. Henry R. Schoolcraft, writing in 1821, said the Algonquian word was chi-kaug-ong; here chi means size or excessive size; kaug by itself means porcupine and when used with chi means polecat or skunk; ong means locality. But the skunk derives its name from the onion or skunk weed, hence Chikaugong should mean the place of the wild onion, not the skunk. In Ojibway, says John Tanner, Indian interpreter, skunk is she-gagh and onion or skunk weed is she-gau-ga-winzhe. In the same dialect kago means big and strong. In Miami dialect skunk is se-kaw-kwaw.

Dr. Milo M. Quaife doubted the signification of onion or skunk when he found the term "Checagou" applied to several other places on the map. For instance, he learned that the French fort, Crèvecœur, on Lake Peoria, was called Checagou by the Indians. He believes the basic meaning was great and powerful, which is compatible with Schoolcraft's definition of size. The term may have been applied to Chicago Portage in the sense of bigness, but when La Salle used it there he merely adopted the Indian word. Since nothing near the Chicago of that day deserved to be called great and powerful except the Lake, and the term was not applied to that, it seems reasonable that the powerful flavor of the wild onion, which grew everywhere, identified the region as Checagou, and that Joutel was accurate.

After dark in peace times the main stream undergoes the most fantastic change. It seems to become the apron of a great stage, part of which is brilliantly lighted, while the extremities of the scene fade into the blackness of the night.

To view it we approach this tall house of stone and glass that cuts the wind like a huge knife on the site of Fort Dearborn and is known as 333 North Michigan Avenue. Its corridor of green marble suggests luxury, and the big bronze doors that lead to its elevators bespeak the opulence of modern business life. We proceed swiftly to the twenty-fifth floor, where the wide windows of a private club, the Tavern, command a remarkable view of river and harbor and the spot where Chicago began.

Far out in the lake a red lamp on the crib, whence Chicago draws its water, blinks on and off. In the harbor, where yachts, motor cruisers and, in time of peace, oceangoing vessels from Scandinavian ports lie moored, porthole and signal lights send long streamers over the water. A wavering line of white reveals the restless waves that lash the breakwater. Far to the south the sky glows red from the furnaces of the steel mills of South Chicago and Gary.

On the north bank two long rows of soft amber lights outline the Navy pier. Closer in a huge neon signboard in brilliant colors celebrates the lure of Baby Ruth.

It is not the light of day that illuminates North Michigan Avenue. It is a light much more intense, and curiously erratic. It throws some buildings into sharp relief, exaggerating their proportions against the sky and, by skipping others, thrusts them into limbo. In the background the far-reaching beacon of the Palm Olive Building stabs the sky. Almost pushed aside by the endlessly recurring lamps of motor cars, the old, decorative Water Tower glows like a golden pillar. To the right as we look up the avenue the workshops of the *Tribune* are a sheet of daylight. But the most startling display lies directly below us. Here the twin Wrigley Buildings stand forth in the glare of many reflectors, their glazed-brick walls accentuating the brightness.

Only the needs of war can darken this proof of the determination of man to defeat the night.

Thus we view the Chicago of our time, a channel for commerce, flanked by the monuments to commercial enterprise and business daring. It would seem that this river has nothing in common with the original water-way of the explorers and voyageurs. Yet sometimes, when the sunlight pales and dusk comes on, a chill wind gives warning of impending change. Silently the lake prepares a shroud to cover time's milestones. In immense, rolling billows a gray mist tumbles toward the houses, spills over walls and roofs, whirls down to blot out doors and windows and upward to toss plumes madly about the pinnacles. The lamps grow dim as the mist thickens; voices speak from mouths unseen and motor horns throw echoes from wall to wall. The bridges, the embankments, the streets and houses, are lost to the human eye.

This is the great act of nature that man cannot change, cannot obliterate. It sends his memory back to first things. The expectant ear hears the sound of paddles falling on the water; the eye of imagination discerns, through a rift in the mist, a canoe carrying an explorer and a blackrobe, facing out to sea . . .

PART TWO

The French Find the River
and the Portage

I

Prayers on the Chicago

THE Chicago was a lazy river, moving slowly
between banks of sandy hillocks, idling among tall reeds,
when the first white men who have left specific records
came paddling down from the Forks in a canoe, turned
the curve of the hill where a sand bar intercepted their
eastward passage and entered the great lake a few hundred yards to the south. They were Jacques Marquette,
a French Jesuit priest, thirty-six years old, and Louis
Jolliet, Canadian-born French explorer, twenty-eight.
They were coming from the Mississippi by way of the
Illinois, the Des Plaines and the Chicago Portage, and
their eyes must have reflected an eager interest in their
surroundings. For they were seeing objects only vaguely
indicated on maps and what they told would help fill
in the contours of the unknown wilderness. Their passage down the river is commemorated by a plaque at the
north end of the east wall of the Michigan Avenue
bridge, which says that they came this way in 1673.

Their story has been told many times and will
be repeated as long as one brick rests on another in
Chicago, for it is a simple and inspiring beginning for

27

the metropolis. Especially significant is the coming of Father Marquette, who represents the spiritual aspirations of man, as Jolliet may be said to represent man's material ambitions. Great as Chicago has grown in wealth and worldly goods, it also has cherished its spiritual possessions.

The waters these men traversed were French; the land was a French possession, for had not Saint Lusson proclaimed, at Sault Ste. Marie in 1671, that all the land adjoining the Great Lakes belonged to the king of France? Neither of these men could imagine that his power would ever be seriously jeopardized, nor could they dream what the future might hold for the land bordering the river they had just left behind.

Marquette and Jolliet were bound for Mackinac on the last lap of a voyage of discovery that began when Jolliet, carrying the authority of Frontenac, brought his friend at St. Ignace, Father Marquette, the permission of his superior, Father Claude Dablon of Montreal, to join him on a voyage to the fabled Mississippi. Leaving the mission of St. Francis Xavier at what is now Green Bay, Wisconsin, on May 17, 1673, they portaged from the Fox to the Miskinsing (Wisconsin) and reached the Mississippi at Prairie du Chien on June 17, 1673. They paddled as far south as the Arkansas and returned by way of the Illinois, stopping at the village of friendly Indians of the Kaskaskia tribe at what is now Twin Bluffs, Illinois. With their help they voyaged up the Des Plaines, portaged across the marshy ground to the south branch of the Chicago and thus appeared at the lonely, wind-swept hill and reached the great water that Jolliet was to designate as the Lake of the Illinois or Missihiganin. By September they were back in Green Bay, having traveled twenty-five hundred miles in four months.

It had been a remarkable voyage and it gave the Chicago the distinction of carrying two of the truly admirable characters of pioneering history—a devout, gentle priest, whose relations with the Indians leave no doubt of his zeal and their recognition of his shining character, and a far-seeing, conscientious explorer, whose records have never been questioned for accuracy. Jolliet suffered the loss of his papers in the turbulent waters of the Sault St. Louis, within sight of the habitations of Montreal, after he had crossed forty-two other rapids without mishap. He was rescued with difficulty from the rocks on which he had been flung but was able to give his superiors particulars that show how thoroughly he understood the geographical importance of the Chicago more than two and a half centuries ago.

"The place at which we entered the lake," he said, "is a harbor, very convenient for receiving vessels and sheltering them from the wind." And recalling his mission, to find a waterway that would connect the Great Lakes with the southern seas, he explained the circumstances of "a very great and important advantage that perhaps will hardly be believed. It is that we could go with facility to Florida in a bark and by very easy navigation. It would only be necessary to make a canal, by cutting through but half a league of prairie, to pass from the foot of the lake of the Illinois to the river St. Louis [Illinois] which falls into the Mississippi. The bark, when there, would easily sail to the Gulf of Mexico . . ."

Those were the prophetic words of 1673. They

were to be echoed by explorers, trappers, traders and military men; they were to be uttered by exasperated bargemen as they tugged at the ropes of boats laden with pelts and pulled them through the reeking marsh, the boggy mud and over the pulverized soil in dry seasons of that link between the lake and the inland waters—the Chicago Portage.

One year later Father Marquette was to become intimately acquainted with the moods, the vagaries, the changing habits of the Chicago. In November, 1674, he began a new mission, this time to the Indians who lived on the Illinois, with whom he had stopped the year before. Leaving with two men, Pierre Porteret and Jacques—later historians have identified him as Jacques Largilier—he moved down the west shore of Lake Michigan to the mouth of the Chicago, landing there December 4, 1674. The biting blizzards of the West had begun. Moreover, Father Marquette was ailing with dysentery. Thus it became necessary for the party to rest on the spot, and on that bleak shore the three men sought shelter and replenished their larder for several days before moving on.

We do not know the exact location of the mouth of the Chicago in the seventeenth century, since the river meandered over the plain south of the hill and entered the lake anywhere between the Lake Street and Madison Street of today. The date, too, is not exactly our own, for the calendar added ten days in the eighteenth century, but this does not effect the spirit of the day, which caused the city of Chicago to decree, on the occasion of the opening of the Lakes to Gulf Waterway in 1933, that December 4th henceforth would be observed as Marquette Day in Chicago. It is a day on which nature may well reproduce the cold of 1674.

The animal life that Marquette and his companions saw along the Chicago that winter would be hard to visualize today. "During our stay at the entrance to the river," wrote Marquette in his Journal, "Pierre and Jacques killed three cattle [buffalo] and four deer, one of which ran some distance with its heart split in two. We contented ourselves with killing three or four turkeys, out of many that came around our cabin because they were almost dying of hunger. Jacques brought in a partridge he had killed, exactly like those of France, except that it had two ruffs of three or four feathers as long as a finger near the head, covering the two sides of the neck where there are no feathers . . ."

He was a holy man, with his life dedicated to the service of the Virgin of the Immaculate Conception; it was his great regret that cold and illness prevented him from celebrating mass on the Feast of the Immaculate Conception at the mouth of the Chicago. He and his companions moved up the river and made camp near the portage two leagues (five miles) from the mouth; this was the place where canoes were usually hauled out; the portage began just west of the present Damen Avenue bridge on the land of the present International Harvester Company. The weather, the bleak prospect ahead and the priest's weakness must have militated to make them winter on the spot.

In the cabin that they built there Father Marquette said mass every day, even when his weakened frame was racked by the disease that was sapping his strength and eventually would take his life. He was unable to observe Lent except on Friday and Saturday of that hard winter.

It was not, however, a lonely spot, but on the main route of Indian travel. Chachagwessiou, a chief of the Illinois, had already met them. Soon parties of Indians came by with furs, eager for French tobacco. Marquette gave them one head of cattle (buffalo) and one deer and observed that they were good traders when they exchanged three robes of ox skin for one cubit of tobacco. When the Indians returned home they told two Frenchmen, La Toupine and a man called the surgeon, about Marquette and wanted to carry him down to them. The surgeon and an Indian came up with blueberries and corn and Jacques went back with them to get corn and such delicacies as the tongues and flesh of two buffalo.

Later the Indians brought meat, pumpkins and twelve beaver skins and made a mat for Marquette; they asked for powder in exchange. Marquette had no powder to give them and told them he did not want them to make war, but he gave them a hatchet, two knives, three clasp knives, two double mirrors and numerous glass beads, which gives some idea of the equipment missionaries carried in their luggage in order to make friends with the Indians. The Illinois Indians camped near him a month, and he sent them with letters to the Mission of St. Francis Xavier.

Marquette was interested in the changes on the river. He records that he saw the tides come from the lake, "which rise and fall several times a day," and ice going against the wind. On March 28th the ice broke up and collected above their camp; on the 29th the water was so high that they had to put their goods in trees and sleep on a hillock. When they began their trip into the Indian country they traveled three leagues up the River and found no portage; the water had risen twelve feet at the place where they began their portage eighteen months before, which would indicate high water in the Des Plaines. They saw many migratory birds—bustards, ducks, geese, cranes. They met the surgeon and an Indian going up with a canoe load of furs, which they were to place in a cache.

At the village of the Kaskaskia Marquette made an impressive effort to convert the tractable Indians to Christianity, and his fervent preaching in honor of the Virgin of the Immaculate Conception was warmly received. For our purpose his chronicle is ended, for he did not return to the Chicago. His illness left him no strength for his labors and in his weakened condition he determined to return to St. Ignace.

His statement that Illinois Indians escorted him thirty leagues and that he followed the coast along the south shore of the lake makes it plain that he did not again attempt the Chicago Portage, but went by way of the Kankakee and the St. Joseph. On that trip north he chose the hill on which he said he would die. His death occurred near Ludington, Michigan, Saturday, May 18, 1675, at the age of 37 years, 11 months and 8 days.

2

The Vanishing Cross of Father
Marquette

THE two most famous sites in Chicago are the south plaza of the Michigan Avenue bridge, where the United States raised its flag over Fort Dearborn, and the land lying between the north end of the Damen Avenue bridge and the point where the South Fork joins the South Branch of the Chicago. The latter area, looking like the back yard of a factory, is hallowed ground, for here, on the best authority, Father Jacques Marquette, S.J., lived during that difficult winter of 1674-75, when, racked with disease, he passed his days in prayer.

Historians did not decide on the location of Father Marquette's rude cabin without controversy. Father Marquette wrote in his Journal that he wintered on the north bank of the Chicago, hard by the beginning of the portage; that here a hillock gave him protection from the spring floods, when he and his companions were compelled to place their belongings on the limbs of trees. I was greatly interested in the present appearance of this site, for I was confident that I should find a chapel commemorating this, for members of the faith "one of the most sacred acres of earth," and that the city of Chicago had suitably recognized this as the first prolonged residence by a white man on the site of Chicago.

Traveling by way of Blue Island Avenue, I found Damen Avenue just east of the plant of the International Harvester Company, which today occupies land that was on the main route of the portage between the Chicago and the Des Plaines in the seventeenth century. The locality is filled with nondescript factory buildings, barns, lumber piles and the scrap heaps of factories. I found no chapel, but the avenue led directly to the Damen Avenue bridge, which bears one of the memorials raised to Father Marquette.

The Damen Avenue bridge was built as recently as 1930, and if the name is unfamiliar to those who once knew the thoroughfare as Robey Street, let me explain that it commemorates Father Arnold Damen, S.J., founder of the Holy Family parish, which contains the site of Marquette's camp. The memorial is a bronze plaque on the bridge, and as it was placed there by the city and not by the church, it emphasizes Marquette's place as an explorer and discoverer rather than as a spiritual guide to the Indians. However, the bas-relief by Emery P. Seidel, from a drawing by Thomas A. O'Shaughnessy, does present Marquette and an Indian chief. Since it was erected during the mayoralty of William Hale Thompson, it also perpetuates the name of his malodorous administration.

Deciding where Marquette had camped was no easy

task for the amateur and professional historians who paced off distances, examined tree trunks and applied Marquette's general directions to the banks of the Chicago River. The first man to get excited over it was Ossian Guthrie, an engineer connected with the Illinois and Michigan Canal, which began near this spot. His father, Arthur Guthrie, built the original pumping station that supplied water to the canal. Ossian Guthrie succeeded his father at the station and was in charge there until 1871. While working at the canal Guthrie became interested in the history of the region. He observed that traders using the portage camped on a hillock of land on the north bank of the river, at that time completely wooded. The trees were ancient, some of them sixty feet high with trunks two feet thick. After consulting Marquette's Journal, Guthrie and one of the stonemasons, James Malholland, would pace the ground until they had determined, to their own satisfaction, exactly where Marquette had wintered.

It is not certain that Guthrie's hill was identical with the one that Thomas A. O'Shaughnessy declared was the site of the camp, for all the hills in this vicinity have been leveled. O'Shaughnessy said that it occupied approximately the site of the present turning basin in the river and that it was 250 feet long, 150 feet wide, and 14 feet high. It was composed of glacial silt, and as the city encroached upon it, it was used in brickmaking. Apparently the hill was visible as late as 1884.

Other investigators had other ideas. In 1895 the Chicago & Alton Railroad announced that Marquette, flooded out of his cabin, had landed near its right of way on March 31, 1675. The site had been located "by a comparison of his Journal with the original engineer levels and surveys." The railroad erected a mound of boulders and a tablet on the spot, and when the tablet was stolen, provided another.

When the Chicago Drainage Canal was opened directly west of Robey Street in 1900, the Chicago Association of Commerce took an interest in the Marquette site and co-operated with the city to erect a large cross there. At that time Robey Street had no bridge and the authorities chose the spot where the street reached the north bank of the river for the memorial. Here, on September 28, 1907, was unveiled a handsome cross of mahogany, donated by the Willey Lumber Company, set in concrete and bearing a long inscription describing Marquette's career. Seymour Currey says the cross was fifteen feet high; reports that it was thirty feet high are believed to be inspired by the 30-foot cross that Father Allouez raised in the village of the Kaskaskia Indians in 1677, two years after Father Marquette's death. This cross did not stand long; it was "maliciously destroyed," say the records. The Willey Lumber Company replaced it with a new cross, which had metal trimmings on its edges and carried the words: "In memory of Marquette and Joliet, 1673." Jolliet never wintered here, but he traversed the portage with Marquette.

When the cross had been standing a few years a report went around that a dredge had brought up a small wrought-iron cross, about three feet high, French in design. This occurred within the memory of living men, yet I have been unable to find anyone who brought up the cross or actually saw it taken out of the river. What did happen was that someone erected this cross

beside the larger cross, and the two stood side by side
for twenty years. The wrought-iron cross caused historians some uneasy moments. They did not believe that
Marquette had burdened his luggage with a heavy iron
cross; besides, he did not mention it. But there it was.
The best explanation they could give was that it re-
sembled the ancient crosses on French graves in the old
burying ground of Cahokia.

When the new bridge was begun in 1930, it became
necessary to remove the crosses. The large cross, which
had suffered the loss of much of its metal trim, was
hung on the side of a red barn near by. In this forlorn situation it hangs today. With the passing of the
men who erected it, nobody in the vicinity assumes
any responsibility for it. Several men near the bridge
pointed it out and then got into an animated discussion
over its significance.

"That's the original cross of Father Marquette,"
said one man. "He brought it down here himself and it
fell into the river and was lost for two-hundred years.
They dredged it up at this very spot."

"It can't be the original," said another man. "That
would have rotted in river water. It's a copy."

"A canoe couldn't carry a cross of that size," said
another bystander. "The cross they dug up was a little
iron cross. I saw it myself."

"Well, if there's such a cross, where is it?"

"All I can say is, it used to be here, but it's gone."

That much is true. The little wrought-iron cross
has been missing since the crosses were removed to make
way for the bridge. Nobody knows what became of it.

But with the junk dealers buying old iron, it isn't hard to guess.

Marquette's spiritual mission has not been emphasized at the bridge, but is commemorated on a handsome monument about ten blocks away—at Marshall Boulevard and West 24th Street, opposite the Harrison Technical High School. Since there is some doubt about the exact location of Marquette's camp, we cannot criticize the placing of this memorial in a more accessible and decorative spot. It was dedicated July 20, 1926. It was erected at the expense of the Ferguson Fund, which is administered by the Art Institute of Chicago for the purpose of beautifying the city. This bronze monument by Herman A. McNeil, with its figures of Marquette, Jolliet and an Indian, is the most exemplary in the Chicago area, for its figures fire the imagination and its legends offer historic information to the young high school students who pass it daily. It is a clear reminder of the spiritual mission of Marquette. Despite the highly advantageous site, the location was criticized in some quarters as an effort to "hide the monument away from public view." These objectors wanted it to stand on Michigan Avenue in Grant Park, as approximately the site of Marquette's first rest, of a few days, at the mouth of the Chicago, in 1674. But where it stands today is part of the ancient portage and within reasonable distance of Marquette's winter vigil.

3

Good Works in the Nineteenth Ward

As I walked back to Blue Island Avenue from the legendary site of Marquette's camp on the Chicago, I meditated on the changes that had come over this verdant land in one hundred years. A century ago the northern bank of the river was still wooded; farms lined the roads, and there was no intimation that the flat, sandy prairie, at times covered with waving grasses, would become the hub of the most congested population in the whole middle continent.

Now the streets were flanked by drab-colored brick buildings and dilapidated wooden houses that seemed to lean on one another; there was evidence, by the piled-up debris, that men were too busy with their own concerns to bother with the day's waste. The stores put on a brave show with advertising placards in gay colors and signs in neon tubes, but the general impression was one of shabby exteriors. I hailed a taxicab to drive back to the Loop and made some remark to this effect to the driver. "You said it!" he exclaimed; it seemed I had picked up

one of the natives of the district, an Irish lad who was
bitter because the neighborhood was running down.

"I know every foot of this part of town," he
spoke out of the side of his mouth as we started up Halsted Street. "I lived here twenty-eight years; I'll show
you the house. See that row? The middle store? Well,
my folks lived in the flat above that and we kids played
under that sidewalk and all around these corners. Look
at it now; it's falling down; the plaster is coming off
the ceilings, but do you think the landlord will repair it?
Not that fellow, not as long as he can squeeze a dollar
out of it."

This was the neighborhood where Jane Addams
had begun her brave experiment in social education by
direct participation in the lives of the lowly; I recalled
that she had spoken of the crowding out of the Irish
and the Germans by Poles, Bohemians, Russians, Greeks
and Italians in this, the Nineteenth Ward, and that great
aggregations of gypsies wintered here. I asked about the
latter. "Yeah," said the driver, "the place is lousy with
gypsies," and there was no mistaking his contempt.
"They hire an empty store and sleep in the corners on
old rags, a filthy lot."

I knew something about them myself, for years
before, when I was a reporter, I had visited a gypsy
family camping in a vacant store in this very neighborhood. The swarthy father was the king—they are always
kings when a reporter calls—and I remember he told
me that his attractive 16-year-old daughter could be had
in marriage for $1,000, but the guy who wanted her
would damn well have to show the color of his money
first. He uttered this royal command while lying on a

mattress on the floor, hands locked behind his head and one leg bent over a knee, and I had kept a mental picture of his fat belly, strapped in with a broad leather belt and wobbling as he talked. The bedraggled, many-skirted women of his household stood around, each with a dead-pan expression, and one urged me to hear my fortune. The only smile of the day came from the high-priced princess, who shrugged her shoulders and said archly, "If a fellow have the money, I marry him." A silly business, one of those curious examples of how the customs of a roving people survive in an American slum, making a momentary splash on a feature page.

When my cab reached the brown, brick buildings of Hull House, at Halsted and Polk streets, I had the driver stop, and sat there and gazed at the plain lines and sharp gables of the institution as a flood of memories came over me. More than any other spot in Chicago, Hull House had seemed the place where the spirit bloomed in good works. It was the leaven in the lump, and no one could estimate the great good it had done, and still did, both practically and as an inspiration to people who fought privilege, political corruption, dishonest acquisitiveness and the ignorance of society's victims. Silently I saluted the memory of Jane Addams, dead since 1935; Lillian D. Wald had called her "the finest expression of the American spirit of democracy." Still filled with the mental image of how Marquette had prayed on his knees every day of that long, icebound winter on the Chicago, within a mile of this spot, I thought that it was fitting that Jane Addams should have come, two centuries later, with her ideal of service and participation, to a locality where the devoted Marquette had offered up so many fervent prayers for the welfare of mankind.

I had been in and out the doors of Hull House both as a student at the university and as a reporter, though never associated with its activities. In my first weeks at the university I went there with a classmate, a friend of Miss Addams. From the first moment Miss Addams exhibited her practical efficiency, and from then on I never entered Hull House without feeling that the spirit of getting things done, without fuss or window dressing, was in the very air of its rooms. The outcome of that first visit was a personal tour of the settlement, and what a tour! Miss Addams, determined to show her young visitors her domain, did not delegate the task; she led the way, but in double-quick time. We raced through the rooms: kitchen, theater, reading rooms, apartments, trying to keep pace with the energetic founder, who explained as she walked and halted only to describe the murals of Lincoln and Tolstoy, both working with their hands.

Later, when I interviewed her at intervals, I came to respect her directness, her calm appraisal; she avoided guesses and dealt with concrete situations, and had a businesslike way of speaking, but always with deep courtesy. It was characteristic that she thought of solving social problems in terms of practical contact; her ideal never kept her in the library, among statistics, for she believed that "nothing so deadens the sympathies and shrivels the power of enjoyment as the persistent keeping away from the great opportunities for helpfulness and a continual ignoring of the starvation struggle which makes up the life of at least half the race."

EARLY TRADERS MAKING PORTAGE BETWEEN

THE CHICAGO AND DESPLAINES RIVERS

When Jane Addams came to the Nineteenth Ward it was a congested district of small shops, saloons, factories, sweatshops and tenements, with many families living in rear houses on the alleys, where a faucet in the yard supplied water to all the tenants and ashes and garbage lay heaped up under their windows. I had wandered in and out of this wilderness behind Hull House with a social worker and had seen washing strung out over the alleys on lines propelled on pulleys, while dust from the ashes swirled up around us.

To bring better housing into this world was a slow struggle, but Jane Addams and her associates put their energies into it. They arrived in 1889 at a melting pot that didn't melt. Huge migrations had crowded one nationality upon another. Italians, Poles and Russian Jews jammed the meager housing facilities. The push-cart markets were only a few blocks away in Maxwell Street. Sweatshops were operated in lofts and basements while immigrant women carried huge bundles of cloth to their crowded homes for work far into the night. Children were exploited as workers; occupational protection was unknown; disease was not controlled. It was in this area that W. T. Stead, the London economist, found the material for his book, *If Christ Came to Chicago*, and co-operated with Hull House, just after the World's Fair of 1893, to stir the civic conscience.

What Jane Addams and Hull House accomplished cannot be put on memorial plaques, for it is merged in the history of social reform. Hull House took its valiant part in bringing about the first factory laws, abolishing sweatshops, fighting civic graft, curtailing child labor. Miss Addams knew how political corruption and exploitation of immigrant labor went hand in hand, and she has described her feeling of personal shame when an opponent of the bill to abolish sweatshops offered to donate $50,000 a year for two years to the settlement if she would withdraw her support of the bill. She supported the 8-hour day and the 48-hour week when the trade-unions were still too weak to win; she stood behind the organization of a juvenile court. The girl who had been thrust out of home because of a misstep; the fiery radicals who needed a hall to blow off steam; the peddlers of foreign birth who were pushed around; the juvenile offenders who were not criminals, found help under these roofs. Jane Addams in turn praised "the kindness of the poor to each other" and recognized that dogmatic social theories have to be tested by experience if they are to alleviate the woes of mankind. Many other settlement houses and social service agencies followed Miss Addams's example in the congested districts of Chicago, important among them being Dr. Graham Taylor's Chicago Commons, Mary McDowell's University of Chicago Settlement, "back of the Yards," and the settlement house of Northwestern University. For her activities on behalf of international peace Miss Addams shared the Nobel Peace prize with Nicholas Murray Butler, and donated the money to the Women's Peace party. Only a short distance from Hull House, near Loomis Avenue, a district of poor habitations has yielded place to a modern housing project of 52 houses and 975 low-cost apartments; I thought it eminently proper that they should be called the Jane Addams Houses.

4

La Salle's Sextant Locates the Portage

AFTER Father Marquette and Jolliet had traveled over the Chicago and the portage, this path became part of the high road used by French explorers, traders and missionaries. Two names dominate the annals—those of René Robert Cavelier, Sieur de la Salle, and his faithful lieutenant, Tonty of the Iron Hand, and their passage on the Chicago is commemorated with a bronze plaque on the Michigan Avenue bridge. What they accomplished in the interior of the state is told in *The Illinois* of the Rivers of America series.

When they first went to the Illinois River they traveled by way of the eastern shore of Lake Michigan and the Kankakee. In 1681 Tonty went north by way of the Chicago and in the late fall of 1681 Tonty and Father Membre were back at the mouth of the Chicago, with a party, and began building sledges to carry them over the icy portage. This must have happened near the head of navigation of the Chicago, where the portage began and plenty of timber was available. On January 4, 1682, La Salle joined them for a trip over the portage to the Illinois and the Mississippi.

In 1682 or 1683 La Salle had built for him, some-where in this neighborhood, a log cabin with a stockade, where furs could be stored under the protection of two men. La Salle dated several letters "Du Portage de Checagou" and in one of them located the portage at 41 degrees, 50 minutes north latitude, which later investigators found to be one thousand feet south of the spot where the present Kedzie Avenue reaches the river and about two miles west of the spot where Marquette camped on the ridge. It is likely that the cabin may have been located here, and this may have been the "fort" on the Chicago, mentioned as late as Wayne's treaty of Greenville of 1796.

Was there a French fort at or near the mouth of the Chicago? Historians have no direct proof, but they do say that Tonty arrived at the "fort of Checagou" in 1686; that Tonty and de La Foret strengthened a fort at Chicago in 1691-1692 and that Desliettes, a relative of Tonty, commanded there and lived there from 1698 to 1702. It is a part of the records that the French had a cache of furs near the mouth of the Chicago, which was robbed by passing Frenchmen; that Garie had a hut on the North Branch, which was known for a short time as Garie's River.

Two letters are important in this period. The first, of June 4, 1683, which no longer bears the place of its origin, contains La Salle's comment on the portage and his objections to Jolliet's plans for a canal. The second letter is his farewell to the men at Fort St. Louis, as he prepared to return to France by way of Montreal— his last farewell, for he never came this way again. It is dated Checagou, September 1, 1683, and is now in the possession of the Chicago Historical Society.

In our generation, when Chicago's industries were rapidly obliterating the old trails, two men with a love for exploring and taking pictures began to trace the route of the French voyageurs that became the highway of a continent. They were Robert Knight, now deputy commissioner of buildings in Chicago, and Dr. Lucius H. Zeuch, a physician, since deceased. They began their tramps into woods and fields associated with historical events, consulting records for directions.

It was a happy moment when their steps led in the direction of the old portage and they put in their vacations on the Des Plaines and the South Branch of the Chicago, despite the mosquitoes. They traced the old lines of Mud Lake. Mud Lake was the name given by early American traders to the district so inefficiently drained by the Chicago. It lay between the present Kedzie Avenue and Summit and included a large slice of what is now the Central Manufacturing District. This area received the floodwaters of the Des Plaines after the spring thaws, and all the water that did not get over the Kedzie divide and out by way of the Chicago was left in muddy pools that sometimes extended as far south as Archer and as far north as Ogden—these being the high ridges along which the first roads ran. The French explorers traveled this area with curses and the missionaries with prayers and there is extant plenty of testimony to its drawbacks as an avenue of transportation. In midsummer it was likely to go bone dry, making necessary a long haul of the boats; in winter it was covered with ice, in spring it was flooded.

Gurdon S. Hubbard, who traveled over the Chicago Portage and through the Kankakee area many times as agent for the American Fur Company, recorded the difficulties of a trip in October, 1818, when he crossed the portage with a dozen boat crews. The muddy region between the rivers was so great an obstacle that for three days the crews labored with the barges, four men propelling a boat with oars while six or eight waded beside it in the mud, with bloodsuckers and mosquitoes making their lives miserable. Hubbard seems to have encountered every kind of weather and to have used every method of transportation; some of his boats were even equipped with rollers. When he went up the Des Plaines with the Illinois brigade of the American Fur Company in the spring of 1819 the water was so high that he could use sails and move easily over the portage to the Chicago regardless of the location of the channel. In 1824 he scuttled his barges, loaded his furs on pack horses and came by way of Mount Joliet and the Kankakee.

Charles Fenno Hoffman, who came in 1834 from New York to tour the West, wrote that it would be easy to drain Lake Michigan into the Mississippi by this route, since 18-ton boats passed over the portage in high water.

Knight and Zeuch had a pretty clear idea of pioneer transportation when they began to trace the original portage route. They could visualize the traders with their packs, bound in pelt sacks, going up the Chicago, hauling out their canoes and then laboriously dragging their heavy loads, taking advantage of an occasional pool to paddle part of the distance. They learned that here, in the wilderness, was demonstrated the inexorable tendency of man to increase his load. The canoes grew in size as their burdens grew, until they were 35 feet long and 6 feet wide and held four tons; then the traders used pirogues with six or seven oars; these were followed by the Mackinaw boat, 40 to 50 feet long, 12 feet wide and 3 to 4 feet deep; by bateaux, 30 feet long, 8 feet wide, propelled by six oars, and finally the Durham boat, 60 feet long, 8 feet wide, 2 feet deep, capable of carrying fifteen tons. Heavier grew the pelts that passed from the interior to the traders at the Chicago, St. Joseph, Green Bay, Mackinac, Detroit and beyond.

All these boats were pulled across the land from the Chicago to the Des Plaines before Jolliet's dream of 1673—a canal—became a reality. Dragging these huge loads left grooves in the earth. But when Knight and Zeuch took up the trail they had to tramp many weary miles over brick pavements, for the wooded, swampy ground was now covered by factories, crossed by clanging trolley cars and bound together by the steel hoops of railroads. But they found the historic trail and the story of that discovery is incomparably told in their book, *The Location of the Chicago Portage Route of the 17th Century*, which they published in 1928.

The portage route was never wholly the same. Marquette and Jolliet seem to have used the portage at Riverside and followed the bank of Mud Lake to the Chicago at the present Damen Avenue. La Salle located it at Kedzie Avenue and the river. In this general area voyageurs left the river and took to the land. In Riverside, seven miles beyond, the portage ended for those moving from Lake Michigan to the Illinois. Sometimes the travelers swung far north to avoid the marshy area, sometimes far south. Knight and Zeuch established that the west fork of the Chicago, a small tributary reaching into the shipping yards west of Damen Avenue, was originally a ditch on the portage route that was deepened in 1852 to help drain Mud Lake. It has been recently filled in.

Mud Lake was finally removed in 1900, when the new Chicago Sanitary Canal began its work and carried the remaining waters of this area down to the Des Plaines. Thus contours known to pioneers have been changed by later generations, but no one is disposed to quarrel over that. Mud Lake spread its miasmic air over a large space now used by houses, streets and factories. But Zeuch and Knight were able to identify a stretch of land that had changed little from historic times. This was a part of Portage Creek west of the old Ogden Avenue dam, which is built across the creek at Harlem Avenue. This part of the creek, they write, is the same as it was when Jolliet and Marquette used it. Even the proximity of three million people has not eradicated the ancient path the pioneers used nearly three hundred years ago.

Today the western end of the portage is suitably marked, through the efforts of the Forest Preserve Commissioners and the Chicago Historical Society. It begins at Harlem Avenue and West 47th Street, and if you approach it by way of Summit you cross a bridge and get a glimpse of the old bed of the Illinois and Michigan Canal, now no longer used. This bridge also crosses the Illinois Waterway of the Chicago Drainage and Ship Canal, which carries all the water of the Chi-

cago River—as I shall describe later. On both sides of
the waterway and canal are farms; to the northeast
huge oil tanks stand against the sky; on the west is un-
cultivated land leading to the portage. The ground
is hilly and the trails are winding. The entrance is
marked by stone walls on each side of the driveway
and the one on the left bears the words "The Chicago
Portage 1673." Stretching ahead are close-cropped
grassy squares with three broad stone steps for each rise
of ground. At the end stands a boulder and on it are
grooves that indicate that once a bronze tablet rested
here. But, alas, the tablet is no more.

Once again we are confronted with the vandalism
that tries the patience of those who mark historic sites.
But removing heavy bronze tablets is not merely the
mischief of rowdy youth; it suggests thievery for gain,
for bronze can be melted down and sold. The tablet was
inscribed with a regard for accuracy and had its place
in the educational scheme when it was formally put
there in 1938. It called attention to the site as "the earliest factor in determining Chicago's commercial su-
premacy" and said the portage was "an early strategic
point in the wars incident to the winning of the Northwest for the settlers."

Behind the boulder alluring trails wound through
the trees to the Des Plaines. Paths led over pools and
the markers showed that at times the water rose six feet
higher. The woods were in their wild state, filled with
underbrush and weeds, but before the path reached Des
Plaines they ended and a hard, coarse bank led down
to the stream. Here the Des Plaines seemed to invite
fishermen, who were wading in the shallow waters.

Near by a Negro was picking berries off a low tree. He looked up and volunteered that he was "gettin' enough berries to make me a little wine. They make awful good wine and when I get my sack full I'm going home." With a grin he indicated the fishermen. "Fish don't bite well today. Seems too hot. Night fishin' is the best anyway. Fish don't like daytime."

The pioneers had discovered that night fishing was best, too.

PART THREE

The American Flag Comes to the Chicago

I

Captain John Whistler Builds
Fort Dearborn

IT MAY not have rained that morning in April, 1803, when Captain John Whistler strode up the sand dune around which the sluggish Chicago struggled to reach the lake. But the chances are that it did—a flurry or two, after a misty dawn, and a gust of wind that tossed the swirling sand into Captain Whistler's neck. That would have been a characteristic welcome by the elements of the landscape that the captain had come to change. For his orders, which had trickled down to him at Detroit from the secretary of war, General Henry Dearborn, were to take six soldiers of the 1st U.S. Infantry, survey a military road from Detroit to the mouth of the Chicago River, and plan to erect a fort—"stockade works aided by blockhouses" was the way the secretary phrased it.

A little rain and a handful of sand wouldn't have hampered Captain Whistler in his pioneering. He had had plenty of outdoor experience. First, as a lad of nineteen, he had marched with Burgoyne to Saratoga, wear-

FROM HIS WINDOW, JOHN KINZIE COULD LOOK

CROSS THE RIVER TO OLD FORT DEARBORN

ing the king's coat. Taken prisoner, paroled and freed, he had sailed back to England, married, and brought his bride to America. Having learned a soldier's trade, he continued as a soldier in the ranks of the young republic. Thus he happened to become one of the fighters who were so badly led by St. Clair and driven out of the Ohio wilderness by the enraged Miamis. After that disaster he marched once more under the canny leadership of Anthony Wayne. At Fallen Timbers, on August 20, 1794, Wayne routed the Indians and the British. The next year he called the Indians to Greenville to hear his terms. That was the council in which the assembled Wyandots, Delawares, Shawnees, Ottawas, Chippewas, Potawatomis, Miamis, Eel River Weeas, and Kickapoos conceded what claims they might have had to a spot in the western wilds described as "one piece of land six miles square at or near the mouth of the Chikago river emptying into the southwest end of Lake Michigan where a fort formerly stood." Nobody remembered what fort ever stood there, but that was of no matter. For with that they also conceded "one piece 12 miles square at the mouth of the Illinois river emptying into the Mississippi; free passage of the portages and rivers connecting these grants."

It was an English-born captain of the United States Army who was to nail down the American right to the Chicago and its portage. This was a defeat for the British who had maneuvered for years to control the fur trade that passed through the valley. Even after the treaty of peace with Britain, General John Graves Simcoe, the British commander, had planned to establish trading posts at the Chicago and other strategic portages. But now the Americans were in possession, and the captain stood on the hill and outlined the stockade and the houses of the fort.

Then he went back to Detroit to get the garrison and his family. He was forty-five years old and neither his meager Army pay nor the hazards of the frontier stopped him from living a full and complicated domestic life. Eventually he became the father of fifteen children. With him on that trip to the Chicago were his grown son, Lieutenant William Whistler, as well as his three-year-old, George Washington Whistler. The names of both became historically important. For Lieutenant Whistler was to command the 2nd U.S. Infantry at Fort Dearborn during the Black Hawk War, from June, 1832, to May, 1833, and thus become the last United States officer in charge there, while George, who played about the palings of the fort until he was ten, was to build railroads for the czar and, in 1834, become the father of James A. McNeill Whistler.

Captain Whistler's family was spared the difficult journey over the erratic Indian trails from Detroit to Lake Michigan. While the troops marched on foot, the captain and his family boarded the U.S. schooner *Tracy,* which also carried artillery and camp equipment. It sailed to the mouth of the St. Joseph River, where it met the troops. The Whistler family took one of the *Tracy's* rowboats to the Chicago, while the troops marched around the foot of the lake. There were sixty-nine officers and men in the contingent that had the task of erecting Fort Dearborn. They pitched their tents on the north bank of the river, while the officers obtained shelter for their families in the trader's cabins. The hill

on which they were to build the fort was eight feet
above the river, which curved around it and, stopped
from entering the lake by a huge sand bar, flowed south
until it found an outlet. Many old settlers said the river
entered the lake at what is now Madison Street. But
that must have been around 1830; in Whistler's day the
mouth seems to have been on a line with the present
Lake Street.

To this bleak hill the soldiers dragged the logs that
they made from trees cut on the north bank. They had
neither horses nor oxen. They built two blockhouses
and a stockade to enclose the grounds, and put a small
blockhouse at the northwest corner and another at the
southeast corner. The main gate was in the south wall;
there was a smaller one near the northwest blockhouse,
and beneath it the soldiers dug a tunnel that opened on
the river's bank, which they called the sally port. As
time went on they built barracks and a small powder
magazine of brick inside the stockade. West of the fort
they erected a two-story log building, with split-oak
siding, for the United States factory, or Indian agency,
and between this house and the fort they placed root
cellars. South of the fort the ground was enclosed for a
garden. The fort mounted three pieces of light artillery.
When Captain Whistler raised the flag of the United
States over Fort Dearborn he could reflect that at last
his adopted country had placed a padlock on the rich
trade route to the interior.

2

Chicago's First Boss

THE trading life that developed on the Chicago was not a matter of sentiment and romance. It was tough and realistic. It involved contradictions of behavior that are still a mystery. The fog that has ob-

POINT DU SABLE FARM, LATER OWNED BY
JOHN KINZIE

scured the earliest transactions at this important post lifts slowly as historians delve among the letters and bills that have come to light in recent years.

For nearly a century Chicago believed that its first settler was a runaway slave, who raised a shelter on the Chicago and then faded into oblivion. Research reveals that Point du Sable was the son of a Frenchman and a Negro woman, a man with a fair education who occupied positions of trust, owned many implements and developed, on the Chicago, a post and farm that paid him handsomely. For many decades John Kinzie, the most influential trader of the early 1800's, was lauded as a beneficent Father of Chicago, the man who had saved the garrison of Fort Dearborn from extermination. Great as his services were, he was often selfish, acquisitive and quarrelsome; his bickerings with Captain John Whistler resulted in the removal of that officer from Fort Dearborn. Although tradition calls Kinzie the successor of Point du Sable in the cabin on the Chicago, he actually took it over from Jean La Lime, the man he later killed in a quarrel outside the stockade of the fort.

Soon after the American Revolution ended Jean Baptiste Point du Sable, a native of the frontier, built himself a cabin on the north bank of the Chicago, opposite its mouth. In 1779 he had been arrested by British scouts at a trading post on the St. Joseph River and taken to Michilimackinac. But so useful was he, and so highly esteemed by the Indians, that the British yielded to the entreaties of the latter and put him in charge of a British trading post near Port Huron.

When the war was over he came to the Chicago, established a trading post and founded a family. His consort was an Indian woman who was known to the French fathers as Catherine. Point du Sable must have lived with her for many years without benefit of clergy, yet held to her loyally, as was often the custom in the wilderness. For the records show that in 1788 he was in Cahokia, where the church had established a mission, and was there married to Catherine, and that two years later his daughter, Suzanne, married Jean Baptiste Pelletier in the same place. It is believed that all returned to Chicago to live, for there is a church record that the daughter of the Pelletiers, Eulalie, was born there October 8, 1796. Another member of the household was Point du Sable's son, who bore his name.

In 1795 Anthony Wayne specifically acquired the land at the mouth of the Chicago from the Indian tribes by treaty. In 1800 occurred the first big commercial transaction on the banks of the Chicago. For a reason still unknown, Point du Sable sold his trading post on the Chicago to Jean La Lime, a trader who had been active on the St. Joseph, for 6,000 livres.

This sale is important. It is a historical event with wide implications. It shows that Point du Sable, far from being the itinerant Santo Domingo Negro described by Juliette Kinzie and other early writers, was a man of property. When Dr. Quaife found du Sable's bill of sale in the archives of Wayne County, at Detroit, which had legal authority over the Chicago area in 1800, he established the extent of du Sable's post and the place he took in pioneer activity. For du Sable sold his house, which was 22 by 40 feet in extent, two barns, a horse mill, a bakehouse, a poultry house, a workshop, a dairy and a smokehouse. He also transferred two mules, 30 head of cattle, two calves, 28 hogs, 44 hens, eight sickles, seven scythes and a large assortment of carts, saws, kettles, axes and other tools. These help explain how he was able to supply the 1790 expedition of Hugh Heward with large quantities of pork, flour and bread and the use of his pirogue for their voyage, by way of the Chicago, the Des Plaines and the Illinois, to the Mississippi. They indicate that the log cabin that stood on a hill adjoining one of today's great highways, Michigan Avenue, was the nucleus of a large farm; that cows grazed over the sandy area to the north and west, that woodsmen felled the stunted oaks on what is now North State Street and farm hands cut wheat and hay on land where the *Tribune's* presses roll. Noteworthy among du Sable's possessions were 11 copper kettles and one cabinet of French walnut, 8 by 4, with four glass doors—a strange object to appear in a cabin in the wilderness.

Point du Sable moved on to Peoria and to St. Charles, Missouri, and there is only brief mention in the records of his later career. But two men associated with the sale of his trading post become a part of Chicago frontier history. They are Jean La Lime and one of the two men who witnessed the bill of sale—John Kinzie. Kinzie was the first boss of Chicago.

Walk across the Michigan Avenue bridge to the east side of the North Plaza and you will come to a wall overlooking a vacant lot, about 20 feet below, now used for parking cars. For many years Kirk's soap factory bordered the river at this spot, an industry that became known for an advertising dodge that contradicted all the established practices of advertising men. For Kirk used to circulate with bars of soap a picture showing a frowsy, unwashed hobo inscribing a testimonial, saying that he had used Kirk's American Family Soap and none other since, a legend that always brought a smile from housewives. For years the Kirk plant prospered in Chicago's front yard, to the exasperation of the Chicago Plan Commission, which wanted to landscape the river's banks but could not oust a going concern.

A historian must suspect that Chicagoans are sometimes careless when they write legends in bronze. Set in the wall that overlooks this parking lot is a tablet that relates that "near this site stood the Kinzie mansion, 1784-1832, home of Pointe du Sable, Le Mai and John Kinzie, Chicago's first civilian. Here was born in 1805 the city's first white child, Ellen Marion Kinzie." Le Mai may have lived briefly there, but his cabin was elsewhere. Kinzie was hardly the first civilian to come here. Historians deny the distinction given Ellen. Most remarkable is the omission of the name of the man who took over the place from du Sable and was supplanted by Kinzie—Jean La Lime. Therein lies the unsolved mystery of early Chicago.

John Kinzie, a son of Canada and a British subject, exploited the commercial possibilities of the wilderness with cunning, and became so versed in the ways of the natives that he was accused of being "a white man gone Indian." Shaw-nee-aw-kee they called him—the Silver Man, because he was supposed to have learned the craft of the silversmith. His progeny married into the families of other Chicago settlers and his blood flows in the veins of many citizens living there today. He was a domineering man, with a quick temper and a sharp tongue.

Kinzie's picturesque story begins with his birth in Quebec in 1763, the son of a Scottish surgeon in the

British Army named Mackenzie. There is a family tradition that Kinzie attended school in Williamsburg, Long Island, but Quaife does not mention it. Early in life Kinzie established himself as a fur trader in Detroit, in Ohio, and at a famous frontier crossroads, St. Joseph, in Michigan Territory, now called Bertrand. At times he was associated in his trading with his half brother, Thomas Forsyth, son of his mother's second marriage.

His marriages throw an interesting light on the vicissitudes of frontier families of the colonial and revolutionary era. He first married Margaret McKenzie, who became the mother of William, James and Elizabeth Kinzie. In 1778, when Margaret was ten and her sister Elizabeth eight, the two were stolen by Indians from their home in what is now Giles County, Virginia, and taken to Detroit. There they married. Years later their father located them and persuaded them to return with him to Virginia. Both left their husbands and remarried in Virginia. Two of Margaret's children by Kinzie eventually joined their father in Chicago; her sister Elizabeth, having married her second husband, Jonas Clybourn, in Virginia, established the Clybourn family in Chicago. Some of Margaret's children by her second husband, Benjamin Hall, also settled in Chicago.

Kinzie's second wife also had a checkered frontier career, and she is of special interest because she became the mother of the Chicago Kinzies. She was Mrs. Eleanor McKillip, widow of a British militiaman who was killed fighting against Wayne at Fallen Timbers. She, too, had been an Indian captive, having been taken from her home near Pittsburgh in 1779 at the age of nine, and she was located by her father in Detroit in 1784. She married Kinzie in 1798 and her daughter by McKillip, Margaret, became the wife of Lieutenant Helm and played a prominent part in Kinzie's rescue of his family at the Fort Dearborn massacre. Margaret McKillip Kinzie's first son, born in Chicago, was John Harris Kinzie, who was to become well known in Chicago life and to bring to the West a cultured flower of the East, his wife Juliette.

When Kinzie came to the Chicago in 1804 he occupied the former du Sable cabin and enlarged it. What it became in later years has been described in detail by Kinzie's daughter-in-law, Juliette, who wrote her account in *Wau-Bun, the "Early Day" in the Northwest*. It was a low, one-story cottage with an attic under the gabled roof that came down over the porch. It sat in the middle of a sandy wilderness like a little New England house, with a front yard, four Lombardy poplars, planted by Kinzie in 1811, and a picket fence. Two tall cottonwoods rose behind the house. In 1830, when Juliette Kinzie arrived as a bride, it was surrounded by a dairy, a bakehouse, a lodging for the French employees and a stable, possibly built by du Sable. From its porch, which faced to the southwest, the Kinzies could look out over the river, with its patches of reeds and wild rice, almost to the Forks; opposite them they could see the northwest blockhouse of Fort Dearborn, the magazine and the barracks, the whitewashed picket fence, the locust trees and the flagstaff, on which floated the flag of the young republic.

Just before coming to the Chicago for good Kinzie figured in a curious episode involving the enslavement of a black man. Kinzie and his half brother, Thomas

Forsyth, started suit to recover a runaway indentured Negro who was, to all purposes, their slave. This may be representative of the way early traders got around the Ordinance of 1787, which provided that there should be no slavery in the Northwest Territory. It also offers indisputable evidence that Jean La Lime was intimately known to Kinzie and Forsyth.

This Negro, Jeffrey Nash, was acquired by a bill of sale on September 5, 1803. On May 22, 1804, Kinzie and Forsyth executed an indenture by which Nash bound himself to serve them for seven years—Forsyth made it out, Nash signed it with his mark, and Jean La Lime witnessed the paper. Nash was to receive "meat, drink, apparel, washing and lodging fitting for a servant," and, in the customary language, bound himself not to waste his owners' goods, or to fornicate or contract matrimony, play dice or cards or visit taverns. The document was filed in Detroit, as the seat of Wayne County, but Kinzie and Forsyth are designated as "merchants of Chicago," which was only partially accurate and may indicate that they meant to make Chicago their headquarters thenceforth.

Forsyth operated a trading post in Peoria from 1802 to 1812. He took Nash to Peoria, where he served a number of years and ran away. It is said that he had a wife and children in St. Louis. Tracing him to New Orleans, Forsyth and Kinzie instituted suit to recover Nash, and the parish court upheld them with a decision that preceded the Dred Scott decision by forty years, holding that a black man could not raise the question of his right to freedom in the federal courts because he was not a citizen of the United States and hence could not bring suit. They produced the contract, which several investigators have pronounced fraudulent.

Nash must have had unusual protection, for he appealed to the Supreme Court of Louisiana, and the high court handed down a judgment in his favor, citing the Ordinance of 1787 as confirming Nash in his freedom, and holding that only a crime would justify slavery. This is said to be the earliest lawsuit involving the Ordinance of 1787, but only by indirection can it be called "Chicago's first great lawsuit," as Eugene E. Prussing did in his study of the case. The whole transaction is associated with Chicago only in so far as it throws light on John Kinzie's relations with Jean La Lime and fills in the career of Kinzie, which is associated also with the events that follow.

3

The Mystery Man of Frontier Chicago

JEAN LA LIME is the mystery man of early Chicago. As the second owner of the trading post on the river, which he bought from Point du Sable, he played an important part in its historical development, yet he remains unnoticed on bronze tablets, his importance ignored by historians. Until about ten years ago he was known as a trader and an interpreter at Fort Dearborn, but little else had been found about him. Then Milo Milton Quaife came upon strange, unexpected evidence.

The document that makes La Lime important is, of course, the bill of sale by which Point du Sable sold his extensive trading post to him for 6,000 livres in 1800. This showed that du Sable had a large stock and that Jean La Lime was able to pay a large sum. The witnesses were John Kinzie and another trader, William Burnett. Where did La Lime get the money to buy the post? Did he buy the post for Kinzie? If so, why did Kinzie hide behind him?

Kinzie may have come to Chicago for pelts, but he did not attempt to live there in 1800. But Jean La Lime was living in the du Sable cabin in 1803, when his associate was Dr. William C. Smith, first surgeon of the troops at Fort Dearborn. Smith called him "a very decent man and good companion." On May 22, 1804, Kinzie and Forsyth made their questionable contract with Jeffrey Nash, the Negro, in which the two partners are called "merchants of Chicago." The indenture was witnessed in Detroit by the man of mystery—Jean La Lime.

In 1804 John Kinzie came to Chicago and took over the trading post. Both Juliette Kinzie, who later married his son, and the bronze plaque at the site say that he took over the du Sable cabin, following Pierre Le Mai. Juliette Kinzie writing the reminiscences of her mother-in-law, Mrs. John Kinzie, said Kinzie "purchased the trading establishment of Monsieur Le Mai, at the mouth of the Chicago River."

In 1808 Dr. John Cooper came to Fort Dearborn to succeed Dr. Smith as surgeon. He says he found four houses, or cabins, on the north bank of the river opposite the fort, and that they were inhabited by John Kinzie, Jean La Lime, Antoine Ouilmette and Pierre Le Mai and his Indian wife. Nothing has appeared about the disposition of the large stock of goods that La Lime bought from Point du Sable, nor is La Lime mentioned again as its owner. He became an interpreter for Fort Dearborn, which suggests that he was reduced in income. But he was a respected man, for Charles Jouett, the government Indian agent, named his son for him.

It becomes evident that Jean La Lime's separation

from John Kinzie was not a friendly matter; that there was bad blood between the two men. La Lime was still at Fort Dearborn early in 1812, for on April 13, 1812, he wrote a letter to Captain William Wells of Fort Wayne—the rescuer of the garrison who was to die in the Fort Dearborn massacre—telling him about the murders committed by the band of Potawatomis on April 6th at the Lee farm on the Chicago River.

Jean La Lime was himself to die before the Indians attacked his colleagues at Fort Dearborn. It must have been one day that spring that John Kinzie left his cabin and rowed across the river to Fort Dearborn. As he walked up the path Jean La Lime came out from the fort and accosted him. They had words and La Lime shot Kinzie, the ball passing through the muscles of his neck. Kinzie pulled his knife, grappled with La Lime and stabbed him to death. Bleeding profusely, Kinzie rushed to his boat, crossed the river, returned to his cabin and had Mrs. Kinzie bandage the wound. Then he hurried into the woods and hit the long trail to the trading post at Milwaukee.

When the fort discovered the killing a squad of soldiers was sent to the Kinzie house to get Kinzie. Their investigation, according to Gurdon S. Hubbard, satisfied them and they "exonerated" him. But they carried the corpse of Jean La Lime across the river and buried it a short distance beyond Kinzie's land, near the present Cass street. Some time later Kinzie, apprised of his exoneration, returned to his home and went about his business. The report says that never again did he mention the fatal fight, but that for the rest of his days he looked after the grave which had a picket fence around it. In 1891 bones and part of a pine coffin came to light at the southwest corner of Cass and Illinois streets and were thought to be those of "the little Frenchman," La Lime. They were "presented" to the Chicago Historical Society by Joseph Kirkland, the author. John Kinzie had other feuds. In 1810 he became involved in a bitter quarrel with the officers at Fort Dearborn, led by Captain John Whistler, who tried to stop liquor being given, against regulations, to the Indians. The fight involved both officers and Indian agents and resulted in the removal, from Fort Dearborn, of Captain Whistler and the principal officers of the garrison. As Dr. Quaife points out, this actually saved their lives from massacre in 1812.

It also led to a challenge. Dr. Cooper was asked by Lieutenant Hamilton to bear his challenge to a duel to Kinzie. Kinzie not only declined to accept it, but cursed the lieutenant so violently that a quarrel between Cooper and Kinzie resulted. Cooper thereafter would have no further intercourse with Kinzie. Fifty years later, when Kinzie was long dead and Fort Dearborn a memory, the aged Dr. Cooper recalled the violent temper of Kinzie and accused him of the murder of Jean La Lime.

Matthew Irwin, government factor at Chicago from 1809 to 1812, throws further light on the animosities of that day. He wrote an official letter to General Mason, head of the department of Indian trade, making not only the charge that Kinzie had murdered La Lime, but also expressing the belief that he was instrumental in bringing about the Fort Dearborn massacre in order to save his own life by destroying the witnesses to his crime. This seems rather farfetched, but the distance that separates us from the frontier post makes it hard for us to pronounce judgment. We should also have to take into account that Gurdon S. Hubbard, who had a reputation for probity, spoke up on behalf of Kinzie in later years.

But it is clear that the La Lime killing was far from a casual quarrel and had important repercussions on the post, where men took sides freely. That it was lost to history must be blamed on the Fort Dearborn massacre in the following August, which wiped out the settlement. When normal trade was resumed years later the death of La Lime was no longer an issue. Yet a curious reminiscence of the dead trader was put on the official records in 1821 when Governor Cass negotiated his treaty with the Indians at Chicago. In that treaty a half section of land was allotted to John La Lime, son of the Indian woman, Nokenoqua. There is small doubt that he was the son of Jean La Lime.

4

Blood and Fire at Fort Dearborn

WHEN the War of 1812 unleashed the fury of the Indians on the western frontier, the pioneer settlement on the Chicago went down on a day of rapine and murder. On August 15, 1812, the garrison of Fort Dearborn evacuated the post and, with women and children in its train, attempted a march to safety. It was overwhelmed on the sands near the present 18th Street; out of the company of nearly one hundred that marched out, 63 died, and perhaps the most terrible episode of that day was the butchery of 12 children who had been put into one wagon for safety.

The story has been told in every history of Chicago and will be repeated as long as the city stands. It belongs to the chronicle of the Chicago, and it shows how far the calamitous War of 1812 extended its horrors. In this outpost it was a fight for trade, for Fort Dearborn protected the American traders who were encroaching on the privileges of the British, who had long cultivated the favor of the Indians with annuities and arms.

Fort Dearborn was alarmed as early as April. On

the night of April 6, 1812, eleven Indians, presumably Winnebagos, fell upon the Lee farm, near the bend of the river, about where Racine Avenue meets the river today, and killed two hands. John Kelso, a discharged soldier, and the Lee boy escaped to give the alarm; they stopped at the cottage of Thomas Burns and added to the fears of Mrs. Burns, who had just given birth to an infant.

John Kinzie was playing his violin in his cabin when the alarm reached the garrison. The officers immediately fired a gun to call soldiers back to the fort, and this warned a corporal and six men who had gone up the river, two miles above the Lee place, to fish by torchlight. When they heard the gun they put out their torches and rowed back in the dark. Soldiers rowed to the Burns cottage, transferred Mrs. Burns and her infant with her bed to the boat and brought them safely to the fort.

The fort now became the center of refuge and agitation. Settlers and stray laborers were organized into a militia company of fifteen. Traders moved their families to the proximity of the fort. Indians came and went. When war was declared that summer and Mackinac fell to the British, the American commander in the West, General Hull, decided that Fort Dearborn could not be held and ordered its evacuation.

There is no dispute that Hull gave the order, but historians have not yet determined whether his wishes were properly expressed in the paper, not in his handwriting, that reached Captain Nathan Heald, the commanding officer, through the agency of the Potawatomi, Winnemeg. The fort was to be evacuated; arms and ammunition were to be destroyed; the goods in the government post were to be distributed to the needy and to friendly Indians. Hull also asked Fort Wayne to help; thereupon Captain William Wells, Corporal Walter Jordan and thirty-two Miami Indians were sent to Fort Dearborn. Fort Dearborn now became a center of controversy. For eight days Heald argued with his officers, with Kinzie, who opposed the evacuation, and with Indians, one of whom fired a rifle in the commanding officer's quarters. On the 13th, all the blankets and calico cloth were given out; liquor barrels were knocked in and the contents poured into the river at night. Only twenty-five rounds of ammunition were saved for each man. The delay gave the Indians time to form their attack.

The soldiers and civilians in the fort marched forth at 9 A.M. on August 15, 1812. Captain Wells, who had been brought up among the Miamis, wore Indian costume, and was in the lead with his Indian band. The wagons with the women, children and baggage were grouped together. Mrs. Heald rode her fine bay mare. It was reported later that the musicians played the Dead March—a prelude to disaster.

When the party had proceeded less than a mile and a half south Captain Wells observed hostile Indians behind the sand dunes, and Heald ordered the regulars to charge them. The Americans were hopelessly outnumbered. Moreover, the thirty-two Miamis immediately took flight. Thereafter the soldiers fought fiercely, individually, against odds. They accounted for many of their enemies, but the toll of their own losses was 24 enlisted men, 12 militiamen, 2 women and 12 children. The women were Mrs. Corbin, wife of a soldier, who fought every attempt to take her prisoner, and her Negro slave girl, Cicely. It is said that Captain Wells killed eight Indians before he was felled and pinned down by his horse; the Indians then killed him and ate his heart in the presence of Mrs. Heald, his niece. The latter was taken prisoner. She had been wounded six times, but when a squaw tried to seize her blanket, she struck her with her riding whip, and the Indians stood by and admired her spunk. The Indians appropriated a silver shawl pin, worn by Captain Heald, and a tortoise-shell comb mounted with gold worn by Mrs. Heald. Years later they were found in St. Louis, and an army officer, recognizing them, bought them and sent them back to the Healds.

During the excitement Mrs. Helm, the wife of Lieutenant L. T. Helm and daughter of Mrs. Kinzie by her first marriage, was dragged from the battle by Black Partridge and thrust up to her head in the waters of the lake, where, presumably, she could not be seen from the battlefield. This famous rescue is depicted in the battle monument, which once stood near the site of the battle but is now sheltered inside the building of the Chicago Historical Society.

At this point we resume the story of the fortunes of John Kinzie. Exciting and tragic adventures fell to other survivors of the Fort Dearborn massacre, but our principal interest is in Kinzie as the major trader on the Chicago. Once more he demonstrated his influence with the Indians. He joined the men escorting the wagon train. When the fighting began his wife was sitting in a boat with her children, expecting to be rowed across the lake to the Burnett trading post on the St. Joseph. In *Wau-Bun* we read that Mrs. Kinzie's party, besides her children, consisted of her nurse, Josette, two servants, of whom Victoria Pothier was one, a clerk, boatmen and two Indians. They did not start, however, and when the Americans straggled back, as prisoners of the Indians, they returned to the Kinzie cottage. Here they were joined by Mrs. Helm, who had been hit by a bullet, which John Kinzie removed with a penknife.

Apparently they did not expect to be molested, but a few days later they were menaced by hostile Indians from the Wabash, and Mrs. Helm had to hide behind the bed in Ouilmette's cabin. These Indians were about to attack the Kinzies when another Indian friend, the half-breed Billy Caldwell, arrived and persuaded the Indians to accept gifts from Kinzie and depart. Soon after Kinzie and his household, including Mrs. Helm, left for the Burnett post.

The war ruined Kinzie. He was said to owe Robert Forsyth and William Smith $30,000. He had lost a fortune in stores. Though in no danger from the Indians, he was now in trouble with the British. Some time later, in Detroit, they arrested him for high treason, put him in irons and kept him for seven weeks on a prison ship off Quebec. He was liberated in 1814, rejoined his family in Detroit, and resumed the work he knew—interpreting and trading. When the war was over Lewis Cass gave him work as interpreter among the Potawatomis.

In 1816, when Kinzie returned to his house on the Chicago, he began energetically to recoup his fortunes. He may have been ruined, but he had credit, for he borrowed $16,000 worth of goods from Robert Stuart. He also had the Indian agent, Charles Jouett, petition President Monroe to permit Kinzie to become a subagent as interpreter at Fort Dearborn, at $2 and two rations a day, "to support himself, Mrs. Kinzie and four fine children." Kinzie, said Jouett, "has a strong mind, firm integrity and invincible courage."

To make his case strong Kinzie described his activities on behalf of the Americans. He declared that he had warned the authorities of Indian hostility and joined Captain Heald in the evacuation. "I marched out of Fort Dearborn with a musket on my shoulder and was taken prisoner with the remaining few that escaped the tomahawk." He paid the Indians $500 in goods to get the release of Heald and Helm. He had twice refused the British offer of a captaincy in the Indian department. He had persuaded the Indians not to burn Detroit and other settlements on the approach of General Harrison and was held for high treason for corresponding with Harrison. He had exposed the British system of bribing the Indian chiefs with gifts and whisky at Malden. And in 1815 he had proposed a plan for achieving peace between the Indians and the government, which included checkmating the British merchants by "small presents to the chiefs" and developing a strong military post at Chicago, "to protect trade and create respect for agents."

This proposal was made in a letter to Governor Cass and shows how well Kinzie knew the value of the river and the portage as a trade route. He said: "The navigation of these waters will in a few years become an object of great importance to the United States, as at present boats of several tons burthen can pass from

Lake Michigan into the Mississippi River, there being only four and a half feet difference in the elevation of the two waters.

"Chicago is all important to the Illinois country, as it is the key of communication and has command of the trade of a vast territory, and whose navigation serves to forward the returns of the merchants to Michilli-mackinac, owing to the difficulty of procuring boats."

He cited the opportunity to mine for coal and lead; he advised that the Indian country be left for the Indians under the control of American agents, and that no whisky be permitted. A shrewd, farseeing man was John Kinzie, whose faith in the commercial advantages of the Chicago post remained firm despite Indian massacre and exile. He came back, took part in the life of the early community as a justice of the peace, and lived until 1828, by which year the westward movement was well on its way.

PART FOUR

The Indian Goes West

Red, White, and Mixed

I T IS not customary to perpetuate the weaknesses of leaders on memorial tablets and monuments. They stress the major virtues, and thus signify the higher estimate man places on nobility and truth. Even in these practical days, when flamboyant praise has given way to records of achievement, frankness stops short of a complete revelation.

Thus we need never expect a monument to describe the pioneer of the western frontier as he actually was. That is asking too much of human nature. But if such a monument were erected, to the wonder and awe of all Chicago it would read like this:

He was a crack shot . . . A good provider . . . Loyal to his woman . . . He drove a hard bargain and stuck to it . . . He reared his own cabin, ground his own meal . . . He got the best of the Indians, the traders and the government of the United States.

But posterity does not commemorate the acquisitive habits of its ancestors. When it raises monuments it celebrates courage, not foolhardiness; enterprise, not speculation; endurance, not ruthlessness. Yet the pioneers did not choose the wilds because they wanted to be alone under the sky. They never thought of themselves as the vanguard of civilization or the standardbearers of empire. They went where they could make a good living, profit by trading, and get public land. They were, for the most part, tough-minded and hardboiled.

After Fort Dearborn was burned in 1812, the Chicago had a respite from the traders and the military. Its waters moved through a region visited by few white men. On the hill at its mouth the charred logs of the old barracks fell to ruin. The brick magazine alone remained intact, like an old mortuary vault. Across the river John Kinzie's poplars still stood and deserted cabins braved the wind that flung the sand into their open doors. Only a few French traders, who helped to rescue the Fort Dearborn captives from Indian slavery, lived on the Chicago during the winter of 1813.

If a lone Indian—Potawatomi or Ottawa—paddled past the hill, he heard no challenge from the soldiers. Likewise he found no American trader ready to buy his beaver pelts. If this was to his satisfaction he may have decided that the intruders were routed for good. This was his mistake. He was merely floating in the trough of the wave that presently would return and fling him far inland.

In the decade of 1820-1830, traders and settlers filtered back into the prairie lands. In the decade of 1830-1840 land speculators dominated the scene. Cook county was organized; Chicago grew from a hamlet to a town. Opportunity and Speculation met on the banks of the Chicago and the city was born. On August 5, 1833, the town of Chicago was incorporated, with only thirteen voters at the polls, twelve voting for and one against the proposal. On March 4, 1837, a charter incorporating the city of Chicago was issued at the Vandalia Court-house and William B. Ogden was chosen first mayor. This chapter deals with some of the high lights and personalities of those hectic twenty years.

The friendly traders were the first to come back to the Chicago. As early as 1813 Jean Baptiste Beaubien and his little four-year-old boy, Medore, stopped at the Chicago and walked over the ruins of the old fort. It was not the intention of the federal government to abandon this outpost, but it was niggardly in its appropriation of money for maintaining it. In June, 1816, the government sent a company of soldiers under Captain Hezekiah Bradley to Fort Dearborn and its rebuilding was begun. John C. Calhoun was secretary of war at the time and there was a hint from Washington that it be called Fort Calhoun, but Fort Dearborn it was on the official records and so it remained.

Even now the government was not disposed to spend money on the post. Although substantial buildings were erected and military routine was observed, the troops were frequently shifted and allowed to dwindle in numbers, and for months the fort was often deserted. At one time Alexander Wolcott, the Indian agent, was in charge of its buildings. But recurring scares of Indian uprisings brought the troops back. After the Winnebagos threatened to make trouble for the settlers on the Rock River in 1828, two companies of the 5th U.S. Infantry were sent to reoccupy Fort Dearborn, with Captain John Fowle as commander. One of his first lieutenants was David Hunter, who became a general in the Civil War, and one of his second lieutenants was Abram Van Buren, son of Martin Van Buren.

These and other names of men who played a part in American history suggest how many future leaders cut their eyeteeth on the Chicago. The story of David Hunter, who lived to the proverbial ripe old age, is an example. Hunter was a competent fellow; he took the job of teaching the children of settlers who lived near the fort. He joined the Kinzie clan when he married Maria H. Kinzie, daughter of John, who had been born in the cabin on the Chicago in 1807. But perhaps the most fateful event in his life occurred when his path crossed that of another lieutenant in 1829.

One day Lieutenant Hunter observed an unfamiliar soldier making his way toward the fort on the north bank. He rowed across the river to bring him to the fort and learned that he was Second Lieutenant Jefferson Davis, of the 1st U.S. Infantry, who had helped lay out Fort Winnebago at Portage, Wisconsin, and was now on an expedition of his own, looking for deserters. The two men could not gaze into the future, no more than all those other potential leaders who chased Black Hawk and his Indians across Illinois three years later. Thus they could not discern that one day General David Hunter, as commander of the Department of the South, would order freed all the slaves in the three states under his military jurisdiction, in opposition to the president of the Confederacy, Davis, and that his order would be revoked by the federal president, Abraham Lincoln, who at that moment in 1829 was digging stumps or splitting rails on an Illinois farm.

Alexander Wolcott represented another type of culture on the Chicago. He was possibly the first Yale man to cast his lot with the young settlement, and he must have been far from the rough-and-ready type of pioneer known to the West. He was appointed Indian agent in 1820.

Wolcott belonged to the capable Connecticut family of that name. He was descended from Roger Wolcott, governor and major general, who led the Continental troops at Louisburg, and two other Alexander Wolcotts, who made reputations at Yale and had careers as surgeon and lawyer. The Wolcott who reached Chicago was born in 1790, studied medicine at Yale and received his degree in 1809. He served as a surgeon in the War of 1812 and then went west.

As Indian agent at Fort Dearborn he had a responsible position. In six months of 1820 he paid out $27,600 in subsidies to the Indians from the federal government, to keep them in good humor. In that period Wolcott collected $1,300 in salary, a large sum in pioneer days. At the same time he paid his subagent $500. This subagent was none other than our old friend John Kinzie.

Wolcott became closely associated with the Kinzies. In 1823, when he was thirty-three years old, he was married to John's daughter, Ellen Marion, who was eighteen. She may not have been the first white child born in Chicago—as the memorial tablet says—but she was the first Kinzie born there. That was the year Wolcott was in charge of the fort, then temporarily without a garrison. We are also indebted to Wolcott's records for the information that the weather was mighty cold along the Chicago in pioneer times. On January 1, 1820, the ice was 14 inches thick in the river; on February 2nd, it was 18¾ inches thick; on January 31st, 22 inches of snow fell.

Wolcott, who died in 1830, when only forty, exerted another indirect influence on Chicago history. It was through him, no doubt, that John Harris Kinzie became acquainted with Wolcott's highly intelligent niece, Juliette Magill. She became his wife, and as the author of *Wau-Bun* bobs up frequently in our history. It was Juliette who described the agency house in which Wolcott lived. It stood on the north bank of the river, near the present State Street, about thirty rods west of the Kinzie house. It had been begun by Charles Jouett, and in the course of years had acquired two additions. According to Juliette Kinzie, it made people laugh to see a house with two wings at the back. We don't know why this should have stirred the amusement of pioneers, whose habitations had no specific style. Maybe it indicates that a break from the conventional creates surprise, even in a settlement of log cabins.

It was in this growing settlement that a new type of native began to make his influence felt. This was the literate half-breed, the man whose mother was a squaw, but whose father, a white man, had given him the white man's schooling. In the Chicago chronicle such men became useful as go-betweens. Several were recognized as chiefs by the tribes to which their mothers belonged. Invariably they profited when the government paid subsidies to the Indians. But in the end their situation was tragic. As long as the frontier was wild they enjoyed life in both red and white camps. When the white life with its fenced-in fields and vested rights became dominant they found the adjustment difficult. Best known of these men was Billy Caldwell, the Sauganash, chief of the Potawatomis.

But the white settlers had no use for the Indian. The story of how he was pushed out of his woods and fields, shoved across the Mississippi, fills many a dark page in American history, but it was the inevitable clash of two incompatible ways of living. As an individual the Indian was often friendly, a hunter, guide and porter, and squaws of his race fitted into white men's cabins without emotional strain. Of one whole tribe, the Illini, nothing but good tidings have reached us, but their friendliness to conversion and trade was offset by their weakness as fighters; they were completely wiped out in the middle of the eighteenth century. The Indians that the Chicago settlement knew wheedled and stole, and with the connivance of greedy whites became steeped in whisky. When the Indians became thieves, the whites reached for their guns. "It is useless to argue with an Illinois Indian hater," wrote the New York author, Charles Fenno Hoffman, who learned that a settler was afraid to send his child to the spring for water and had to plow with a heavy rifle near at hand.

The competitive, volatile society of the 1830's swept the Indian aside. It ordered him off its town lots, pushed him off its roads, moved him out of sight. Youthful Chicago saw it done; it refused to be its red brother's keeper. It shared the determination of the farmers to get rid of the Indian, but to do so it had to turn against some of its best, most trusted and useful Indian friends.

If Indians could not get along with the whites, it was also true that they could not get along with other Indians; the tribesmen had many animosities. These were even carried over to the white settlers. Thus we have record of an indignant protest by Frances R. Howe, whose grandmother, Monee, inadvertently had been called a Potawatomi by some careless miscreant. The protest, reflecting indignation and pride of race and position, reads: "I am pleased to be able to contradict the statement that my grandmother was a Potawatomi. Such an idea would be enough to disturb the peace of her last repose, did she know of it. She hated the Potawatomis with a perfect hatred, disliked their costume, disapproved of their customs, considered their dialect a detestable jargon. Her father was a French gentleman; her mother was a woman of the Ottawa tribe . . ."

There is one Indian story that provides a most amusing variation from the usual tale of strife between whites and Indians. It rests on the statement of Edward Gay Mason that Father Louis Vivier, a priest at Kaskaskia, in 1752 wrote a letter describing the adventures of a famous Indian chief named Chikagou. Chikagou was taken to Paris, where he was lionized. At Versailles the Duchess of Orléans gave him a snuffbox, which he brought back and exhibited to the Indians. This incident should lend itself to balladry. The spectacle of the great chief Chikagou taking snuff on the frontier from a box given him at the fabulous court of Louis XV is too good to be overlooked.

Not all the white men who came to Chicago in

these years expected to get rich quick on land deals.
A notable exception was the young Jeremiah Porter,
Presbyterian dominie, who saw Chicago as a promising
field for harvesting souls. Like other young men he
looked to the west for his opportunity. On a schooner
going to Sault Ste. Marie he met a man who had heard
that the government was about to build a lighthouse at
the Chicago River and who had decided to open a board-
inghouse there. At Sault Ste. Marie Porter and his young
wife came to board at the house of Henry R. Schoolcraft, who dramatically described his travels in the Chicago area and told Porter that he had heard that John H.
Kinzie, Indian subagent at Fort Winnebago, was going
to lay out a town. When Major John Fowle was ordered
to go from Sault Ste. Marie to Fort Dearborn, Porter
accepted the major's suggestion that he accompany the
troops as chaplain.

Thus Jeremiah Porter arrived in Chicago's momentous year—1833, when the little settlement was just
pulling itself together after the Black Hawk War and
the cholera scare and getting ready to bulge. Porter
observed the lazy Chicago flowing between grassy banks,
making a half circle around Fort Dearborn and issuing
into the lake half a mile south. His schooner could not
land its passengers for some time because of the turbulent lake. Arrived at the post, the young minister observed that there were some taverns and cabins but no
churches.

Porter lost no time getting started on his mission.
The carpenter shop at the fort was cleared for services
and on May 19, 1933, Porter preached his first sermon.
He found lodgings and a room for study on the unfin-

ished second floor of a store at South Water and La Salle streets. In June he organized the congregation of the First Presbyterian Church with nine settlers and twenty-five men from the garrison.

All around him he heard talk about the prosperity that would come to the farmers when a canal was built. But not all men present had visions of riches. When an optimist declared that the settlement would have five thousand inhabitants in five years, an army man rebuked him. "That cannot be," said he, "for there is no back country to sustain a city." The army man could not see the wood for the trees.

Almost immediately the river began to play a part in the religious life of the community. There was the wife of Dr. J. T. Temple, for instance, who decided that baptism in the Christian faith demanded immersion. She goes down in Chicago history as the first to take the plunge. We may well imagine that most of the three hundred settlers at the post came down to the banks of the river, south of Fort Dearborn, in what is now Michigan Avenue, to see the lady baptized. There was also another attraction. Mrs. Temple drove to the spot in the first stagecoach ever seen in Chicago. As the minister immersed the lady he appropriately repeated a text from Acts 8:38: "And he commanded the chariot to stand still: and they went down both into the water . . . and he baptized him." Jeremiah Porter had a sense of humor.

After that the river helped hundreds to enter the faith and Chicago often saw groups of converts dipped into its waters at State Street. Joseph H. Balestier, of the Brattleboro Balestiers, who lived in Chicago in the late 1830's, said: "Converts were baptized in shoals, generally in cold weather in a sort of cove or slough which came in from the river near State Street."

Jeremiah Porter had one dip that he didn't relish. He was returning home one night that winter from the north side and walking across the ice, carrying a lantern in one hand and a hymnbook in the other, when he fell into a hole made by icecutters. Handicapped with a long cloak Porter had his troubles getting out, but he survived, saving both hymnbook and lantern.

2

The Great Pacificator Arrives

ONE morning in the summer of 1827 Gurdon S. Hubbard was having breakfast at the Kinzie's when the lusty voices of men singing a boat song drifted down the river. "That's Lewis Cass," said Hubbard. Pretty soon Cass pulled up in his Mackinaw boat, twelve men handling the oars and one steering. Cass said he had portaged to the Wisconsin from Green Bay to get to the seat of the threatened Winnebago rising, then had proceeded to Jefferson Barracks at St. Louis and ascended the river on a steamboat carrying troops to Fort Snelling. At the mouth of the Illinois Cass and his men left, put their boat back into the water and rowed up the Illinois and the Des Plaines, portaged to the Chicago. They had completed the round trip in thirteen days, rowing sixty to seventy miles a day.

The speed and energy with which Lewis Cass acted was characteristic. Though Illinois was now a state, Wisconsin was still part of his Michigan Territory. He knew how open to attack were the isolated settlers who had begun farming the prairie land. Fort Dearborn was undermanned. Cass's urging sent Hubbard on horseback down the Sauk trail to Danville, where he collected fifty mounted men and hurried them to Chicago. The Potawatomi half-breed chiefs sprang to his support; Billy Caldwell and Alexander Robinson, the latter known to his people as Chechepinqua, persuaded their tribes to remain quiet, while the friendly Shabonee wore out two ponies dashing to the Ottawas to keep them from making common cause with the Winnebagos.

Lewis Cass, who used the Chicago frequently during the two decades following the War of 1812, was now thirty-eight and had been governor of Michigan since 1813. He comes into the chronicle of the Chicago, not only because he held Indian councils here, but because he was in constant touch with John Kinzie. That Cass found Kinzie useful in treating with the Indians and later supported his claims for government help speaks well for Kinzie's capacities. At different times Cass employed John and his son John Harris as agent and interpreter.

Of all the leaders who visited the Chicago in the first thirty years of the nineteenth century, Cass had the strongest intellect and the best administrative ability. Claude G. Bowers, reviewing his innovations on the frontier—organization of schools, efforts to encourage and protect settlement, and far-flung precautions to keep the Indians in check—calls him an empire builder with sagacity, courage and imagination. Cass was a subordinate when General William Hull surrendered Detroit to the British, and he resented it as a cowardly act. He knew how much the British had contributed to Indian uprisings and it prompted his lifelong antagonism to British policy. Cass became Jackson's secretary

of war in the big Cabinet upheaval of 1831. He was
also a senator and a candidate for president, losing to
Zachary Taylor. His last important federal post was
secretary of state under Buchanan. His extraordinary
public career covered a wide range of activities and he
survived the Civil War and Lincoln, dying in 1866 at
the age of eighty-four. Cass Street, on the north bank,
commemorates his name and runs near the spot where
he negotiated with the Indians in 1821. To me his most
interesting trait was his reading for self-education. He
was the only frontier leader who kept a number of
books in his boats when he traveled into the interior.

The Winnebago scare had brought troops back to
Fort Dearborn, so that it was not deserted when the
Black Hawk War broke out in western Illinois in 1832.
Once more the half-breed chiefs were called upon to
hold their tribes in check, and for the most part they
succeeded. But although the war was waged with the
Sac and Fox nations, the Winnebagos and Potawatomis
were seriously disturbed. Fear of roving bands terrified
the settlers as far away as the Chicago area.

One of the panic-stricken communities was that of
Walker's Grove, or Plainfield, between Joliet and
Aurora. Stephen R. Beggs, a Methodist minister, made a
fort out of his house for the settlers, but when news of
the Creek massacre of May 22, 1832, reached them, they
decided to seek the protection of Fort Dearborn. When
they arrived, they found the fort had no quarters for
them. The account of their treatment, as given by
Beggs, blames the officers. He relates that several families were compelled to live in one room fifteen feet
square. The house was struck by lightning, which, as

is usual in such cases, resulted in the precipitate birth of an infant. Indeed, the crisis seems to have caused an unusual spurt in the population of Walker's Grove, for fifteen babies were born to badly scared mothers. On one occasion refugees were turned out of a room because a major needed it. But Beggs did manage to bring religious guidance to the soldiers. Amid the rolling of drums the militia was called to fall in near one of the houses of the fort. Beggs stood on the steps and preached on the text: "Lamb of God, who taketh away the sins of the world."

When the Black Hawk War broke out, Cass had just became Jackson's secretary of war. He advocated rushing General Winfield Scott to the scene with reinforcements from the regular army. Jackson didn't approve of Scott, who was a National Republican, but he found Cass's advice useful because he was politically opposed to General Gaines, the commander in the West. The Illinois situation was desperate. The home-grown militia under Stillman had turned tail, thereby perpetuating his name in Stillman's Run. Also they refused to follow the Indians over the border into Wisconsin, because they were not obliged to fight outside their own state. So chaotic were defense arrangements that General Henry Atkinson gave them their discharge, though the war was far from over. Lincoln was one of the militia youths in that encounter, and Jefferson Davis was with the regulars.

On July 10, 1832, General Scott arrived at the Chicago. He had two nicknames; his opponents derisively called him Old Fuss and Feathers, but his friends glorified him with the resounding title of the Great

Pacificator. The temptation to ridicule Scott because he came too late to do any fighting is great, but undeserved, for en route he had faced an enemy more deadly than the Indian. That was cholera.

Scott arrived on the first steamship ever to anchor at the mouth of the Chicago. This would have made a sensation in ordinary times, but now there were hardly any traders left to welcome it. They had heard of its calamitous cargo and fled to the prairie. Only the garrison was at hand to help unload the cargo of sick and dying.

Scott had set out from Fortress Monroe with nine companies of regulars and picked up a handful of newly commissioned officers of the class of 1832 at West Point. At Buffalo he leased four steamboats, the *Sheldon Thompson,* the *Henry Clay,* the *William Penn* and the *Superior.* He put troops on the first two and supplies on the others and sailed July 2nd. Cholera broke out on Scott's ship, the *Henry Clay,* at Detroit. He transferred his staff to the *Sheldon Thompson* and sent the West Pointers home. At Fort Gratiot a lot of sick men had to be landed, while others took the opportunity to desert into the woods. When Scott reached Chicago one officer and fifty-three privates had died and many were ill. Scott had worked tirelessly among the men en route. Now the sick men were unloaded and taken to Fort Dearborn. Those still well removed the dead and buried them in a pit near the river and what is now Wabash Avenue. Often soldiers who had buried their comrades were stricken a few hours later and taken out and buried the next day.

At Fort Dearborn General Scott met Major Wil-

liam Whistler, for once more a Whistler was in charge
of the post that Captain John Whistler had organized
in 1803. The fort had been evacuated in 1831, but
when the Indian trouble threatened Major William
Whistler was ordered to proceed from Fort Niagara to
Fort Dearborn with companies G and I of the 2nd U.S.
Infantry. He was the son of Captain John and a second
lieutenant when Fort Dearborn began its troubled
career, and he was to command there until May, 1833.

By the end of July the cholera had subsided and
Scott hurried to the front. By that time General Atkinson had chased the Indians beyond Prairie du Chien.
Scott took charge when the fighting was over and only
the treaties remained to be imposed. He did that at
Fort Armstrong, on Rock Island, and signed the treaty
that pushed the Sac and Fox Indians beyond the Mississippi on the site of Davenport, Iowa. He also negotiated a treaty with the Potawatomi and Winnebago,
who agreed to move west, but didn't.

Cholera broke out at Fort Armstrong and here
General Scott published a famous order, in which he declared that alcoholism must be associated with the spread
of cholera, and ordered that "every soldier, or Ranger,
found drunk or sensibly intoxicated, be compelled, as
soon as his strength will permit, to dig a grave at a suitable burying place, large enough for his own reception,
as such grave cannot fail soon to be wanted for the
drunken man himself or some drunken companion."
Scott was on the right track when he declared that
cleanliness of person and camp and care in preparation
of food would help prevent disease, but he did not know

that boiling the water would have freed the camp of contagion.

The last of the Indians to make trouble for the whites were the Winnebagos. In 1839 they refused to move out of Wisconsin to the lands that had been allotted them in the West and gave the settlers a good scare. Once more General Scott was called upon to meet the chiefs with whom he had negotiated the treaty at the end of the Black Hawk War. With his faithful servant, Black David, he sailed from Buffalo to Green Bay, but being unable to get transportation to Fort Winnebago, took a steamer down to Chicago and then went by stage to Madison, Wisconsin, over the old road now known as Milwaukee Avenue. Scott tried to mollify the Indians by telling them to stay in Wisconsin and to move out the following year, but the Indians refused. Scott returned to Chicago and while there made a special point of commemorating the anniversary of the battle of Lundy's Lane on July 25th.

3

The Man Who Took the Fort

LIFE along the Chicago in the early days would
have been pretty dull but for the Beaubiens. These two
brothers from Detroit, John and Mark, brought a bit
of Gallic spirit to a community of hard-bitten traders
chiefly engaged in driving sharp bargains. Gay and un-
predictable, with music in their souls, John and Mark
never were able to master the frontier game of money-
grubbing. When they tried to be shrewd, they became
amusing failures. But they helped teach school and make
music for dances; John brought the first piano to Chicago and Mark fiddled contentedly from youth to old
age.

John Wentworth, editor and politician, loved Mark
and his fiddle and saw to it that Mark left his fiddle to
the Calumet Club, which he had entertained on occasion. "He inherited the art in the natural way," said
Wentworth. "When one string broke he used three,
when another broke he used two, and when a third
broke he played on one."

Although John and Mark were American born,
they had been brought up in a small French Catholic

community in Detroit and had many French character-
istics. Their grandfather had emigrated from France to
Detroit, where their father was born. John was Jean
Baptiste Beaubien in those days. He saw Mackinac surrender to the British in the War of 1812, just as his
brother Mark, who was then twelve, saw General Hull
surrender to the British at Detroit. I have already mentioned how John visited the ruins of Fort Dearborn with
his little four-year-old boy, Medore, whose mother was
an Indian squaw. John came to the Chicago to live in
1819, when the American Fur Company, worried because rivals were cutting into its trade, sent him there
to remedy matters. John Crafts had been intercepting
the Indians at his place on the river near the old Lee
farm. John Beaubien must have been an adroit fixer, for
in 1822 the American Fur Company appointed Crafts
superintendent with John as his assistant, and it is not
unlikely that his geniality had a lot to do with this
compromise.

A few years later Mark, now twenty-six, visited his
brother and decided to make his home on the Chicago
too. He brought his family from Detroit and put up a
log cabin at the southeast side of the Forks, to be designated in later years as Lake and Market streets, and
now on Wacker Drive. He took out a license to run a
tavern and got permission to operate a ferry, with the
proviso that he transport free any citizen of the
county.

This litte log cabin, twelve feet square, was to as-
sume an important role in the history of Chicago. For
a few years later Mark built a substantial house across
the street, and when Father Saint-Cyr came to Chicago

SAUGANASH TAVERN

to organize the first congregation of the Roman Catholic Church, Mark Beaubien gave him the use of the little cabin. Here, on May 5, 1833, Father Saint-Cyr celebrated his first mass, and laid the basis for the parish of St. Mary's, which built its church soon after on the north side of Lake Street, west of State.

The tavern that Mark Beaubien built on the lot now called the southeast corner of Lake Street and Wacker Drive, became famous as the Sauganash. It was a wooden structure with clapboard sides, on the familiar plan of a central hall with rooms at each side, and had a second story. While he was building it his friend Billy Caldwell, the half-breed Indian who was one of the best educated men in the Chicago settlement, asked him what he was going to name it. "I am going to name it after a great man," said Mark, calling it Sauganash after Caldwell's Indian nickname, which means Britisher. This building, which remains famous in Chicago history as one of the substantial inns of stagecoach days, is always associated with Mark Beaubien, yet he did not run it after 1834, when he sold it to John Murphy. From then on Mark kept moving restlessly between Chicago, Peoria and other towns, apparently no longer interested in starting new enterprises.

But it was John B. Beaubien who was to startle the Chicago community with a feat that left the shrewd New England traders gasping. On May 28, 1835, John, who had become a colonel of militia and later adopted the title of brigadier general, walked into the office of the United States receiver of public moneys, Edmund D. Taylor, and calmly announced that he was buying the Fort Dearborn reservation under the law of preemption of public lands. Since the prevailing rates asked by the government were $1.25 an acre and costs, John put down $94.61 and demanded title to the land.

The land agent was flabbergasted. He had no precedent to go by and didn't know what law applied to the situation. The Fort Dearborn reservation was government land and no longer in use for military purposes. Colonel Beaubien lived on it. When the last troops had marched away a few years before, the War Department made plain that it did not intend to continue a military post there. No attempt was made to protect the remaining buildings from the wind and rain that battered at the roofs and shutters. The land agent was at a loss. He took Beaubien's money and gave him a receipt.

Colonel Beaubien was jubilant. He had bagged a rich claim. Measured by what lots were selling for on Lake Street that very day, he was on the way to become wealthy. He had bagged fifty acres of the finest land, right in the heart of a community seething with land speculation. We can imagine him swaggering down the street, announcing his purchase and showing his receipt, and enjoying the excitement that drew the pious from their churches, the housewives from their ovens and the two-bottle men from the dramshops.

Chicago had a population of 3,265 that year, and probably a thousand or so additional speculators whose offices were in their saddlebags. How they received the news is not hard to imagine. They thronged around the colonel and asked dozens of questions. Who put the fort on sale without public notice? How could one man buy it secretly? Who set the price? Did the colonel intend to run a fort of his own, drill the militia and mount guard? Or did he intend to tear down the fort and sell town lots?

In the meantime the agent had been running around, getting advice from officials. He had given Beaubien possession, so now he went into court with an action of ejectment. It would have been easier to deny Beaubien the fort in the first place and refer the whole matter to the War Department. But the agent had let that opportunity slip by. Judge Thomas Ford of the Cook County Circuit Court decided, on the evidence before him, that the purchase was legal, but that Beaubien could not take possession until he had a patent from Washington. The agent then appealed to the Supreme Court of the state, which reversed the decision. Colonel Beaubien then took the case to the United States Supreme Court which threw out the purchase. On December 18, 1840, Beaubien was invited to call at the land office and get his money back, without interest.

Harriet Martineau, the famous English traveler, was visiting in Chicago when the Beaubien sensation was on, and made mention of it in her book on western travel, thus: "A poor Frenchman, married to a squaw, had a suit pending, when I was there, which he was likely to gain, for the right of purchasing some land by the lake for $100, which would immediately become worth $1,000,000." Not exactly accurate, but indicating the gossip of the time. The incident led the United States to sell the reservation. It was learned that it contained 53¼ acres and that the river had bitten off 3¼ acres in the coure of winding around the hill. When sold the land brought $1 a front foot or $106,042. That would have been a juicy plum for the colonel. The southern end of the reservation became Fort Dearborn Park, where Lincoln was to speak. It was eventually used as the site of the present public library.

The Beaubiens never accumulated much money, although some of John's half-breed Indian progeny received subsidies from the government in the Indian treaties. But as they grew older provision was made for them by their friends. Strange to say, they were associated to the end with the Chicago River. In 1854, when the lighthouse was no longer in use, John Wentworth prevailed on the government to let John live there. When he died in 1863, Mark took up his residence there. He died in Kankakee, Illinois, in 1881, when he was eighty-one years old. His life had spanned the whole development of Chicago, from a sandy plain with a log cabin to an immense industrial city, the air heavy with the black smoke of factory chimneys.

4

The Big Pay-off

Henry R. schoolcraft was an observant man
with a scientific mind; his books bear witness to his
scholarly labors in the wilderness. Longfellow drew on
him for his legend of Hiawatha. In 1832 Schoolcraft
found the source of the Mississippi and named it Lake
Itasca. But before that happened he was a traveler on
the Chicago. In 1820 he accompanied Governor Lewis
Cass's expedition as a mineralogist around Lake Michigan and became acquainted with the Chicago Portage.
Arriving at the mouth of the Chicago in canoes from
Green Bay the party found a village of ten or twelve
dwellings and sixty people, with a garrison on "the
south shore of Chicago creek, 400 or 500 yards from its
entrance to the Lake." This places the 1820 mouth of
the River considerably farther north than Madison
Street, where some settlers placed it in the 1830's. The
"creek" was eighty yards wide and had a sand bar at its
mouth. The party ascended eleven miles in boats and
barges, making a portage of seven miles to the river
Plein—that is, the Des Plaines—and going by way of
Mount Juliet, a hill known later as Mount Joliet,

which shows that the Chicago Portage was difficult. Yet Schoolcraft was impressed by the beauty and fertility of the country around Chicago; he thought it had an elevation "which exempts it from the influence of stagnant waters and a summer climate of delightful serenity" and he added that it "only requires the extinguishment of the Indian title to the lands to become one of the most attractive fields for the immigrant."

This matter of honoring Indian titles was an indication of the conflicting policies pursued by the federal government toward the Indians. They must have baffled the red man, and they certainly contributed to his corruption. Why the frontiersmen were so ready to make treaties with the red man whom they had fought, defeated, abused and crowded out is not always clear until we see the hazards involved. The settlers were strung along a wide frontier and had to depend on Indian goodwill. The British were on the border making a practice of giving annuities of money and goods to loyal Indian tribes, both to keep the tribes as military aides and to get them to favor the British in selling furs. The Americans fought the Indians and then signed treaties with them, taking their lands but giving them cash, goods and annuities, the latter probably frontier insurance to get them to stop roving and marauding among the settlements. The fact that the whites and half-breeds also profited handsomely by these treaties leads to the conclusion that this was one reason why the practice persisted so long.

One of the most active negotiators of the Indian period was Lewis Cass. Cass was one of the commissioners who negotiated the Treaty of Prairie du Chien

in 1829 with the Indians of the "three fires"—the Potawatomis, Chippewas and Ottawas. John Kinzie and
John B. Beaubien were witnesses. Billy Caldwell, the
Sauganash, who became a chief of the Potawatomis
through his mother, received a handsome handout, including the 1,240 acres on the North Branch of the
Chicago, of which the nucleus today bears his name and
exists as a public park.

Lewis Cass was governor of Michigan in 1821 when
he held a council with the Indians at Chicago and negotiated a new treaty to get the Potawatomis out of lower
Michigan. This was the council at which Henry Schoolcraft was present. The council was held on the north
side of the river, with an "open bower" for the council
house. On August 17th Governor Cass made his speech
to the Indians, of whom three thousand had assembled.
Two days later they refused his terms, but by August
29th every chief had signed. The reason for their conversion may be found in Alexander Wolcott's statement to Cass, that it was done by the "bribery of the
chief men."

The treaty provided for a generous donation by the
United States. The Potawatomis were to receive an an-
nuity of $5,000 for twenty years; the Ottawas an an-
nuity of $1,000 "for ever." The sum of $1,500 a year
for ten years was given the Ottawas, and $1,000 a year
for fifteen years was given the Potawatomis for the ex-
penses of blacksmiths and teachers. Traders and half-
breeds were generously remembered. John B. Beaubien
witnessed the treaty and received a half section of land
for each of his two sons by an Indian squaw. John
Burnett, the trader of Bertrand, had married the sister

of a Potawatomi chief and received two sections, while his children received one section each.

The meeting was marked by the usual excesses. Cass denied the Indians liquor at first, and finally yielded. When liquor was given them there were ten murders in twenty-four hours.

The Black Hawk War brought to a head the determination of the West to get rid of the Indians. Illinois settlers were especially eager that there should be no more war scares. Even the so-called friendly Indians, who had taken no part in the Sac and Fox disturbance, were often a nuisance. They were lazy and shiftless around the settlements; they drank firewater to excess; they disregarded boundaries and plantings. It might be said that the traders made a pretty profit out of their dealings for pelts with the Indians and encouraged them to spend their goods for drink, but such advantages were offset by the trouble the Indians made for the settlers.

As long ago as 1825 John C. Calhoun, then secretary of war, had proposed a vigorous policy of dealing with the Indians to President Monroe, urging their removal to land west of the Mississippi. Monroe passed the idea on to Congress, without action. Now Andrew Jackson was president and part of his policy was the opening of public lands to settlers. He issued a call for a council of Indians of Illinois and the territory of Michigan, the latter embracing Wisconsin, to meet September 10, 1833, at Chicago. Governor George B. Porter of Michigan was designated to propose terms of removal to the tribes. A cabin on a hillock near the Kinzie house, on the north side of the river, was chosen as the council house.

By September the Indians began to arrive with their squaws and children—twenty-four chiefs of big and little tribes being entitled to sit in council, including the headmen of the Potawatomis, Ottawas, Chippewas, Kickapoos and Miamis. They came on foot and on horseback, with their braves riding furiously on their ponies, kicking up the dust and yelling, and the squaws trudging after with drags loaded with camp gear. They made camp all around the village.

The traders were ready for them. Expecting the usual generous handout by the government to the Indians, the merchants had laid in a special stock of gay cloth, blankets, ornaments of all kinds. Shanties were hurriedly thrown up on South Water Street and stocked with tobacco and whisky. It was going to be a great chance to sell goods.

Charles J. Latrobe, an Englishman who was touring the West, happened to witness the meeting and record his impressions. He saw the commissioners and their attendants housed in plank huts on the north side of the river and the storekeepers, lawyers, doctors in half a hundred clapboard houses on the south bank. With a certain amount of disgust he grouped together the "horse dealers, horse stealers, rogues, creditors, peddlers and grog sellers," and found the whites more pagan than the red men. The Indians had painted their faces with chalk and black and vermilion paint. In the chaos of mud and rubbish some men were betting on races, some engaged in grouse shooting, others in brawls, and drunken, whining Indians were all over the place. Two Indians fought a duel for the daughter of a Chippewa chief on the sand lots of the north bank and died from the wounds inflicted on each other.

Governor Porter made the principal harangue, addressing the chiefs in the bland, parental manner assumed by white officials when they dealt with the unruly children of the forest. He said that "as the Great Father in Washington had heard they wished to sell their land, he had sent commissioners to treat with them." The Indians replied that "their Great Father in Washington must have seen a bad bird, which had told him a lie, for far from wishing to sell their land, they wished to keep it."

The usual delays ensued, and when Latrobe tired of the confusion in the village he liked to stroll "toward sunset across the River and gaze up the level horizon, stretching to the northwest over the surface of the prairie."

Governor Porter outlined the government's terms and asked the chiefs if they were satisfied. They answered, "No. We shall dance tomorrow." On the following day a horde of Indians, nearly naked and painted in fantastic colors, pranced and whooped their way along South Water Street from the fort. They stopped before each door to beg for handouts, and the Reverend Jeremiah Porter, who gave them crackers, said they looked "like the very incarnation of evil." They wasted time until September 24th, when the arguments of the half-breed chiefs, who were more white in their outlook than Indian, persuaded one after another to sign the treaty.

The terms were generous, even wasteful. In place of the four million acres of land that the Indians theoretically occupied, they were to receive five million acres on the other side of the Mississippi and the settlers thought that an easy way to get rid of them. They were to be moved at the expense of the government, which agreed to put $1,000,000 annually into schools and to educate farmers and mechanics. The first payment was to be $90,000 in goods, the next $56,000 in silver half dollars, for the Indian valued most highly the clinking coins. In addition the government cut a melon for the traders and half-breeds who presented claims, giving some of them land and others annuities. The Kinzies received about $20,000 between them, supposedly in compensation for losses in the War of 1812. Victoria Pothier, who had been in the Kinzie house at the time of the massacre and later married the half-breed chief, Shabonee, received money; so did her brothers, Jean and Thomas Mirandeau, and sisters, Jane and Rosetta. Beaubien's wife and children were remembered once more; Ouilmette's wife and children received money and land; Mrs. Helm, who had been rescued from the Fort Dearborn massacre, received $2,000. The half-breeds Billy Caldwell and Alexander Robinson cashed in once more, with lump sums and annuities. The Great White Father was generous, but historians now consider many of the claims dishonest.

The government's agents now went among the Indians and threw half dollars on the blankets spread out before them. We can imagine what smiles the flood of silver brought to the faces of the expectant natives, but their pleasure could hardly have exceeded the joy of the grogshop men, to whom the clink of coins meant large profits. Some Indians had as many as four hundred half dollars tossed in their blankets. That the traders put many temptations in their way is evident without documentary proof. The braves went on a drinking orgy. They quarreled and drew their knives; they mounted their ponies and dashed madly over the prairie; finally they tumbled into the dust in a drunken stupor. The white men were not satisfied with getting the half dollars; they even whisked away the Indians' blankets.

Not every white man in Chicago was trying to get hold of the Indians' silver half dollars. The Reverend Jeremiah Porter did not only deplore the rowdy, sinful doings; he called his congregation together and prayed mightily. Whether this body included settlers who were turning a pretty penny in sharp trading history does not say, but it is quite likely. If we look at this affray with the eyes of Jeremiah Porter, we see the Indians filthy and untamed, yelling and whooping from the effects of gin, or sleeping bleary-eyed in the town ditches. The congregation shudders at this "desecration of the Sabbath" and is at one with the pastor, who takes his text from the Scripture: "And he kneeled down, and cried with a loud voice, Lord, lay not this sin to their charge." And while they kneel in prayer a lone Indian, detached from the rabble and curious about the ways of white men, lounges in the open door and unconcernedly twangs a Jew's harp.

But for Jeremiah Porter there was a silver lining. Some of the saloonkeepers, eager to garner the Indians' silver, had sent afar for extra cargoes of whisky. A schooner with fifteen barrels arrived at the mouth of the river. But so strong was the high wind that disturbed the lake those September days that scows were unable to bring the cargo around the bar before the Indian orgy was over.

In August, 1835, Chicago saw the final act in its Indian history. At that time about one thousand tribesmen assembled to collect their subsidies and were given blankets, tobacco, powder, rifles and money. They met in a council house on the north side, listened to harangues and staged brawls. On August 18th, eight hundred braves staged a howling war dance that frightened the spectators, many of whom were new to the West. John Dean Caton, in *The Last of the Illinois,* has left a description of that episode. The warriors, said he, were naked but for loincloths. They had painted red vermilion stripes edged with black points on their bodies; their hair was gathered in scalp locks; they wore hawk and eagle feathers and brandished tomahawks and war clubs and pounded with sticks on hollow vessels. From their north side camp they moved west over the old bridge at Kinzie Street, then south to the Lake Street bridge and crossing it with weird yells and howls, they gave their wildest demonstration in front of the Sauganash. Its second-story windows were filled with women. With bloodshot eyes and perspiring bodies, expressing "fierce anger, hate, revenge and cruelty," the Indians pranced forward, head and face thrown up and back arched, or squatted in their dance, making threatening gestures toward the white women in the windows. "It seemed as if we had a picture of hell itself before us and a carnival of the damned spirits there confined," wrote Caton. The scene was repeated at the Tremont, and then the procession broke up in front of Fort Dearborn.

It took several years to move the Indians west of

the Mississippi. Chicago's half-breed chiefs assisted in the evacuation. When they came to choose their residence most of them went into exile with the tribes. Billy Caldwell, who had many friends in the Chicago settlement, chose the lot of the Indian and turned his back on the acres given him on the North Branch of the Chicago. Medore (or Medard) B. Beaubien, son of John B. Beaubien and an Indian woman, and married to the daughter of Chief Laframboise, said, "I would rather be a big Indian than a little white man." We are tempted to look on this as an expression of loyalty to the simple, though unwashed, sons of the forest, did we not know that it had paid these men in cold cash to follow the red man's trail.

Not all the Indians left for good. Alexander Robinson, called Chechepinqua, became a sort of grand old man of the Indian days, surviving until 1872, when he is supposed to have reached the hoary age of one hundred and ten. His conversion to temperance was one of the triumphs of the Chicago Temperance Society; in a spectacular gesture he confronted a whisky bottle as his deadly enemy and smashed it with a tomahawk. Unfortunately, there were other bottles at hand and he became a backslider. He lived on his acres on the Des Plaines, now perpetuated in the Chechepinqua forest preserve, and lies buried in the family graveyard near West Lawrence Avenue, now suitably marked by the authorities.

The lot of Shabonee, the Ottawa chief, who rode furiously to keep his tribe from joining Black Hawk, was less fortunate. Despite his services to the pioneers he was just a filthy old Indian to the homesteaders who overran his acres. It is said that once, in his old age, he tried to camp on land that had belonged to his tribe. The irate farmer who had plowed the lands saw him as a disorderly trespasser and ordered him to move on. Shabonee died in Morris, Illinois, in 1859, eighty-four years old. He had seen his people dispersed and knew that the eager, grasping white man had no time for the easygoing, hand-to-mouth life of the frontier.

PART FIVE

The Ditch That Made Chicago Grow

I

The Canal or the Railroad?

O N July 4, 1836, the town of Chicago, which had about four thousand people, not counting land speculators who were arriving like locusts, celebrated Independence Day in the fashion of the time, which was to be noisy and bibulous. Amid the booming of cannon and the firing of horse pistols the townspeople crowded aboard two small schooners and one small steamboat, the *George W. Dole,* which was to tow them, and moved up the river to the spot where the South Fork joins the South Branch, to see the first spade of earth turned for the new Illinois and Michigan Canal.

The southwest bank of this confluence was the place where the canal was to start and was called Canalport. On that day, and for many days thereafter, it was the center of national attention and the visual evidence of Chicago's commercial expansion. One hundred and five years later I stood as near the spot as I could without falling into the river. I could find no vestige of the land, no indication that a famous canal had ever existed there. Time and man had obliterated it.

From the land where the spade was turned the

crowd could see, not far to the west, the head of navigation of the Chicago and the spot, presumably, where Father Marquette had passed his arduous winter. There, too, was the beginning of the portage and the eastern end of Mud Lake, which the canal was to displace as a route of travel. The crowd had no doubt that it would be the road to wealth. They had come from miles around, on foot, on horseback and in cumbersome farm wagons. Among them were merchants who hoped to sell more flour, tools and lumber; boatmen who hired out heavy draft horses to pull barges; land lawyers who were piling up as much as $500 a day in fees.

It was a great day, filled with the promise of rich pickings. Fifty years later men who were now old settlers recalled, with glee, a minor incident of the celebration. As the crowds refreshed themselves at the clear waters of a spring someone poured whisky and lemons into the pool. For years the veterans caressed their memories of those Pierian waters.

Most emphatically Chicago wanted the canal, but the original impetus to build it came long before there was a settlement, and later the money came from elsewhere. From the days of Marquette, Jolliet, La Salle and Tonty in the seventeenth century men talked about cutting a waterway through the land between the Des Plaines and the Chicago and thus overcoming the long land haul. In the dawn of the nineteenth century the young republic caught the canal-building fever and called the route through the Chicago Portage one of the keys of the continent, necessary to connect the Great Lakes with the Gulf of Mexico. While the early French traders valued it as a means of getting their furs to market, the early American strategists saw it as a military necessity.

Washington officials had debated the uses of the canal ever since Secretary Albert Gallatin of the Treasury Department recommended it in 1808. The Indian treaty of August 24, 1816, was specifically drawn with this water route in mind, for it extinguished all Indian titles to land ten miles north and ten miles south of the Chicago and by going as far west as the Fox and Illinois rivers covered also the portage. Major Stephen H. Long reported to the War Department in 1818 that the canal could draw water from the Des Plaines. When Illinois was made a state in 1818 its boundary was moved from the bend of the lake to a point ten miles north, so that the outlet of the canal and its harbor at the mouth of the Chicago might be within the confines of the state that owned the canal. Governor Shadrach Bond proposed the canal to the State Assembly. Military judgment also favored the canal and John C. Calhoun, secretary of war, recommended it against the judgment of President Monroe. In that year two engineers, Graham and Philips, carried their surveying chains over the canal route and recommended that the canal be fed by water from Lake Michigan. In 1822 Congress authorized the canal, giving its route and ninety feet of way on each side from the public lands.

This was good news to the pioneers, but they had no money. The public land, however, was vast in extent. They asked Congress to give them land to sell, for they thought the canal might cost over $600,000—perhaps as much as $700,000. Their estimate was based on the first survey of the route by Justus Post and René Paul in 1824. It was far too modest. In 1827 the government authorized the sale of every alternate section of the public land. In 1830 the sales started, with disappointing results.

J. M. Bucklin, an engineer with canal experience, tried to determine where a canal with a depth of four and a half feet would get its water. He saw two possibilities—either to draw it from Lake Michigan by way of the Chicago, after lowering the bed of the canal below that of the river at Summit, or from the Calamic, now Calumet, by way of a swamp with an unwieldy name. Ausogananashkee Swamp the pioneers called it, but their descendants have made short work of it; they call it the Sag. The Chicago River plan, cutting through rock, would cost $1,500,000; the Calumet plan, $160,-000, for the stretch of eighteen miles; the advantage was obviously with the Sag.

Suddenly a new obstacle appeared—the railroad. News of it flew across the country with the wind. The eagerness with which backwoodsmen and prairie farmers accepted its possibilities, without ever having seen it in action, suggests the readiness for new devices in a fluid society. Here, too, was the love for invention. In 1831 only a few primitive railroads were running on the Atlantic seaboard. Few pioneers in Illinois had ever heard a locomotive whistle. Yet in that year the General Assembly instructed the canal commissioners to find out from their engineer "whether the construction of a railroad is not preferable or will be of more public utility than a canal."

Only a few months before, the canal commissioners had described the possibilities of Chicago to the legislature, advocating the "construction of a safe harbor at the mouth of the Chicago River." They said the town possessed many advantages; it occupied "the only eligible site for a town on the Lake shore, within the limits of Illinois, surrounded by a beautiful champaign fertile country, surpassed by none in the richness of its products, and from the long experience of its inhabitants, is decidedly healthy. Its prominence in a commercial point of view has already prompted merchants from the northeastern part of the state and the northwestern part of Indiana to take their produce to Chicago, ship for Detroit, Buffalo and New York, and return by the same route, as the safest and cheapest." The shipper saved $1.25 per hundred weight in costs and gained ten days in time. "The circumstance of Chicago being located at the head of the contemplated canal will make it the future depot of all the surplus products of the country on the Illinois river and its tributaries."

Chicago shippers did not have the railroad fever. To them water routes meant prosperity; the railroad was superfluous and got no support. The canal meant rising prices for land. Vaguely across the years come echoes of the fears of men who wagered everything on the roseate promise of the canal. They must have shaken in their knee-top boots when the legislators began to say, "Maybe we ought to use that money to build a railroad."

Bucklin, the engineer, was realistic. He took several years to study comparative costs and routes and in 1833 reported in favor of the railroad, which would cost $1,000,000, where the canal would cost $4,000,000. The drought of 1830 convinced him that the waters of the Des Plaines and the Calumet would not be sufficient in dry seasons. There also were leakage and surface evaporation to take into account.

A railroad could run from the Forks of the Chicago, thirteen miles straight southwest along the north end of the portage to Laughton's Ford on the Des Plaines, then proceed along the right bank of the river to the Illinois. His explanation shows how primitive early railroad building was. He suggested a single track of iron rails resting on stone sills, and advised steam power instead of horses because horses's hoofs spread the roadbed and affected the rails. Governor John Reynolds had a horse-drawn railroad, six miles long, carrying coal from his mines near East St. Louis, the first in Illinois.

You would have expected the canal commission to support the canal, but actually it advised the legislature to build the railroad. The state dismissed the commissioners and asked the government if it could use the canal money for railroad purposes; Congress agreed. For several years nothing happened in the legislature, but in Chicago trade grew so rapidly that merchants began to clamor more loudly for their canal.

Before the canal came, heavy wagons hauled farm products into town, while cattle and hogs were driven in on foot, often from long distances. In 1833, for instance, Gurdon Saltonstall Hubbard, whose name recalls the Gurdon Saltonstall who located Yale University in New Haven, drove in three hundred hogs for packing. Cattle arrived daily; in the season of 1842-43 Archibald Clybourn, who had established his packing plant on the North Branch, packed nearly three thousand head of cattle for shipment to Buffalo.

The rich soil of Illinois started producing so rapidly that by 1842 the Chicago market was glutted with farm products and farmers began their perennial complaint that they weren't getting enough for their wares. Chickens sold for 5 cents each; eggs were 4 to 5 cents a dozen; potatoes 10 cents a bushel; flour was $3 a barrel; lard, $3.50 for 100 pounds. It is difficult to estimate what these amounts, paid in a frontier community where money was scarce, would represent today, but the dislocation is obvious and has persisted for one hundred years.

To get to the Chicago market farmers traveled many weary miles in lumber wagons and prairie schooners. Farmers from the southern part of the state brought apples, butter, hams and bacon, and other farm supplies. Often they traveled hundreds of miles to reach the market, camping along the trail, doing their own cooking. They bought coffee, salt and cloth for their own use. The prairie schooner was a familiar sight at Chicago up to the time of the coming of the railroad in 1852. When these covered wagons carried heavy loads they were often hauled by five or six yokes of oxen; the drivers referred to themselves as "the crew" and when they got ready to return home they "set sail."

This expansion of trade in Chicago made better transportation an immediate necessity. It became evident that the canal was the sensible project. By 1835 the state officials agreed; a new commission was appointed and a public loan of $500,000 authorized. In June, 1836, contracts were let for the first section, the Summit division, a cut providing a canal 60 feet wide at the top, 36 feet wide at the bottom, and 6 feet deep.

The digging of the canal called for backbreaking labor by brawny men. The engineers advertised for shovels, carts and barrows and teamsters with wagons. In 1836, 350 laborers were hired and first were put to work building shanties for them to live in. By the end of 1838 over 2,000 men were shoveling dirt along the Canal. At first raw labor was scarce; the contractors, who had expected to pay $20 to $26 a month, soon were offering $40 a month per man and $80 per yoke of oxen. Farm boys from New England, strong fellows who had worked on the Erie Canal in York State, immigrants from Ireland just off the boat and workmen hired in Canada arrived to dig the ditch. In a few years the news spread and the canal attracted so many laborers that wages dropped to $16 per man and $45 per yoke of oxen. But every summer the canal had men on the sick list, for the miasma of the bottom lands and the mosquitoes brought fever in their train and canal digging became known as an unhealthy job.

All along the route of the canal and through the valley of the Illinois men began building mills of stone and wood and hammering together runways for the water. Mills that our generation considers picturesque in ruin were needed for prosaic jobs—to grind meal and cut lumber. Every hamlet that had access to water power built a mill and soon this busy institution of a more self-sufficient economy was clanking away by dams and pools. Listed among the factories of Chicago in 1846 was one that made French burr millstones—a task long since buried in limbo. When the state appealed in 1843 to the London bondholders for a new loan to complete the canal, it estimated that the canal would drive two hundred and twenty millstones of four and a half feet in diameter, and if water power were sold at a yearly rental of $500 per run the annual returns would yield $66,000, sufficient to pay the interest on $1,100,-000 of the canal debt.

After the canal was begun the state got a foretaste of its actual cost. Estimates had to be revised upward again and again. At times canal lots sold rapidly; at other times they found no market. When the land boom collapsed in the financial panic of 1837, the ubiquitous speculator lost his shirt. The state suspended specie payments. Canal contractors had to issue orders for payments and use them as currency. In a few years the canal debt was over $4,000,000 and the state was figuring on potential assets—timber above the earth, lots on the surface, coal and stone beneath the earth. It placed great reliance on its 230,476 acres of public land, which it hoped to sell at $10 an acre, if the customers came.

Soon the engineers were saying that it would cost $8,000,000 to complete the canal and clear the Chicago River. But on July 4, 1836, Chicago said, "Hang the cost!" The canal was on its way.

2

Chicago Meets a New Member
of Congress

In ten years the whole shipping situation in Chicago changed. From a village where wild speculation in land lots attracted the gamblers of 1836, Chicago became, by 1847, a big depot for imports and exports. In 1836, when the canal was begun, tools, farm implements and supplies valued at over $300,000 reached the port of Chicago, but the exports were only $1,000.64. By 1842 this disproportion had been righted; imports were valued at over $659,000 and exports at over $664,000.

Thus, before any possible use could be made of the canal, Chicago had become an important shipping center. Enormous quantities of wheat, lard and tobacco were being loaded on lake vessels. Lead from the mines at Galena, carried overland in wagons, was reaching Chicago. Maple sugar, which the French explorer Joutel had found near the Chicago in 1688, was now being shipped east. But, although sawmills were operating all over Illinois, Chicago was still importing huge quantities of cut lumber, clapboards and shingles by sailing vessels from the northern woods. And in 1843, when Chicago had 7,580 inhabitants, the town imported 2,-585 barrels of whisky.

The harbor was crowded with brigs, schooners and propeller barges, called propellers for short. A vast traffic was developing on the Great Lakes, where seven hundred steamships were active by 1847. Vessels had to anchor outside of the Chicago because of the danger of being thrown on the beach, and much of the unloading was done by lighters. The federal appropriation of $25,000 in 1833 had sufficed to cut the sandbar and build two 500-foot piers, but the river kept filling up and the piers were inadequate. Ships needed protection from storms in port.

As the shovel of the diggers tackled the final miles of the new canal and the prospect of a vast increase in commerce confronted Chicago, the merchants became vociferous in their demands for harbor improvement. But their arguments were heard with little enthusiasm in far-off Washington, where numerous eastern senators and representatives had home ports with similar needs. The River and Harbor Appropriations bill already went deep into the pork barrel. President Monroe, who had been a friend of frontier development, had signed the first lake harbor bill, but in 1846 President Polk vetoed the harbor bill as "comparatively unimportant." He was conserving money for the Mexican campaign.

His act was a challenge to the Chicago shippers to make their wants heard. The city now had sixteen thousand inhabitants, all of whom would be described today as live wires. Conscious of the prairie, it called itself the Garden City, after its motto, *Urbs in Horto*. Its needs led to an important maneuver—the calling of the River and Harbor Convention for July 4, 5, 6 and 7, 1847. This was Chicago's invitation to the East to come and see. Invitations were sent to members of Congress and other influential men in the eastern states. Friends tried to induce Daniel Webster to come; they knew of his interest in the Middle West. In June, 1837, he had come to Chicago after buying a farm near Peoria; Chicago had paid a tribute to his eminence by sending a delegation of citizens to greet him as he reached the Des Plaines end of the Chicago Portage and escort him in state to the Lake House. Webster could not attend the convention, but promised to support the bill and declared that Chicago "is the seaport of Illinois." Thomas H. Benton wrote that the junction of two great systems of water would create "an incredible amount of commerce, destined to increase forever."

To accommodate the convention a sailmaker was hired to build a large tent and seats for four thousand were installed. Present and an active supporter of the appropriation was Horace Greeley, editor of the New York *Tribune* and called "the star speaker of the vast assembly" by one of the observers. He had come with a party of three hundred from New York, which included Thurlow Weed. So large was the crowd, and so inadequate were the hotels, that some delegates were provided with berths in ships on the river.

The River and Harbor Convention brought to Chicago a rising Illinois political leader—Abraham Lincoln, the only Whig representative from Illinois in Congress. The Chicago *Journal* wrote of him: "This is his first visit to the commercial emporium of the state and we have no doubt his visit will impress him more deeply, if possible, with the importance of, and inspire a higher zeal for, the great interests of river and harbor improvements. We expect much of him as representative in Congress, and we have no doubt our expectations will be more than realized, for never was reliance placed in a nobler heart and a sounder judgment. We know the banner he bears will never be sullied."

If this was actually the first visit of Lincoln to Chicago, it demonstrates how little Chicago had affected the political life of Illinois up to this time. Yet Lincoln, entering the State Assembly two years before the construction of the Illinois and Michigan Canal began, had been a consistent supporter of both canal and railroad projects, together with Stephen A. Douglas, and knew all the arguments for developing local improvements with federal money.

One of the strongest arguments against the appropriation of federal money for improvements on the Illinois River came from David Dudley Field of New York, who took the stand that any improvements inside a state should be paid for by the state. He was consistent in declaring that no federal money should be used to improve the Hudson above the port of entry. Lincoln was asked to reply to him. In his fifteen-minute speech he made a good impression. Greeley, seeing Lincoln for the first time, wrote his newspaper that he was "a tall specimen of an Illinoisan, just elected to Congress from the only Whig district in the state." This was the last time Greeley was to rely on the mails for his correspondence. In January, 1848, the telegraph came to Chicago.

FRINK & WALKER'S STAGE CONVEY

ASSENGERS UP "ARCHEY ROAD"

Within the year Lincoln was to repeat his argument on the floor of the House of Representatives. Rising on June 20, 1848, to criticize President Polk's veto of appropriations for internal improvements, Lincoln said:

"The driving of a pirate from the track of commerce on the broad ocean and the removing of a snag from its more narrow path in the Mississippi River can not, I think, be distinguished in principle." He declared that improvements on the Mississippi and its tributaries were next in importance to maintaining the navy and that the Illinois and Michigan Canal would be of general as well as local benefit. "Nothing is so local as not to be of some general benefit."

General Lewis Cass might have been expected to support harbor improvements, for he had been closely identified with the development of Chicago and the West. But he was now in national councils and opposed the harbor plans. In 1848 he was to be nominated by the Democrats for president on a platform that included opposition to federal support of internal improvements.

Most remarkable, as a portent, was the speech of Governor William Bebb of Ohio, whose remarks foreshadowed the industrial strife of the future. "Vain will be your canals and railroads, your river and harbor improvements," he warned, "if the condition of the toiling millions be not thereby or therewith sensibly ameliorated—if they shall still be constrained to delve twelve to fourteen hours per day for the bare necessaries of physical life." Bebb worked for the 8- to 10-hour day many years before the Knights of Labor, the Railroad

Brotherhoods, and the American Federation of Labor agitated this reform; many years before Eugene V. Debs ran the railroad strike for better wages and shorter hours.

Chicago put on a good show. All the delegates wore badges of different colors, Illinois choosing red, white and blue. The big event was the parade of July 5th, when marchers and floats urged the need of river improvement. To top the parade came an exhibition by the brave fire laddies in helmets, red shirts, high boots and spick-and-span apparatus filled with gleaming brass.

Long John Wentworth, mayor, representative in Congress, editor and orator, worked for harbor appropriations for years and tells an interesting anecdote of a meeting with Henry Clay in 1851. Senator Clay had supported the harbor appropriations bill and come from Washington to New York with Wentworth, in order to take a steamer to New Orleans. Wentworth suggested that the next time Clay went home he should travel by way of the Great Lakes. Clay replied, "I never go where the constitution does not go. Hence I must travel by salt water. Make your lakes constitutional. Keep up the war until your lake harbors get their deserved appropriations and then I will come out and see you."

3

When the Canal Was New

IT took twelve years to complete the Illinois and Michigan Canal, and when it opened, in 1848, Chicago had twenty thousand people. The officials clambered on board the canalboat *General Fry* and made the first trip from Lockport to Chicago on April 10th. But a few days later the canal served its real purpose, when the *General Thornton* passed the length of the canal, from La Salle to Chicago, with a cargo of sugar from New Orleans, bound for Buffalo. It seemed like the realization of the president's somewhat bombastic message of the December before, when he had declared for a waterway between the Atlantic and Pacific with the paradoxical slogan: "Rend America asunder and unite the binding sea."

Rates on the Canal at first were 6 cents a mile for passengers, 3½ cents a mile for freight and 3 cents a mile for coal. Lumber was charged one cent a mile per one thousand feet. But the articles listed for shipment contained some curious products of the West: wood ashes, beeswax, sumac, marble dust and ginseng. I have seen the berries of the ginseng plant, used for medicinal purposes, in the woods of Illinois, but I doubt that there is much marble dust being shipped today.

Soon the tolls began to clink into the cash box, and by the end of May the canal had taken in over $6,000; in July it was over $11,000, and in September over $21,000. The winter months were a loss and freshets on the rivers helped curtail the receipts; yet the canal earned $80,000 the first year and bettered that the second.

Without getting too deep into figures, we may observe the effect of the canal on Chicago as a "freight handler, stacker of wheat." In 1847 Chicago's imports and exports had been practically even, favoring imports that ran a little over $2,500,000; but in 1848 imports jumped to over $8,000,000 and exports suddenly reached $10,700,000. Here was proof of what the Chicago shippers had contended—that they needed the Canal to tap the interior. Ten years before Chicago had imported pork from Ohio at $10 a barrel; now it began exporting in tremendous quantities, and prairie-fatted beef that bore Chicago brands were soon in great demand in Liverpool and London, for the superiority that had come by careful curing.

Easterners with an eye to quick profits from land speculation were not all convinced, before the canal opened, that Chicago would sustain its mushroom growth. In 1843 a writer in Freeman Hunt's *Merchants Magazine* of New York City weighed the claims of four promising lake towns—Cleveland, Detroit, Chicago and Maumee, and asked "which of these will be greatest in 1890?" The answer was that, even though Detroit was the largest in 1843, "it does not seem to be as probable

that within 47 years it can even approximate, in population or wealth, to the comparatively old and well-
peopled territory that comes within the range of the
commercial influence of Maumee"! Maumee was the
terminal of a canal that now lies in ruins on the outskirts of Toledo. After the Illinois canal opened the
editor still stood pat. "The canal is not as productive
as anticipated," he wrote, "and the probability is that
it never will be."

In 1851, when Chicago's first railroad was organized, the canal had a warning of the competition that
was to blast its hopes and bring it to an end. But in the
1850's the railroads were not yet powerful enough to
throttle the canal; the country was growing too quickly,
producing too much, to hurt any one form of transportation. Products arrived in Chicago in three ways—
by canal, by railroad and by teams, and the last was far
from negligible.

Some of the allocations of products were curious.
Thus, the canal moved only a negligible quantity of
wheat in the early fifties, but of corn it moved two-
thirds of over three million bushels that came into Chicago, for the Illinois ran through the heart of the corn
region. Similarly, wool moved by canal far exceeded
that by trains or teams. Huge quantities of lumber were
shipped into the interior, for everybody was building,
and the mills of the north continued busy for a long
time supplying every form of cut lumber for the flat
prairie lands of central Illinois.

Chicago had a long time to wait for a railroad.
Although a survey for a line from North Dearborn
Street to the Des Plaines was made in 1837, it was 1851

before the Galena & Chicago Union started trains on the route that was to become the great Chicago & North Western in 1864. It was 1856 before the Illinois Central completed its "branch" to Chicago—the main line ran from Cairo to La Salle. Chicago did not invest in railroads in the days when the canal was supposed to be the key to its prosperity. Most of the railroad capital, not a part of subsidies, came from foreign investors. But a large share of the bond loans for the canal came from London, too.

Chicago was so engrossed in the canal project that it took no part in the early railroad construction. This coincided with the first digging on the canal. The Northern Cross Line, a segment of the Illinois Central, ran for 24 miles from the Illinois River at Meredosia to Jacksonville. Its first locomotive, shipped from the East by water, was lost en route and never recovered; the second, the Rogers, went by sailboat from New York to New Orleans, and then by steamboat up the Mississippi and Illinois rivers. It made its first trip in November, 1838, out of Meredosia. In 1842 the line was extended to Springfield, and by 1847, before Chicago's great hope, the canal, was opened, the Northern Cross had gone begging and was sold for $21,500. Rails also were used, with mule power, by Governor Reynolds for his coal railroad near East St. Louis and by Charles Collins for a four-mile railroad running out of Naples, Illinois. When the Galena & Chicago Union finally started running over its first eight miles in 1849, it was drawn by its first locomotive, the Pioneer, which had been built by Baldwin and reached the port of Chicago strapped on the deck of a Great Lakes brig.

In September, 1860, Albert Edward, Prince of
Wales, a smooth-faced youngster of good manners who
danced freely with democratic society and made himself agreeable everywhere, was taken by Mayor Wentworth to see one of the wonders of Chicago. It was the
great pumping station, the Hydraulic Works, that stood
on the neck of land, long since dredged out, where the
South Fork enters the Chicago. That machinery, which
one historian described as "a monstrous engine and a
powerful pump," impressed the Prince of Wales, and
well it might, for there it was pumping water out of
the Chicago into the canal.

Arthur Guthrie built the works, coming west in
1845 to design a device that would take water from
Lake Michigan out of the Chicago River so that the
canal might have enough, and his grandson, William
H. Dunn of Glencoe, who recalls many of the legends
of Chicago's beginnings, says these were the first works
ever erected for such a purpose. The big stone building
that housed the works was ready when the locks opened
in April, 1848. Ossian Guthrie, the engineer's son, ran
the works until 1871. In 1888 Chicago built a new
pumping station and a new lock for two boats, and the
station was operated until the Sanitary District opened
the new Drainage Canal in 1900.

The original canal divided into two branches, like a
Y, just before it came to what is now Ashland Avenue.
The North Branch was the main canal and had a lock
with gates and abutments of limestone. These gates
separated the waters of the canal from the South Fork
of the Chicago. The South Branch of the canal ran a
short distance east of the present Ashland Avenue and

stopped short of the South Fork; it was a dead end for barges that were loading or unloading goods.

The South Branch of the canal was on a line with the present Fuller Street, which was laid out in 1855. Running into Fuller is Lock Street, which stops short at the river. Originally a wagon road that ran north, along a terrain that for a few years became the village of Locks, it was lost when all the land east of it was dredged out to make the large turning basin where the South Fork joins the Chicago.

When barges were brought into the South Fork to enter the canal, the first set of gates was opened and the barge went into the lock; the gates were then closed and water was pumped into the lock to raise it to the level of the canal, which was a few feet higher than the Chicago River. In the early days horses and mules were used to tow barges and the ground was packed solid by their hoofs all along the route. Later tugboats came into use.

As soon as work began on the canal shacks sprang up along its route and big wooden barracks were hammered together for the laborers. Finally a line of shanties and frame houses stretched along the north bank of the lock canal and became known as the Levee. There were saloons, boardinghouses, grocery stores and stables and they took care of the wants of brawny men, teamsters, bargemen, tugboat crews, freight handlers. Biggest of the frame houses when the canal was opened was the Canal House, which for something like fifty years served as the center of canal life.

What a noisy, brawling crowd surged over this terrain more than ninety years ago! Mule skinners coming off the towpath; teamsters arriving with heavy loads, unhitching their horses and putting up at the Canal House; barges arriving with goods and passengers. Frink & Walker's stage standing by to convey passengers up Archer Road to Chicago's taverns. Boys hopping on and off canalboats, hooking a ride, to the accompaniment of noisy outbursts from the boatmen.

Here passengers embarked with mixed feelings of apprehension and delight on such "palatial" boats as the 1850 packet, *Queen of the Prairie,* which had a cabin 50 feet long, 9 feet wide and 7 feet high. When coupled with three other barges it was pulled along at the rate of six miles an hour by a steamboat or by horses on the towpath. It is said that the *Queen* could accommodate ninety passengers, but when we consider that nine feet is the width of the average living-room rug, and seven feet the height of the average basement, we suspect there was little comfort for ninety human beings, unless they were scattered through the three barges. For this dubious luxury they paid $4 per hundred miles, including meals. But the great drawback was the time, for it took 22 hours to proceed from Chicago to La Salle, a distance of 103 miles. No doubt this included long stops for unloading freight. Obviously the West did not grasp the meaning of the slogan for the new age that Dr. Bethune announced in his Phi Beta Kappa oration at Harvard in 1849: "Minutes, not miles; 'How long?' instead of 'How far?' "

These passengers must have suffered many discomforts, especially in the hot summer nights when the mosquitoes flourished. But the hardest lot was that of immigrants and homeseekers who had dared the long trip. Sometimes cholera broke out among them. The dead were hurriedly buried on the banks of the canal and when the boat returned to Canalport the captain read aloud the names of those who had died en route. The story of immigrant courage and stamina in the development of the continent is a record, not of high, reckless adventure, but of dogged patience and persistence. It has never found its proper historian.

4

Bridgeport and Archey Road

ONE sunny Sunday afternoon I was wandering about the Ashland Avenue district below the river, looking for vestiges of the canal terminal, when I came upon the Archer Avenue bridge. This venerable structure, one of the old-fashioned swing type that must have been erected about the time the canal was filled in, crosses the South Fork about a block east of the point where Archer and Ashland avenues intersect. I walked, as usual, into the bridgetender's house. There was no reason for suspecting that tugs and barges would be whistling for the bridge that day, but the bridgetender was on the job, talking with two friends from the neighborhood. His house was small, but cozy, and his brass electric switch had a high polish, showing long and frequent usage.

I asked about the canal and Bridgeport, and he warmed up to the subject. For he had grown up in the neighborhood, and the two men with him belonged there too. Bridgeport was the Irish village that grew up on both sides of Archer Avenue, and became larger and more populous with the years. It is still there—just

across the waters of the South Fork, opposite the site of
the canal, which was Canalport. Bridgeport is bounded
by the river on north and west, by West 31st Street on
the south and by Halsted Street on the east. Its individ-
uality is apparent at a glance, for its streets have never
conformed to the directions followed by Chicago streets,
which run toward the cardinal points of the compass.
Bridgeport's streets point northeast and southwest and
the reason is nobody's business. It was a huddle of houses
when the canal workers arrived, became a village in
1845 and in 1860 was swallowed by Chicago, but never
digested.

The bridgetender had vivid memories of the old
days when all Bridgeport was Irish and good for a solid
Democratic vote. But things are changing now, he said,
just as the whole countryside has been changed by the
dredges in the river. A lot of the old Irish families have
moved away and Poles are taking their places. The
bridgetender pointed down the fork to where the big
basin joined the Chicago and to the huge railway bridges
that carried trains where once the canal ran. "They tore
out all sorts of old houses to build those bridges," he
said.

"Wasn't that where Piper's icehouse stood?" inquired one of the men, pointing to the abutment of an
enormous railroad bridge.

"It was," he replied: "I remember it as a boy. That's
all gone now. But if you're looking around, there's still
one of the old canal houses standing. This man lives in it.
We call it the statehouse."

That, of course, was something to see, so I set out
to look for it. When I found it, I saw at once that it

was a survivor from another age. For it stood where nobody would think of erecting a house today. It was a two-story brick dwelling, with the colors of brick long since turned to the smudged clay of the original soil. Slabs of limestone, now yellow like old parchment, had been used for doorsteps, foundations and window sills. There were sheds, a woodpile and a kitchen garden. Beside it lay the outlines of a rock foundation where another house had stood.

The significant thing about it was its location. It stood on the low ground east of Ashland Avenue, on a bit of bank this side of the South Fork. It faced toward Archer Avenue. On the extreme south of the spit of land on which it stood were the remains of a slip, with some broken piling. And this, of course, was the original level of the canal. The house had faced one of the old roads. It was all that survived of the old terminal except memories and the records in the canal office at Lockport.

Archer Avenue, first called Archer Road, was a wagon route before the canal came. The Irish used to call it Archey Road. It was one of the two original highways that ran straight southwest from Chicago on the high ridges not usually covered by water, and was planned in April, 1831. The other was Ogden Avenue, which led from Chicago north of the river to Laughton's Ford on the Des Plaines and was the main highway for stagecoaches to Ottawa and the prairie towns.

Finley Peter Dunne's famous Irishman, Martin Dooley, was nourished down Bridgeport way. Dunne's original inspiration was a saloonkeeper on Dearborn Street named James McGarry, but when Dunne began introducing Mr. Dooley into his sketches in 1893 he hunted up John J. McKenna, a Bridgeport politician, and made the rounds of the Bridgeport saloons with him, listening to the brogue. McKenna was a unique character, in that his political prestige was based on the fact that he was the only Republican leader in Irish Bridgeport. In one of Dunne's stories a character says: "Did ye ever go to McKenna's? No? Well, sir, of all th' places! Ye go down Madison street to Halsted, an' down Halsted to Archey road an' out Archey road past packin' houses an' rollin' mills an' th' Healy slew an' potato patches till ye get to McKenna's."

The big Chicago thoroughfares that try to penetrate Bridgeport are Throop and Loomis, which cross the Chicago on bridges and almost immediately get terribly befuddled. Throop turns southeast and loses itself; the Throop that emerges south of 31st Street is about seven blocks out of line. Loomis is another headache for any postman just transferred from a place where streets know where they are going. All around are streets with old Irish names: Quinn, Farrell, Keeley, Bonfield, Grattan, Crowell, Haynes, Arch, and even the swamp at the east is Healy Slough. The Keeleys gave Chicago a police chief; Bonfield was named for the family of John Bonfield, who was captain of police at the Haymarket the night the bomb was thrown in 1886; William H. Dunn says that from 1840 on houses went up for families with the good old names of Healy, Sheehan, McKenna, Mooney, Ryan, Boone, Foley— names long since scattered to the environs as their sons grasped the dynamic opportunities of Chicago.

Let us pause to recall Bubbly Creek, for its site is

famous, its reputation notorious, in Chicago history. It has been denounced in countless editorials, sneered at in unnumbered aldermanic speeches, and ridiculed in many ironic sallies by newspaper wits. Bubbly Creek was the derisive name given for fifty years to the Stock Yards Slip—actually the East Fork of the South Fork, beginning just below West 37th Street in the Stock Yards area. If we cared to proceed up the malodorous South Fork, we would pass on the right bank a little distance above the Archer Avenue bridge a plant used by Armour—the main Armour plants, however, are more than ten blocks south. There would follow other plants closely packed together, built of brick so weathered that all the color has gone out of them. Thence the fork turns west into the heart of that great labyrinth of industry—the Central Manufacturing District. But just before it turns we would observe a channel leading straight south, obstructed by a dock wall, and that the channel beyond was being filled in. That channel was Bubbly Creek. Filled with greasy sewage poured into its waters indiscriminately by the Stock Yards plants on its banks, Bubbly Creek was said to have a scum so thick that a steer could walk on it without sinking. As for the odors, these were closely allied, yet men worked in this atmosphere, processing the meat of the nation, and half a century passed before the city, the Union Stock Yards plants, the trustees of the Central Manufacturing District and the Sanitary District co-operated to "abate the nuisance." Now the Racine Avenue pumping station of the Sanitary District speeds the outflow through its sewers and Bubbly Creek moves into limbo, whence none will care to call it back.

The fortunes of the canal rose and fell. Before the railroads came it was on the highroad to prosperity; after the 1860's it fought a losing battle. In the 1890's it was slowly giving up its life. In those forlorn days after the World's Fair, George Ade was writing a daily feature about Chicago, "Stories of the Streets and of the Town," for the Chicago *Record* and John T. Mc-Cutcheon was illustrating it. They visited the old canal, which still had sixty barges plying between Chicago and the Illinois but was now something of a relic. The Canal House was sagging. The Bridgeport pumps were emptying "black water" into the canal. The mark of decay was on the great hope of the West.

"The Canal House," wrote George Ade, "leans wearily forward on its supports. Its windows have been torn out and the front doors are nailed over with boards. The warped clapboards have been worn black by wind and weather. Nothing is needed to complete the ruin. Only a few years ago a man reopened the front room as a saloon. The old Canal boats creeping by were surprised to find a new gilt sign on the dingy front, but they were not surprised when one day it disappeared and the boards were again nailed over the front. Every square-fronted building in the row stands vacant, with rough boards nailed against the doors and windows. Sometimes for half a day at one time no living thing is seen along the deserted water front. The greatness of the levee lives only in memory."

The result for which so many men had hoped and slaved—to make possible the passage of boats from the Great Lakes to the Gulf of Mexico—seemed won when a boat loaded with sugar from New Orleans came up the Mississippi and Illinois rivers and reached Chicago by way of the canal and the river on April 23, 1848. But the depth of six feet was inadequate for any but shallow barges. Soon barge captains and shippers were complaining that the canal was not big enough to carry goods at a profit. Presently their complaints were being taken to the state legislature. The canal needed more depth—more water. It was impossible to pump all the water—it would have to reach the canal by gravity flow from the Chicago. On February 15, 1865, after the canal had been in operation for seventeen years, the State Assembly granted permission to the Board of Public Works of Chicago to lower the bed of the canal at Summit and dredge the river to reverse the current and force sewage down to the Illinois.

This operation was completed July 18, 1871, when the river's current was reversed and its mouth became its source. The chief reason for providing this new flow of water in the canal was not to help traffic but to expedite the flow of Chicago's sewage. Thus the canal, the dream of men of two centuries, began a task that could only be considered ignominious for an artery of commerce. But the needs of mankind change, and man uses nature to his best advantage. Whatever the character of the new service, it was highly important. It had taken six years to prepare the canal for it and cost $3,000,000. But that was just the beginning of another expensive chapter in the history of the canal. For in ten years the canal was judged a menace to the general health and completely inadequate for its huge task and once more engineers began to plan how to make it double its work for mankind.

PART SIX

The Prairie Names a President

I

Political Excitement on the Chicago

In May, 1860, the loudest yell that anyone had ever heard coming from human beings, rent the air on the banks of the Chicago River. The river had never known anything like the shouting, cannonading and beating of drums let loose at the Forks. Not since the Indians in their mad snake dance shrieked their barbarous farewell twenty-five years before on that very spot had there been such unholy noise—especially on the open lot on the river's bank at Lake and Market streets. Across the road, on the southeast corner, vacant since the Sauganash tavern burned down, stood a new wooden structure, an immense barn of yellow pine, adorned with bunting. Outside was a cannon that barked at intervals. Up and down Lake Street marched bands in gay uniforms with chicken feathers in their hats. But the yelling came, not from the Indians, but from civilized whites—the common people who were nominating Abraham Lincoln for the presidency.

Nobody knew how many strangers jammed the dusty streets of Chicago the week of May 13, 1860. Chicago had 112,000 people now; some said 45,000 visitors made the walls bulge this historic week. They came from Maine, Boston, New York and Philadelphia in special trains at half the regular fare; Boston men paid $35 and New York men $33 for the trip. They came in lumbering democrat wagons from the farm country, on horseback and even on foot. Mixed with the crowds were the immigrants who were regularly arriving from northern Europe, some on their way to the Mormon empire.

Politicians and hangers-on packed the forty-two hotels that Chicago had advertised and found some of them improvised from boarding houses. They paid $2 to $2.50 in the first-class houses, which included meals. The big hotels were as good as those of the East and included the Tremont, the Richmond, the Briggs, the Sherman and the Hyde Park. Several had furniture of solid oak and walnut and dressers with marble tops, and water, aided by a hand pump, flowed into zinc bathtubs. As early as 1843 the City Hotel had advertised "warm, cold and shower baths always in readiness," but no one has recorded his experiences with them.

Chicago had been preparing for the Republican National Convention for weeks. The Stephen A. Douglas Democrats had made a tremendous racket with a cannon on May 7th; the Republicans now prepared to outdo them with noise. They held the Chicago Light Artillery ready for salutes, arranged for rockets and flares, and urged a general illumination of houses with lanterns, especially on Michigan Avenue, which could be seen from trains on the pier—the stilts that carried the tracks of the Illinois Central to the station at Ran-

dolph Street. When the special train from Buffalo arrived with fifteen hundred from New York and the
East, it slowed down and took twelve minutes to pass
up the long pier, so that the visitors might be impressed
by the fireworks; rockets saluted it at Jackson Avenue
and guns boomed for it at the station. Chicago's Republicans belonged to a young, fighting party; they were
energetic and fired with enthusiasm. They paraded on
the slightest provocation. The Young Men's Republican
Club, the Swedish Republican Club, the Cameron-Lin-
coln Club, the Mechanics' and Workingmen's Club were
some of the best, but the Wide Awakes, part of a nation-
wide organization that had been born in New York in
1854, made the biggest demonstrations.

With banners flying, bands playing and voices
hoarse from shouting, the delegations from the East
converged on Chicago. Cities were still in the making
and rival citizens tried to shout one another down with
bombastic claims to civic greatness. Whenever a train
stopped the delegates boasted bibulously of their native
attractions. Gilmore's Brass Band of Boston came with
the New England men on the Michigan Central. The
Philadelphia Cornet Band came with the Pennsylvanians.
The Maine delegation arrived triumphantly on the
Grand Trunk, having "annihilated space," as their song
said, in two days, moving with the speed of the sun
"from the Gem of the Sea to the Queen of the Lakes."
These lines were sung to the tune of "The Star-Spangled
Banner," which challenged the bards of several states to
produce new verses. To its high notes the New Yorkers
sang, or tried to sing, these inelastic lines:

Our labors shall cease, when New York's foremost son,
The ablest of statesmen, the purest of men
Shall proclaim to the nation our victory won . . .

Whereas the Pittsburgh men, raising their voices
to the same tune, asked in a rush of patriotic fervor:

Oh, men of the land! What is North? What is South?
One mother has nurtured us, tenderly, kindly . . .

Horace Greeley was at the Tremont, shuffling
about as if he wore carpet slippers; hobnobbing with
politicians in his double task of getting the news for the
New York *Tribune* and putting William H. Seward
and Simon Cameron on the sidelines. This strategy
played into the hands of the Lincoln managers, but as
he was supporting Edward Bates they did not consider
him an ally. In 1858 Greeley thought Lincoln's views
disruptive and prodded Elihu Washburne to get Lincoln to withdraw from the senatorial race before the
nomination; Greeley's views and Seward's had been
identical and their interference in Illinois politics had
made bad blood in Chicago. Greeley failed to get a place
on the New York delegation and qualified as a delegate
from Oregon, at the other end of the United States.
Now he was in mortal fear that Seward would be nominated. He knew New York methods and thought
Seward's men had gained the inside track at Chicago.
These were the days when a man could be individual in dress; he was recognized the rest of his life
by the cut of his coat or the trim of his beard. Greeley's
whiskers were familiar to everyone, but this time his
favorite white coat was missing. The reason, which the

New Yorkers were quick to circulate, started people chuckling behind his back. It was related that Greeley's 12-year-old daughter professed to be a medium, who received presents from spirits in her room, even when doors and windows had been securely locked. Greeley was skeptical but agreed to test the supernatural by exchanging rooms with her for a night. Bolting the door and putting bricks up the chimney hole he sat down under the blazing gas jet to read his favorite newspaper.

He was wearing his white coat. During the night he fell asleep. When he awoke at dawn he found that he had been disrobed and that his white coat was gone. It had not been found prior to his departure for Chicago. The playful crowds snickered as he shuffled in and out. One afternoon the snickers rose to a gale of laughter as he made his way through the Tremont. On his back hung a silk Seward badge that someone had pinned on him.

New York was solidly behind its governor and senator, William H. Seward, and confidently expected to nominate and elect him because of the split in Democratic ranks over the slavery issue. The Democrats thought he would pack the Supreme Court with "Black Republicans," although his policy was conciliatory. Known as Old Irrepressible, his supporters were called Irrepressibles; the nickname derived from his speech at Rochester, two years before, in which he said that there was an irrepressible conflict between slave holding and free labor. With the country's love for nicknames this word had been applied to him at once.

William M. Evarts had come with the Seward delegation and Thurlow Weed, known as "Lord Thur-

low," was pulling the wires. The delegation was booked
at the Richmond House at Michigan Avenue and South
Water Street, where it held high jinks. It boasted a
band, decked out with epaulets, gold braid and scarlet
and white feathers in the caps. The spectacle of the band
leading the delegates to the convention in the dust of
Chicago's streets and playing the current ballad, "Oh,
isn't he a darling?" has been preserved. The New
Yorkers adopted a heartiness that surprised the bluff
Westerners; they slapped men on the back with a loud
"How are you?" and declared they were not going to
be "too damned virtuous." They were said to have
"oceans of money," which they spent on entertainment.

The other candidates were in a trading position.
Simon Cameron, a machine politician, was trying to ride
into power with Pennsylvania's support, the main aim of
which was opposition to Seward. Salmon P. Chase had
Ohio push his claims; he was certain that he was of
presidential stature; even more certain was his daughter.
The Illinois Republicans were not unaware of the pos-
sibility of capturing the votes of both states. They were
putting the old log-cabin spirit into their fight, and
although by no means certain of victory were in no
mood to accept defeat before the battle.

2.

Abe Lincoln Becomes the
Rail-Splitter Candidate

OLD ABE had a new nickname; he was now the
"rail-splitter candidate." It was only a week old, for it
was applied to him for the first time when the Republicans of Illinois endorsed him for the nomination
at their state convention in Decatur on May 9th. For
this Richard J. Oglesby was responsible. Dick Oglesby,
like Lincoln a farm boy and a Springfield law student,
had cast about for some homely anecdote to build up
for a popular slogan. When John Hanks told him that
he used to split rails for farm fences with Abe thirty
years before, Dick had an idea. He took John out to
the farm near Decatur where Hanks pointed to the
rails. Oglesby tied two under his buggy, brought them
home and hid them in his barn, as if they were secret
evidence.

When the convention met Oglesby dramatized the
rails. Two men marched down the aisle holding aloft a
rail apiece with a big banner between them. The banner
announced that the rails were two of thirty-thousand

split by Hanks and Lincoln in 1830, and called Lincoln the rail-splitter candidate. They seem to have surprised Lincoln as much as anyone. He looked them over and admitted that he might have split them; at least they looked like rails that he had split. That started the rail business. Now there were two in the Tremont Hotel, the object of studied interest by men who had seen fence rails all their lives. The office of the Chicago *Press and Tribune* had four of them. Within a week after the Chicago convention Decatur's farmers had a new by-product. They were expressing old fence rails to Republican headquarters all over the country at $10 a pair. The fence dwindled but the supply never really gave out. Moreover printers were advertising for one thousand agents to sell lithographs of Lincoln splitting rails. William H. Seward had never split rails. He had no calluses on his hands. He wore long coattails and took snuff. Malicious characters said snuff had ruined his voice.

The lanky candidate of the Illinois Republicans did not come to Chicago for the convention. He moved between his house, his law office and the editorial sanctum of the *Illinois State Journal* in Springfield. Sometimes he played handball at fives, knocking a ball against a brick wall. William H. Herndon, who was in Chicago, said Lincoln played ball and drank beer with the boys, that he "hoped and despaired" in Springfield. But the feverish campaigning in Chicago left Lincoln undisturbed.

When a friend commiserated him in 1858 on his defeat by Douglas for the Senate, he replied, "You are 'feeling like hell yet.' Quit that—you will soon feel better." To Jesse W. Fell he remarked, less than a year before the convention, "I do not think myself fit for the presidency." During the debates with Douglas he told Henry Villard that Mary wanted him to become senator and president, and chuckled at the thought of "such a sucker as me" becoming president. While the politicians were pulling wires he remained aloof and said, "Make no contracts that will bind me." The *Press and Tribune*, edited by Joseph Medill, Lincoln's champion, declared he had "no pledges to redeem, no promises to make good." But Lincoln's managers didn't let that stand in the way of votes they needed.

Lincoln came to Chicago on legal business growing out of the vagaries of the Chicago River—the famous "sand-bar case"—on March 23, 1860, and this seems to have been his last appearance there before the convention met. At that time he stayed at the Tremont House and sat for Leonard Volk, the sculptor. W. S. Johnson had brought suit against William Jones and Sylvester Marsh in the United States Circuit Court to determine title to a tract of land north of the north pier of Chicago harbor, developed by an accretion of sand after the pier was built. Lincoln was one of the lawyers for the defense. In order to establish the shore line of the Kinzie addition in 1833 John H. Kinzie was called to testify, and Isaac N. Arnold, counsel for plaintiff, asked, "How long have you resided in Chicago?" Lincoln interjected, "I believe he is common law here, as one who dates back to the time whereof the memory of man runneth not to the contrary."

It was also on this occasion that Lincoln comforted the wounded feelings of his client, Jones, with

"Don't be discouraged, Mr. Jones; there are those who are better lawyers than gentlemen." Arnold was a brilliant man, an author of parts; he had been associated with Kinzie in antislavery agitation and was one of Lincoln's strong Republican supporters. After the hearing Arnold gave a dinner to the judge, Thomas Drummond, and counsel, and Stephen A. Douglas is said to have been a guest. It was at this dinner that, amid good-natured raillery, Lincoln and Douglas joined in drinking the toast: "May Illinois furnish the next president." Within a few weeks both men were nominees for the presidency.

It is a strange tale, the political history of Lincoln and Douglas, who disagreed over the slavery issue and yet were not very far apart. Both spoke often in Chicago, and when Douglas opened his campaign for the Senate in July, 1858, in front of the Tremont House, Lincoln spoke in reply the next night. Douglas had come to Jacksonville in 1833 and was admitted to the bar in 1834, the year Lincoln was elected to the state legislature. Lincoln took his seat in 1835; Douglas entered it in 1836, and one of the few acts on which both agreed was the support of the Illinois and Michigan Canal and the charter of the Illinois Central Railroad, of which Douglas became chief promoter. In 1837 Lincoln voted for the completion of the canal to Peru and for thirteen hundred miles of railroad. Douglas reached the national House of Representatives in 1843; Lincoln, in December, 1847.

The Lincoln supporters were the most ambitious, active and sleepless men at the convention. Guided by the astute advice of David Davis, Leonard Swett, O. H.

Browning, Norman B. Judd, and having an ardent spokesman in young Joseph Medill, editor of the Chicago *Press and Tribune*, they glued themselves to the coat lapels of delegates, whether friendly or hostile. They had been agitating the nomination of Abraham Lincoln for two years and lining up delegates whenever they were visible. Encouraged by the troubles Stephen A. Douglas was having to keep the southern Democrats from splitting apart, the Republicans had great hopes of winning the 1860 campaign, and the Lincoln supporters had hopes of winning the East. But their opposition was strong. They had to defeat the formidable strength of William H. Seward of New York and hurdle the obstacles raised by such favorite sons as Simon Cameron of Pennsylvania and Salmon P. Chase of Ohio. Getting Chicago named as the convention city was a Lincoln victory engineered by Norman B. Judd.

3

Making History in the Wigwam

FOR Chicago the hammering that went on in the Wigwam was sweet music. The house was hastily constructed, but served its purpose. The word "wigwam" was an old political term; the tribe of Tammany used it in New York. It had been applied also to the tent under which the Decatur convention met. The Chicago Wigwam had a frontage of 100 feet on Lake Street and 180 on Market, with three double doors, 20 feet wide, on Market Street, facing the open lot on the banks of the Chicago River. Windows in the upper story lighted the gallery. There were narrow square ornamental towers projecting a few feet above the roof line, surmounted by flagstaffs at the two Market Street corners. Arched panels on both the Market and Lake Street sides bore the words "Republican Wigwam." The roof was supported by wooden pillars and was nearly flat, save for a skylight. The building backed up against the brick wall of a three-story building, which served as the fourth wall of the Wigwam.

It had cost nearly $7,000 and the builders were $2,000 short, so they announced a money-raising housewarming for the evening of Saturday, May 12th, at which Joshua Giddings of Ohio and other Republican orators were to speak. We may well imagine the buzz of excitement among the spectators as they entered the largest hall Chicago had ever built. It had seats for

THE REPUBLICAN WIGWAM

ten thousand and standing room for four thousand—there were no fire laws in those days.

The arrivals saw a rectangular hall, with long rows of seats facing east, and smaller rows built at right angles on the north and south sides. The gallery followed the rectangular lines of the building on three sides. The spectators faced an immense stage, capable of holding six hundred. At each side of the stage were committee rooms. The speakers stood on a dais on rollers. At the back of the stage was the brick wall, painted in panels to represent arches with Greek statues under them, a decoration then widely used. At the back of the stage hung a large gilt eagle. Most of the lumber was unplaned pine and large square posts supported the roof and gallery and obstructed the vision, but audiences of that day took pillars for granted.

Considerable decorating had been done. Red, white and blue bunting and flags were festooned along the gallery and the coats of arms of the states, against a background of evergreen twigs, ran around the hall. The pillars in front of the platform held busts of great Americans supported by figures of Atlas. The hall was lighted by gas burning in open jets.

When the doors were opened there was a headlong rush by the public that had stood packed in front of the three entrances for hours. Women were to have first call on the galleries, but "gents" would be admitted if escorting ladies. Resourceful stags devised means at once to crash the gates. They paid schoolgirls 25 cents to see them safely inside. Once the men were in the girls went out to repeat the performance and one girl, offered 50 cents for taking a man in, confided that she had already taken in two at each of the three doors. An Irishwoman with a basket of clothes was pressed into service, but when one man presented himself with a squaw, who had been selling trinkets outside the building, the policeman on duty demurred. "She's not a lady," he said emphatically.

Except for the tense battle over the slavery issue, the convention of 1860 was the prototype of many Republican conventions that were to follow. There was the ruction over seating delegates from southern states who had no constituents to speak of; there was the attempt of favorite sons to hold on to their votes until they could drive a bargain for jobs; there were local issues and sectional jealousies, such as the fear of the predominance of New York. There was the battle over the wording of resolutions that today seem to have no great dissimilarity. There were charges of machine politics, bribery and corruption. And the managers had so arranged the seats of the delegates that the Seward men were in front, the Lincoln men in the middle and the doubtful, favorite-son states in the rear, so that they could be visited easily by the Lincoln men. And there were plenty of political dopesters present too, for sixty correspondents had been admitted.

The delegates of 1860 stood midway between the pioneer republic and the modern world power. The War of 1812 had been fought in the days of their fathers. There was a visible link to early American days when George Ashmun of Massachusetts, the permanent chairman, was presented with a gavel made from the wood of Perry's flagship *Lawrence,* which fought in the Battle of Lake Erie, and thundering applause when his famous lines, "Don't give up the ship" and "We have met the enemy and they are ours" were spoken in the Wigwam.

The delegates were in each other's hair as soon as credentials were reported. The Seward men wanted Texas and Virginia delegates thrown out, but failed. Mention of Mississippi, Louisiana, Alabama, South and North Carolina brought laughter and hisses. David Wilmot of Pennsylvania attacked the presence of delegates from the slave states who had no constituents. This led Armour of Maryland to call Pennsylvania too cowardly to bear the Republic banner and, since Wilmot had received the vice-presidential vote at the hands of Kentucky in 1856, "so docile as to sneak under the flag of the People's party." Eventually twenty-four states, two territories and the District of Columbia were recognized; the big delegations were New York, 70, Pennsylvania, 54, Ohio, 46, Massachusetts, 26, Indiana, 26, Virginia, 23, Kentucky, 23, and Illinois, 22.

It is hard at this distance to understand why the venerable Joshua R. Giddings of Ohio should have been affronted because the resolutions did not specifically quote the Declaration of Independence, but we have to read it in the light of the controversy over slavery, which was by no means a clean-cut issue. The original passage said the maintenance of the principles of the Declaration of Independence and the Constitution were essential to the preservation of our republican institutions, but that didn't satisfy Giddings. He wanted it to state specifically that the convention endorsed "the self evident truths that all men are created equal; that they are endowed by their Creator with certain inalienable rights; that among these rights are life, liberty, and the pursuit of happiness."

"When you leave out this truth you leave out the party!" declared Giddings.

But he was voted down, and thereupon, like a spoiled child, he determined to secede. He rose slowly, put on his hat, and started to leave the hall. Delegates rose to plead with him, but he shook them off. The New Yorkers clutched his coattails. Then the handsome young orator, George William Curtis, member of the "Black Republican" delegation from New York, came to his rescue. In a voice that Carl Schurz heard ring out like a trumpet call, he declared:

"Gentlemen, this is a convention of free speech and I have been given the floor. I have but a few words to say to you, but I shall say them, if I stand here until tomorrow morning." And he asked, "Is this the party of freedom met on the border of the free prairies to advance the cause of liberty and human rights?"

In the end the resolution was revised to meet the objection of Giddings and the party declared in the historic words that all men are created equal and entitled to liberty—for that stated the lifelong opposition of the abolitionists to slavery in any form.

There were two kinds of oratory at the convention. No one could have bettered the flow of thought and language of Carl Schurz and George William Curtis, but typical of platform harangues was this outburst of Delegate Anderson of Massachusetts:

"We are Republican in Massachusetts, with one hundred thousand. We come to this convention from Bunker Hill, from Concord, from Lexington, from Faneuil Hall, from the shadow of Old South Church. We hold a purpose firm and strong to rescue, before we die, the whole arch of American liberty from the grasp of the Philistines who hold it. Whether in victory or defeat there we stand, and as the Apostle said, 'having done all,' there we still stand!"

But more eloquent, more urbane, was Carl Schurz, the handsome, brilliant, German-born orator from Wisconsin. He was only thirty-one, but he had an engaging manner and a literary style. In the United States only eight years, he was already a leader in his party; he had worked for Frémont in 1856; had been nominated for lieutenant governor of Wisconsin when still a few weeks short of naturalization in 1857; had spoken in Chicago for Lincoln in the senatorial campaign against Douglas in 1858. Now he was chairman of the Wisconsin delegation and pledged to Seward, whom he called "the intellectual leader of the political antislavery movement."

He had vivid memories of his first visit to Chicago six years before. He had come because the West had "the joy of growth," but Chicago had an "unhandsome" look. Footsore, tired, he sat down on a curb and saw troops of rats coming out from under the wooden sidewalks in the gaslight, some of them running across his shoes.

Once he had seen the tall, lanky lawyer from Springfield enter a railway coach amid greetings of "Hello, Abe!" from his friends. He saw him as a clean-shaven man with deep furrows in his face, wearing a stovepipe hat, a white collar turned down over a black necktie, carrying a gray woolen shawl, a cotton umbrella and a black satchel—"uncouth and grotesque."

The platform was adopted the second day and the slavery issue occupied most of its seventeen planks in one form or another. It declared against disunion, but also against armed intervention in a state's affairs; it was against the Lecompton constitution and federal interference, ditto; it criticized extravagance and corruption in Washington, as tomorrow's Republican platform will once again; it declared against the institution of slavery in new territories; endorsed the abolition of slavery and the due process clause; it was against the African slave trade; it critized the veto of the prohibition of slavery in Kansas and Nebraska. And in the

remaining planks the convention favored statehood for
Kansas, a tariff to protect industry, homestead protection, river and harbor improvements, a railroad to the
Pacific and a daily overland mail, and opposed any
change in the naturalization laws.

On Thursday, the second day, the Seward men
were confident that they had the nomination in the bag,
and toward the end of the afternoon they urged that
the voting begin immediately. The opposing delegates
were by no means ready to agree. They made motions to
adjourn. This threw the convention into turmoil. Determined to press for nominations and balloting, the
Seward men defeated the first motion.

Then the chairman announced that the tally cards
had not yet arrived, but were expected in a few minutes. In the ensuing lull the delegates began to feel the
pangs of hunger and a speaker suggested that it was time
for dinner. It was fatal to the plans of the Seward managers, for it inflamed the appetites of the tired delegates. When "a voice" made a new motion to adjourn
to the next day it was carried. The Seward men left for
a sumptuous dinner at the Richmond House with
friendly delegates as guests. So sure were they of success
that they had a hilarious evening, consuming over three
hundred bottles of champagne. Horace Greeley, their
opponent, was so impressed with their show of strength
that at 11:40 P.M. he wired the New York *Tribune* that
Seward would be nominated in the morning.

Even the Lincoln men were glum, and Joseph
Medill wrote an editorial for the next day's newspaper
in which he appealed "despairingly" for the nomination
of Lincoln. But tradition says that the decisive work
was done during the night. David Davis was tirelessly

lining up delegates for Lincoln. He and his colleagues
had their own strategy: First, to get the agreement of
certain delegations that Seward could be defeated. In
this he won the support of Pennsylvania, New Jersey
and Indiana. Then to get a show of accretion of votes
for Lincoln on the second ballot, to impress the favorite-
son states and convince the wavering, and in this Vermont, Delaware and New Hamphsire agreed to join.
Then they began working on Pennsylvania.

The noise made by the Seward men had convinced
Ward Hill Lamon that he must pack the hall with
Lincoln men. He had observed that a crowd of roughs
headed by Tom Hyer, a pugilist, made the big noise for
Seward. There were plenty of leather lungs in Illinois
to draw on. With the help of an Indianapolis man
named Connor, Lamon gained the ear of Connor's
friend, Hersey, who had printed the tickets of admis-
sion and enlisted him in a nice job of forgery. A large
supply of extra tickets was hurriedly printed; during
the night young clerks signed them with the names of
the officers of the convention and Lamon's men distributed them to Lincoln men, with instructions to enter the convention the moment the doors opened. The
maneuver succeeded; while the Seward men paraded to
the hall behind their band, the Lincoln rooters rushed
the doors and the latecomers learned to their dismay
that the hall was practically filled. When the battle was
over the Seward men, forgetting their own tactics, com-
plained that it was won by overwhelming noise. At
about the same time young Joseph Medill was pointing
to Lincoln's "fifty-one years of perfect integrity" and
exclaiming, "The age of purity returns."

4

The Convention Yell Becomes
an Institution

FRIDAY, May 18th, was the day of din at the
Wigwam. The racket began when William M. Evarts
of New York nominated William H. Seward. Evarts
stood at the beginning of a conspicuous career; he was
to become the defender of Henry Ward Beecher in the
Tilton alienation suit; he was to save Andrew Johnson
from being removed from the presidency by the Radi-
cals; he was to help put Rutherford B. Hayes in the
presidency over his friend Samuel J. Tilden. When he
spoke there was great applause.

Then Norman B. Judd nominated Abraham Lincoln. The applause increased. After that speakers placed
in nomination Dayton of New Jersey, Cameron of
Pennsylvania, Chase of Ohio. Then Caleb B. Smith of
Indiana, the orator with a lisp, seconded the nomination
of Lincoln. A terrific noise broke loose. When it had
subsided there was a mild reception for the name of
Bates of Missouri, and then Blair of Michigan rose to
second the nomination of Seward. This was notice to

the Seward cohorts, who filled many of the seats, that they must outdo the din for Lincoln. The yelling became earsplitting, the noise outrageous. Murat Halstead wrote to his Cincinnati newspaper: "No Comanches, no panthers ever struck a higher note or gave screams with more infernal intensity."

When John McLean was nominated, the convention had time to catch its breath, but not for long. Delano of Ohio, speaking for a portion of the Ohio delegation, which was supposed to be for Chase, seconded the nomination of Lincoln. Maybe this was a complete surprise; maybe the supporters of Lincoln had been goaded to greater efforts by the Seward support. The yell that followed was another step upward (or downward) in the use of the human voice. Halstead had to surpass his own superlatives. "Imagine all the hogs ever slaughtered at Cincinnati giving their death squeals together," said he, "and a score of big steam whistles going, one at 160 pounds per inch . . ."

No, there was nothing unanimous about the Wigwam convention. Thirteen candidates received votes on the first ballot. There were 465 votes in the convention and it took 233 to nominate. Seward received 173½, Lincoln, 102, Cameron, 50½, Chase, 49, Bates, 48. There was one vote for Charles Sumner and one for John C. Frémont, the standard-bearer of 1856, now completely out of the running. Lincoln received one-half of the Maine votes and seven out of ten from New Hampshire. Vermont voted for its native son, Senator Collamer.

If the first ballot showed the lay of the land, the second must have convinced the Seward men that there had been dark doings in the night. For, while Seward gained 11 votes, making a total of 184½, Lincoln gained 79, rising to a total of 181. When Vermont gave all its votes to Lincoln "the New Yorkers started as if an Orsini bomb had exploded." But the bulk of Lincoln's new support came from Pennsylvania, which shifted all but two votes from Simon Cameron to Lincoln. This makes cryptic Lincoln's remark in Springfield, after his nomination, "When the second ballot came I knew this must come," for there was political scheming behind the Pennsylvania switch that Lincoln did not approve openly.

Early in the battle it was known that Pennsylvania, despairing of electing Cameron, was ready to make a deal to stop Seward. Cameron had sounded out Lincoln some time before, but met with the flat statement that Lincoln would not bind himself by promises. During the convention David Davis was said to have promised Cameron the Treasury Department; Lincoln telegraphed that he would not be bound by a bargain. This made the managers in Chicago angry and several expressed their indignation with "Damn Lincoln!" It is inconceivable that an astute campaigner like Lincoln should not have recognized political trading, but he was already on record against spoils politics—having denounced it in his speech before the Republican convention that nominated John Wentworth for mayor of Chicago in 1857—and the record shows that he persisted in his protests, despite the compromises he had to make when he took office.

What actually happened was revealed when Joseph Medill wrote Walter Q. Gresham, later Cleveland's secretary of state, a letter published by Mrs. Gresham in the biography of her husband. In a passage that its author seems to have written with a chuckle, Medill says:

"After the convention adjourned on the second day before a ballot, while Thurlow Weed was leading a street parade for Seward, we went to the Pennsylvania delegation and made a deal whereby Simon Cameron, Pennsylvania's choice, would be withdrawn after a complimentary ballot, the vote of Pennsylvania cast for Mr. Lincoln, and in the event of Mr. Lincoln's election Simon Cameron would be made secretary of war. The next day, when the convention met, my anxiety was great, for Pennsylvania was the trump card in the deck. It became intense after the first ballot, when the chairman of the Pennsylvania delegation asked that Pennsylvania might retire for a consultation. By the time Pennsylvania was reached on the second race, her delegation had returned and the chairman announced, in a beautiful speech, that, having sought divine guidance, Mr. Cameron's name was withdrawn and Pennsylvania's vote was cast for Mr. Lincoln. And yet we had bought them the night before."

Two other commitments were made to hold Indiana: Caleb B. Smith to become secretary of the interior and William P. Dole commissioner of Indian affairs.

And then came the fateful third ballot. As the count advanced, it was observed that Seward held most of his original strength, but did not gain, whereas Lincoln added one state after another, until the buzzing undertones carried the words: "Lincoln's the coming man!" Seward received 180 votes; Lincoln bagged

231½ and needed only a few more to get the nomination.

Who was to deliver them? "In 10 ticks of a watch" as Halstead said, the man of destiny arose: Carter of Ohio. Because his pivotal act raises him for a brief moment from obscurity, his portrait has been preserved: "a large man with rather striking features, a shock of bristly black hair, large and shining eyes, terribly marked with smallpox and an impediment in his speech." He said:

"I arise—eh—Mr. Chairman—eh—to announce the change of four votes from Mr. Chase to Mr. Lincoln."

Enough to nominate! When the Lincoln men caught his words there came "a noise like a rush of wind"—the boys were just taking in breath for a big outburst—and then a wild, insane, unearthly shout, the climax of all the vocal demonstrations of the day. The delegates tore loose the standards of the states and held them aloft, all except that of New York; they waved portraits of Lincoln. A man appeared at the skylight and tried to find out what had happened, so that he could signal the cannoneer; finally, the secretary with the tally sheet made him understand; he left yelling: "It's Old Abe. Hallelujah!" and the cannon boomed the news to Chicago.

New York's delegation remained solemn and funereal. William M. Evarts mounted the secretary's table and in his best legal manner expressed his regret at the defeat of Seward, then, "in melancholy tones," moved to make the nomination of Lincoln unanimous. But most of the orators that seconded were by no means subdued: Carl Schurz defied "the whole slave power and the whole vassalage of hell"; Blair of Michigan made the best speech. When the convention met again after dinner to nominate a vice-president, the choice going to Hannibal Hamlin of Maine over Cassius M. Clay on the second ballot, most of the boys were on the streets parading or in the bars shouting and singing. The Tremont fired a salute of one hundred guns from its roof; the *Press and Tribune* displayed the four rails that Lincoln had split, two hung with tapers, while tar barrels and bonfires burning in the streets added to the frenzy of victory.

Hoarse from singing "Glorious, o'er all the ills of life victorious," the bleary-eyed delegates arose the next day from their uncomfortable beds on hall floors and billiard tables and tumbled into their special trains. George Ashmun and the group named to notify the candidate entrained for Springfield, taking with them the Philadelphia Cornet Band. Old Abe, who had been playing handball and talking things over with the editor of the *State Journal*, prepared to receive them in his parlor, wondering how badly the boys had sewed him up against his wishes.

Chicago and the Republican party buckled down to win the election. The publishing house of Follett, Foster & Company announced that it had employed a young writer named W. D. Howells, "who is favorably known by his poetical contributions to the Atlantic," to write *The Life and Public Services of Abraham Lincoln and Hannibal Hamlin*. An attempt to give dignity to the campaign and to frown on the railsplitter type of publicity was to be seen in their announcement, which said: "The taste of Mr. Howells will avoid any effort to distort Mr. Lincoln into the rough, half-horse, half alligator character, whose chief virtue consists in his having mauled rails, as it seems to be the anxiety of trading politicians to represent him, but he will present him in his proper character as a specimen of true American manhood, one who has worked out an honorable position by the force of his own intellect and energy, who has fought the battle of life on his own muscle and, with no aid from the accidents of fortune, has fitted himself to occupy the highest position in the nation." The life and speeches would cost $1, but you could get the life alone for 25 cents.

Not long after the convention, the Wigwam became the scene of a concert for the benefit of the victims of the great tornado that had cut a swath from Lee Center, Illinois, straight through to the Mississippi and into Iowa. But there were people who said that it could not have rivaled the big wind of the convention.

PART SEVEN

The North Branch

From the Marshes of the North Shore

About twenty-five miles northwest of the Forks of the Chicago, in the marshy glades and valleys behind the ridge that separates the fairest northern suburbs from the open prairie, rises the North Branch of the Chicago River. While still a brook meandering through the woods and fields it is joined by two other streams, the Skokie and the West Fork of the North Branch. Then, properly identified by cartographers as a river in its own right, it moves for miles through its ancient channel, undisturbed by serious improvements until it reaches the heart of Chicago's North Side.

Far longer than the South Branch, it also flows through a larger variety of changing scenes, a panoramic history of human activity. For ages it drained the area behind the ridge and provided water for Indian villages and settlers' farms and sawmills, moving through groves of scrub oak, ash and maple, along banks heavy with hawthorn and wild flowers. Once deer drank at its pools and fish leaped over its rocks. Today it still runs by woods where migrating birds feed undisturbed, flows through pastures where cows lie chewing their cud, moves in rural settings dominated by monastic towers reminiscent of Old World vistas. It finds its way through villages where the public garage still occupies the blacksmith shop that it displaced, where asters and phlox bloom in gardens behind picket fences, barefoot boys wade in muddy pools and cyclists trundle over tiny bridges. From such pastoral scenes it reaches the crowded suburbs and congested factory areas, places where houseboats cling precariously to their moorings, towboats with barges churn the waters, creaking bridges turn, factories spew their waste into the channel and ponderous railroad trains make the low banks tremble.

Once the North Branch met the main stream at the Forks and flowed out to Lake Michigan. Now it is augmented by water taken from the lake at Wilmette and, joining the water coming from the lake at the Forks, continues south into the Chicago Drainage Canal, the Illinois River and the Mississippi. Thus, it becomes, actually, the continuous Chicago. But by tradition and the evidence of maps it is the North Branch, and thus it will remain.

To find the true origin of the North Branch, we proceed to the lovely village of Glencoe, built on the high sand cliffs above Lake Michigan. Almost at its northern line the Dundee road runs straight west. We follow it across the Sunset Ridge road and past the Illinois Golf Club grounds to reach the Somme Preserve. Here, a few rods north of the Dundee road, the North Branch comes sneaking out of the marshy land. Its trickles have been discerned as far north as Highland Park. Flowing south as a shallow brook through the long grass, through Northbrook and Northfield, it reaches the Memorial Woods, adjoining the Wilmette Golf Club, where it is joined by the Skokie River, which drains a low, marshy area known as the Chewab Skokie, lately converted into lagoons.

The Skokie is the region of the tall, waving grasses, the breathing ground of the plover and the mallard and the paradise of the big, Jersey-size mosquito. At least it was until the Forest Preserve Commission evicted the mosquito as a public nuisance. I made its acquaintance years ago, for once I built my house amid the prolific ash and the sturdy oaks of Winnetka, and the Skokie was less than two miles to the west, verdant and miasmic, but good to look upon in the sunset. On rare occasions a strong, westerly wind carried clouds of mosquitoes into our Arcadia and they made the most of their opportunity. Immediately there was great talk about emergency measures among our much-bitten village fathers. The favorite method was to spray the Skokie marshes with crude oil to kill the larvae, which also ruined the grasses. When the Forest Preserve Commission took charge it drained the stagnant pools and led the waters into lagoons.

If I were going out to the Skokie to meditate on how its waters eventually would flow past the tall buildings of Chicago's Loop, I would walk west along Tower Road in Winnetka. But I wouldn't get far, for just before reaching the open country I'd stop at the converted log house of Anita Willets Burnham and pull the latchstring to find out what new wonders had been discovered by this alert and undaunted painter lady.

This house sits on what Anita calls a "woodsy little lot," and it cost her exactly $7; that is, she paid $25 for

ANITA'S HOUSE

it, and then the woman who lived in it on the prairie paid her $18 rent, which makes the net cost of $7, doesn't it? Some pioneer built it many decades ago and there is a tradition that once it sheltered the water-soaked survivors of the *Lady Elgin,* which went down off Grosse Pointe with three hundred members of a Milwaukee political club, the Union Guard, homeward bound from a Chicago rally for Stephen A. Douglas in September, 1860. Anita has added to it, but the nucleus is still an early Illinois log house, with a Dutch oven in the fireplace and a sanded floor, standing right in the heart of Winnetka, where substantial citizens have architects plan their houses. Anita describes it in her book, *Round the World on a Penny,* which has been selling steadily for eight years because she keeps on talking about it. She blames me for advising her to use that title, for her conscience tells her that the trip cost more than a penny, but I say that is a figure of speech. Anyhow, this house and the lot on which it now stands are on the edge of the Skokie and the Skokie is full of wonders.

One of these wonders is that wild flower of the Skokie, the trillium. Of course trilliums grow in every wood, but Anita's trillium is something special. She calls it the double-double trillium. Actually, it is a triple, or nine-petaled, trillium. First come the familiar three petals that you find in your woods; then three petals above them and three petals above them. Finding it in the woods is like coming upon a gardenia blooming among ferns. Anita found it blooming in the leaf mold and caught her breath and marvelled. She still catches her breath when she tells about it.

"It was certainly a beautiful sight," said Anita. "I wanted to preserve it. I told the botany teacher at the New Trier High School about it. He said he had never seen such a flower, but supposed it was a trillium grandiflorum. He saved some of the seeds and planted them, but the next spring there was no trace of any plant.

"I was downhearted about it, until, near the very spot where I found the original, I found another double-double trillium in full bloom. This time I was more careful. I wrote to an eastern nursery about it, and they replied at once that they would like to have it. What would I take for it? So I thought it over and said $10. Do you think that was about the right sum?

I said No.

"I don't either—now," said Anita. "I know I should have asked $20. They wrote back so fast that I knew I had made a mistake. They told me to mark the spot where the trillium grew, wait until August, then dig up the roots and send it on by air mail. I did. It was a slimy nothingness when I sent it on.

"Last spring one of the children came running, shouting: 'There's another double-double trillium in the woods, mother.' I hurried out, and there, sure enough, it was. So I was happy again. I wrote the nursery and asked if they wanted another. They replied No; their plant had bloomed nicely and they were getting ready to propagate it. You see?"

I have never seen a triple trillium and I doubt that Otis Swift, the hetman of the Yosians, who tramp the woods, ever saw one. Anita can paint its wonders, for she has painted the magnolia blossoms of Majorca, the magenta hibiscus of India, the lotus flower of China,

the columbine of Winnetka, and the wild grasses of the
Skokie, just beyond her house.

They call this flat, marshy domain the Chewab
Skokie, and here the roving bands of Potawatomis and
Miamis came to catch ducks and to fish. Once all these
waters found their way into the North Branch of the
Chicago; now drainage systems divert some of them.
The marshes are going; here, for over eight years, thousands of CCC boys, working under the National Park
Service and for the Forest Preserve Commission, have
been building huge lagoons, to control floods and, by
creating a channel, remove the stagnant water where
the mosquitoes breed. At one time thirty-five hundred
were employed here; now the work in the Chewab
Skokie is practically complete, but there is still something to be done in the West Skokie.

Lagoons have been built between Tower and Wil-
low Roads in Winnetka, where I used to drive. Islands
closed to picnickers have been created as refuges for
game. Here the tall grasses shelter mallard ducks and
pheasants, while muskrats build their homes along the
banks. Stocking the lagoons with native fish of the
region, the commission provides recreation for the fisherman. Here he will find bluegills, black crappies, white
crappies, large-mouth black bass, bullheads and breeder
bass. In time canoes and rowboats may be rented and
small sailboats will use the lagoons.

One more tributary of the North Branch remains
to be accounted for. This is the West Fork of the North
Branch, which starts at the county line, considerably
north of the Dundee road, runs through the west woods
of the Somme Preserve, traverses the religious com-

munity of Techny and is crossed by Dear Love Road; skirts the Techny Fields Golf Club, flows through Glenview and the North Shore Polo and Hunt Club and the Glenview Golf Club, and finally joins the North Branch just south of Simpson Street in the grounds of what is now the Northwestern Golf Course. No doubt it was the augmented supply of water that made a pioneer named Miller build his sawmill in this locality.

And now the tributaries of the North Branch are united. But don't begin calling for your canoe yet. Better keep on hiking. The North Branch is deceptive. Sometimes it has plenty of water for all purposes; sometimes, in a season of little rain, it falls lamentably in strength, depth, width. Besides, we are going to find the channel filled with rocks. But throughout its route, the North Branch is picturesque. Its associations are both aristocratic and democratic. No other river absorbs so many lost golf balls. It flows through exclusive golf clubs and clubs that serve the people. It has along its course more recreation grounds than any other stream in the world.

2

From Wigwams to Houseboats

THE North Branch is a winding river, and how
it winds! Anyone attempting to lie along its northern
banks would get curvature of the spine. There were no
great spring floods on the North Branch, so it could
not sweep aside the boulders that stood in its path, but
had to go around them. Thus, the Indian who followed
its course would face the sun one moment and have it
at his back the next. That never disturbed the Indian,
who had plenty of time, and today it is one of the allure-
ments that lead hikers to its carefully plotted trails.

When the North Branch leaves the grounds of the
Northwestern Golf Club and enters Morton Grove, it
reaches the wooded region that was once the home of
Indian villages. After Linné woods come the Miami
woods, once the site of many wigwams. Then it enters
land that has become part of the peoples' playground.
Here the plots are called Jane Miranda's Reserve and
Victoria Pothier's Reserve—part of the latter is used by
the Bunker Hill Golf Club. Jane and Victoria were
pioneers, members of the household of John Kinzie, and
Victoria Pothier (or Porthier) recalled, late in life, how

she was one of the girls saved by Mother Kinzie from the horrors of the Fort Dearborn massacre in 1812. This land is called a reserve because it came to them in the division of spoils in 1833, when the Kinzies were reimbursed by the government for their losses of twenty years before.

Passing through Victoria's land the North Branch enters the extensive Sauganash, or Billy Caldwell, Reserve, and here, too, the name is a reminder of old Potawatomi days. For Billy Caldwell was the popular interpreter and chief whose father was in the British Army at Detroit and whose mother was a squaw, and he was called the Sauganash because that means Britisher in the Algonquian tongue. Billy Caldwell rose to become chief of the Potawatomis and received, as part of his dole in the big distribution of 1833, over 1,240 acres of land of which this reserve is a part. That he ever lived on it is unlikely, for he sold it as soon as he could. Today, it contains one of the popular swimming pools of the North Side—the Emmett Whealan, while its nine-hole golf course often see players tee off at one a minute in a continuous procession, as many as eighty-two thousand players having been counted on the course in one season.

In these reserves we will encounter chattering troops of Boy Scouts and Girl Scouts, and less organized hikers in tan shirts and shorts, tramping the miles of the hiking trails along the banks of the river. It is not difficult to play Indian here, for these trails follow the very paths where the red man walked in order to reach the deeper pools where fish abounded. This general area was frequently a summer village site of the Miamis and Potawatomis; in the late fall they struck camp and dragged their belongings inland, to get away from the wintry blasts of Lake Michigan.

Devon Avenue, which runs through the Billy Caldwell Reserve, marks the northern limits of the city of Chicago. The larger part of this reserve is in the city, running as far south as Foster Avenue, and at the lower end of the reserve runs the old Indian boundary line. Throughout this area the North Branch follows its original channel, winding around, doubling back, in complete disregard of man's attempt to hurry rivers to the sea.

The river is crossed twice by Foster Avenue. Then it skirts the edge of Samuel Gompers Park, an oasis of thirty-eight acres, with rustic bridges and a band stand. It runs south of the Bohemian National cemetery and cuts through the diminutive Eugene Field park, a small area surrounding a field house. But small as it is, it is the seat of useful activities for the neighborhood, and its classes in Americanization are a help to the lads with foreign antecedents. A short block north of the river at Foster Avenue stands the Chicago Parental School, and a few blocks farther east the river passes by North Park College, conducted by the Evangelical Mission Covenant of America.

At West Winona Street the North Branch stops playing around the stones and skipping among the trees and grows up. Here it is reinforced by the larger North Shore Channel, created by the Chicago Sanitary District. This channel draws water from Lake Michigan on the outskirts of Wilmette, eight miles north, and pours it into the North Branch to speed storm waters and sewage and help make it navigable.

The North Shore Channel is one of the three major inlets devised to draw water from the lake and supply the drainage canal with sufficient flow. It was cut through the meadows west of Evanston thirty years ago, and is now followed down to Devon Avenue by Mc-Cormick Boulevard. Its control locks lie under the Sheridan Road bridge at Wilmette. The intake is controlled by four horizontal screw pumps, capable of moving 250 cubic feet of water per second, but since 1938 the government restriction on water has made it necessary to shut down all except one pump, which runs for an hour and rests for two or three hours, according to the seasonal precipitation. Thus, only 70 cubic feet of water per second are moving through the pumps and sometimes that is not enough to keep the river clear of scum.

The North Shore Channel has one other purpose: it permits owners of sailboats and motorboats to reach Lake Michigan from any point on the North Branch where boats can find a haven. For this purpose there has been built beside the pumping station a lock 140 feet long, 28 feet wide, and 11 feet deep.

The Sanitary District canal begins at Lawrence Avenue. Just north of River Park Street, on the east bank, lies River Park, a breathing space of thirty acres where young engineers may experiment in an amateur radio station, girls may try archery and square dancing and youngsters may hear lectures on nature lore. A short distance below River Park, the river passes through the smallest of the parks—Buffalo Park Sunken Gardens, an open space with a buffalo fountain, less than seven-tenths of an acre in size.

Then comes the region of the houseboats. They

were still moored to the banks near the Irving Park Boulevard bridge when I visited the locality, but there were threats from the authorities that they would have to go soon because they impeded the channel. To me they were the logical successors of the Indian wigwams of other centuries, the last vestige of makeshift living, although some of their denizens had held fast to the same moorings for years. From the bridge they seemed shabby and unkempt, with their tarpaper sides, flat roofs and tiny stovepipes, but artists who came to paint them found them picturesque.

To the landsman houseboats are objects of mystery. They share the fascination of the old-time shanty that boys used to build in vacant lots. What goes on inside these curious domiciles? A woman who had lived near them for years spoke of their inhabitants in low tones. "Nobody knows what they're up to," she said. "Why shouldn't they live in houses like everybody else? My sister and I have been living here for years." Her voice dropped almost to a whisper. "Do you know, we've never seen a light on one of the houseboats?"

One observer said they were a nuisance. "They get out of paying taxes," he said, "so what use are they?" Another maintained that they paid a small fee to the city and a mooring fee to the owner of the land. "Where would they get the money?" asked the first.

Close at hand, however, the mystery diminished, but the picturesqueness increased. Several boats had flower boxes and window curtains and their "front yards" were swept clean. Steps built into the bank led to planks that covered the few feet of water between the bank and the boats. Some of these bottoms had been

HOUSEBOATS ON THE NORTH BRANCH

barges used for hauling. When they became too old to be useful they were bought by people who prefer the water to dry land.

It was evident that economy was one reason. One houseboat had a little shed with a pile of coal and wood ready for the winter. The woman who owned it said her place was comfortable the year around. "Cold in winter? Of course not. When I make a fire the place gets so hot I have to open the windows." This was understandable in view of the low ceiling and four little rooms on her boat. She had lived there seven years and had tied up to the east bank because "there's more scum on the other side." An inspection of the river gave small reason for this preference. Curiously enough, she had several electric floor lamps and wall fixtures, but there were no bulbs in them.

Near the east bank, south of the boulevard, a number of workmen were cutting the grass. One of them volunteered the information that this was Paul Revere Park. That, too, is the name given this little area on the maps. But deeply embedded in the lawn lay an iron marker, with the words "Lincoln Park."

With an increased water supply, the North Branch now enters the workaday world, for it has become navigable and must carry sand, stone and lumber barges as well as pleasure craft. South of Irving Park Boulevard it flows through two parks—California at the right and Mid-City Golf Course at the left. Then it reaches the Addison Street bridge and becomes a neighbor of two enterprises that bulk large in the district, but have nothing in common. One is the great Lane Technical High School, built on a site of thirty-one acres, with an enrollment of nine thousand, larger than that of many universities. The other is Riverview Park, a huge amusement enterprise, which makes but indifferent use of the river. Blazing with floodlights and giving forth the characteristic roar—a compound of noise from roller coasters, bands, loud-speakers and other mechanical contrivances—it entertains the American who wants to be shaken up physically by curious devices, enjoys dancing and eats popcorn, ice cream and hot dogs and takes his fun amid thousands like him.

3

The River of Boyville

THE North Branch is the river of Boyville. Many a man who now sits at a manager's desk in the Chicago Loop has memories of barefoot walks on lazy afternoons along the banks of the North Branch. To recall those adventures, I sought out John Drury, whose book, *Old Chicago Houses,* proves his love for Chicago lore. John grew up in Gross Park on the Northwest Side, and his river was north of Riverview Park, a section free from factories and not navigable when he knew it.

There may have been cockleburs among the weeds in those days and cinders along the paths, and insects and pestiferous flies swirling about a boy's bare legs, but in retrospect the period, for John and his contemporaries, has a fascination akin to Mark Twain's love for the Mississippi. But it differed from all other streams in that no majestic steamboats plied its waters. Only an occasional sandsucker, with a barge loaded with sand from the lake, moved up as far as the building material yards south of Riverview and added to the huge piles of fresh yellow sand deposited there. Occasionally a motorboat stirred the gummy surface, but ordinarily the river remained undisturbed.

With no steamboats to challenge the youthful imagination, the boys tied their hopes to the locomotives that clanged their bells throughout the Northwest Side. But the river had "the lure of far places." It was the goal of Saturday afternoon hikes. The boys tried to fish, but fish didn't bite as they had in pioneer days when Charles Cleaver paddled up the river at night, burned strips of hickory bark to light up the water, and speared the muskellunge, which often reached a length of five and a half feet.

"Only the more daring of our gang would ever go in swimming," said John. "They always had to keep their mouths and nostrils closed when doing any fancy underwater stunts. I never went into the water myself because I could not swim. This swimming was a source of apprehension to the good mothers of the North Side, for often a boy would get cramps and drown. The sight of policemen in a rowboat dragging the river bottom with hooks was enough to keep me away from the river for weeks. If some of our gang wanted to go swimming without trunks, the spot was one of several clay holes near the Addison Street bridge, where excavations had been made for bricks. We were forbidden to go there, but we went just the same.

"The old rheumatic Diversey Avenue bridge used to provide us with 'rides,' " said John, "for we would stay on when it opened for a barge. But today the surroundings have changed. The old North Branch as I knew it is gone. Yet only a few years ago I had an experience that revived my memories and tickled my fancy for Americana. For with my wife I attended, one cool August evening, an old-fashioned showboat performance. Seated in the gaudy *Dixiana,* as it tugged at its mooring ropes near the old Diversey Avenue bridge, we had lots of fun hissing the villain and cheering the hero in *No Mother to Guide Her.* And between the acts, the beer in the bar whetted our appetites for further homely doings on the stage. During the intermissions I looked out over the quiet river and thought of the good times I had there as a boy, when there seemed to be sanity, order and security in the world."

The old-fashioned swing bridge of steel and wood that spans the North Branch at Diversey Parkway is way behind the times. For many years, while it carried the heavy teams and trucks of industry in a district of lumberyards and factories, nobody criticized its fitness. Now it appears crude, unkempt and ugly in a neighborhood that has had its face lifted. For the factories have receded and trees and green parkways now lead up to the bridge. A concrete wall runs along the east bank of a large turning basin in the river and thirty-seven acres on the east bank have become a show place of modern dwellings—the trim, rectagonal houses of the United States Housing Project, erected by the WPA and named in honor of a great social worker, the Julia C. Lathrop Homes.

Standing on the parkway leading to the bridge, I beheld below me a greensward with young shrubbery only recently planted. Children were tumbling on the grass and a little dog was yapping at their heels. Near the houses men idly turned the voluminous pages of Sunday newspapers. The 29 houses of the projects, capable of sheltering 925 families, extended for some distance north and south of Diversey along the river. They advertised apartments to let, but from appearances few were unoccupied. To the north rose the towers of Riverview. To the south I beheld a vista of smokestacks and brick factories, most of them idle, deserted. Over their roofs I caught a glimpse of the round dome of the Polish cathedral.

On the west bank some effort had been made to landscape the approach, but below the bridge the scene had not changed much. Directly below me was a barge advertising smoked fish; here also were moored a small schooner and several other pleasure craft. On the bank was a boatyard, where several boats propped up with timbers were having their sides slapped with paint by men in undershirts and a woman in slacks.

A fellow traveler of the moment stopped and joined me in the pleasant occupation of river gazing. We stared at the water, which was glazed with a thick greasy surface like unskimmed broth. A white fox terrier ran up and down barking. Suddenly he turned to the water and waded in. Then he waded out. He was now a black-and-white fox terrier.

The man beside me waved his hand. "All scum," he said.

"Is the water always like that?" I asked.

"Pretty nearly always," he repiled, "unless it rains. They won't let us take enough water out of the lake. You know why? The British stop us."

"Why the British?" I asked.

"They say we are draining the Great Lakes. With all that rain we had last month, too. The British want the earth."

I recalled that the Northwest Side had been heavily settled by Germans decades ago. Maybe some of their resentment still lingered.

"How's sailing here?" I asked.

"No good on the river, but with a kicker you can take the boat out on the lake. That's where those fellows think they're going. They'll be calking and painting all through June and July. Then they get a few rides in August. Then the high winds start and they have to go back home. Look at that river. All scum."

I decided he was spoiling a fine, sunshiny morning and left him.

The apartment houses on the east bank started me thinking about the way men used the earth. First these were farms; then city lots, with occasional white houses with shady front yards; then the factories came and covered many acres with brick. Now the factories were going and the dwellings were coming back, chiefly apartment houses. Extending for nearly a mile along the east bank was the site of the former Deering harvester plant. William Deering started his farm implement works here in 1870 and developed one of Chicago's great industries, occupying eighty-five acres by the time his plant became a unit of the International Harvester Company. For many years the brightly painted red and green implements were here loaded on boats and trains for shipment to America's farms. Today this activity has been removed to the central plant of the International at Blue Island and South Western avenues. Some of the ground has been cleared; a few old buildings still present bleak walls and smokeless chimneys to the eye. Around them are dilapidated houses that will have to go in the rebuilding of Chicago.

4

Goose Island Past and Present

THERE is a fabuous land in the heart of the North Side, which, so the guardians of local lore will tell you, has given more of its sons to the Chicago police department than any comparable area. It is known far and wide as Goose Island, though that name is not recorded officially on any map. The tugboat captain, guiding his barges down the North Branch, will look up when he passes North Avenue and nodding his head to the left bank will say, with a smirk: "There's Goose Island." And it will appear a wilderness of gray, rectangular factory buildings and lumber piles, like the rest of the industrial blocks around it, and you will wonder why its plain name has stirred the imagination.

But if you walk its streets and, overcoming a distaste for the odors that pour from the steaming windows of the tanneries, find a little frame house between the shops and make inquiries of its tenant, you will learn something about the past and present of the island. Its natives will tell that one hundred years ago it was but a neck of land east of the North Branch, a thumb stuck into the river's course. When the Irish immigrants came

GOOSE ISLAND ONE HUNDRED YEARS AGO

from the old sod they made it an oasis of cottages and cabbage patches and planted elms and cottonwoods. In the back yards the newcomers kept chickens and pigs, and in front of their little frame houses they staked out a cow and let it eat the rank grass. Everybody had geese. The geese patrolled the streets and alleys and waddled down to the river's bank. Over five hundred Irish families lived on this neck of land before the factories came.

In the 1850's William B. Ogden, the first mayor of Chicago, who had a finger in many a commercial pie, owned some of this land through the Chicago Land Company. He used its clay for a brickmaking enterprise. The clay pits, the low land, and the bulge suggested a canal cutting off the neck and converting it into an island, and the North Branch Canal now runs from North Avenue to Chicago Avenue. That's why the island is Ogden Island—but try to tell that to a policeman.

"Ha! Ha!" he will say. "That's Goose Island y're talking about."

How does he know? Didn't Goose Island provide the cream of "the Force"? Didn't it turn its sons into firemen, streetcar conductors and ward bosses, and put one of them in the mayor's chair? That was William E. Dever, who as a lad worked in the Griess-Pfleger tannery.

John Drury, who has tramped all over this locality in his search for local legends, tells me that he asked Sergeant James Mullen about the old days on Goose Island. Sergeant Mullen perked up at once. His father, John Mullen, had been so popular that the compatriots called him the mayor of Goose Island. That was a title not lightly bestowed. But Sergeant Mullen contemplated the present with regret.

"Before the factories and the railroads came," said he, "life on the island was a little bit of heaven. With a little bit of hell thrown in, for spice."

It was tough, even on policemen. Didn't Mrs. Herlehy throw a cop right out of her cottage when he came to arrest her husband for raising a row? The men gathered in Jack Butcher's saloon told that tale for years and doubled up with laughter. They settled their own disputes with fists, and bystanders knew enough not to interfere. The island was never a haven for prohibitionists, either. Many a kid who grew up to play a constructive part in Chicago's business life recalled the days when he rushed the growler at Johnny Langan's.

The lads on the island got rid of surplus energy in many ways. They had a swing, thirty feet high, improvised baseball diamonds and swimming holes. When they grew up they went to work in the factories. From the earliest days carpenters hammered planks together for boats and barges at the southern tip of the island, and as time went on the shipyards expanded. The father of Finley Peter Dunne plied his hammer and saw in the yard of Fox & Howard on the point.

The tanneries logically followed the early packing plants of the North Branch. Then the town spread and brick factories crowded the cottages of Goose Island. When a box factory, a varnish factory and a glue and fertilizer plant were established, the garden spot was doomed. Industry had begun its march. A tannery strike with rioting in the streets was different from the traditional fisticuffs of men settling an argument on Saturday night. And the noise of trolley cars, bumping and banging their way across the island in Division Street, was unwelcome to housewives and demoralizing to geese.

A few cottagers still live on the island and discuss it with proprietary interest. One of them, a woman with considerable resentment against mainlanders, had her own version of how the island got its name. "My mother told me," she said. "'Twas one night a gentleman, who had been a bit too friendly with the bottle, lost himself and fell asleep in some unknown place. When he woke up he was surrounded by hissing geese. 'I must be on Goose Island,' said he, and that's how it got its name." She paused and then identified him. "'Twas a gentleman from Chicago," she said.

There is a marker on the stone and steel bridge over the North Branch that identifies this district as Kilgubben. It says an area contained within Kinzie, Franklin, North Avenue and the river was formerly so designated because it was "a squatter settlement of hardworking Irish immigrants." The resident of Goose Island was contemptuous of such misinformation.

"Squatters indeed!" she said. "They were honest farmers, they were; they came from Ireland and they stopped in Maine first. Who ever heard it called Kilgubben?"

The application of the term is a matter of dispute among local historians. In the first place, it should be spelled Kilgubbin, after the original district in Ireland. Then, according to Charles S. Winslow, it was a name for a settlement farther south, approximately running from Kinzie Street to the main river. Authorities also

say that the term "Goose Island" was first applied to a
sand spit at the Forks, better known as Wolf Point. But
the truth is that all these names were loosely applied to
the locality where the Irish immigrants lived.

In the early days of the twentieth century Goose
Island became associated indirectly with an episode
famous in American literature. In *The Pit* Frank Norris
bases his story of a sensational corner in wheat on the
one directed by Joseph Leiter. It was broken by P. D.
Armour, whose ships filled with wheat moved south-
ward in time. On Goose Island P. D. Armour built five
elevators to make future corners in wheat impossible.
The elevators are gone now—most of them burned
down, and the debris of one of them smoldered until a
few years ago, when a city engineer officially pronounced it out.

"We used to have a fire house on the island, Engine
Company No. 10," said a native, "but when the building had to be torn down the city refused to build a new
one."

In more recent times Goose Island has become the
basis for fiction. Robert J. Casey, who has roamed the
world from Easter Island to Burgundy, from the Mag-
inot Line to Tobruk, found Goose Island, right under
his nose, suited to his purpose when he wrote *The Nib-
lick Murders*. In a bantering mood, his newspaper col-
league, John Drury, burlesqued the globe-trotting of
the ubiquitous Casey in *The Great Goose Island Expedition*.

With Goose Island as the center, we draw a circle
on Chicago's map, and let it reach as far south as the
Forks, as far east as the lake, and then go a correspond-

ing distance into the heart of the crowded Northwest Side. Between the river and the lake at this point lies a gigantic laboratory for social study—an area in which human beings engage in every sort of occupation, honest and devious, where poverty lurks in shaky, leaning frame buildings set flush with the street and wealth looks out over the blue reaches of the lake from the high-rent apartments and substantial mansions on the gold coast.

If you walk a few blocks east of the river at Goose Island, in the center of a district heavily populated with Italians, you will reach Oak Street and Cleveland Avenue, known during the Prohibition era as Death Corner. For here one bootlegger after another hit the sidewalk or slumped down in his car as his rivals filled him full of slugs from sawed-off machine guns. Not a long walk away is the garage where the fatal St. Valentine's Day massacre brought to a climax the hoodlums' disregard of the law.

When Frederic M. Thrasher made his studies for *The Gang* he found evidence that the Mafia and the Black Hand still carried on their extortions among immigrants in this section, though the American-born sons and daughters of the community were taking high honors in the schools. When he went west of the river to Milwaukee Avenue, a section predominantly Polish, he found a gang to every block. These gangs were not all malicious though they got into fights with rivals and sometimes became a general nuisance; most of them were small groups of boys in their teens who played in the streets and alleys. In this general locality Nelson Algren found the material for his memorable tragedy of adolescence, *Never Come Morning*. To provide healthy activities for these youngsters Chicago developed its playgrounds and parks, initiated hundreds of sporting events—baseball, swimming, tennis, handball—and added miles to the great stretch of sandy beach of the lake, which today lures the boys from street corners.

5

To the Forks of the Chicago

Moving south from Goose Island, we come to the Chicago Avenue bridge, the focal point for one of Chicago's pioneer industries, the mail-order business. Here, on the east bank, on both sides of the avenue, rise the many-windowed, eight-story buildings of Montgomery Ward & Company, packed with merchandise of every description. Founded in 1872 by A. Montgomery Ward and George A. Thorne, it rose to prosperity because it enabled the farmer to buy goods cheaply by mail and express from a catalogue.

When good roads and the automobile brought the consumer to town, it adapted itself to the chain store system. One of these huge retail stores is located in the main office building, above which rises a tower bearing the figure of a woman poised in flight and known as the Spirit of Progress.

Early in the twentieth century Montgomery Ward had a Spirit on the top of the Ward tower on Michigan Avenue above Madison. The rural population of the Middle West, hurrying to Chicago to spend its profits, usually had three objectives: the stock yards, the Board of Trade, and the Ward tower. Customers mounted its dizzy heights in deadly fear of losing their chin whiskers in the cutting breeze.

One day a group stood below the building staring up at the tower and when asked the reason someone replied that an eagle was sitting on the figure and preening his feathers in the unruly Chicago wind. Nobody had seen an eagle in this region outside of the zoo, but the suggestion made a sensation. The vivid imagination of a Chicago reporter was needed properly to put this event on record and he was found in the person of Wallace E. Smith, one of the brilliant news hawks of his day, later author of *Viva Villa* and successful as a Hollywood scenarist. As Wallace rose to the occasion the crowds grew and traffic had to be regulated. The story of the eagle interested the public for several days. If it was an eagle, nobody saw it fly away.

Montgomery Ward & Company shares with Sears, Roebuck & Company the distinction of making Chicago the center of the mail-order business. Sears, Roebuck, which has its headquarters near Douglas Park, on the West Side, was founded in 1886 by Richard W. Sears and brought into national prominence by Julius Rosenwald, a poor boy who never forgot the underprivileged. The vast philanthropies of Rosenwald were constructive. He stressed the need of education and supported numerous Negro schools in southern hamlets, built the Y.M.C.A. for Negro lads and endowed the fund that bears his name. His sturdy, practical Americanism is one of the brilliant pages in Chicago's record.

Men who work in this area are still talking about the day, more than ten years ago, when an airplane crashed just east of the railroad yards of the North Western on the west bank of the river. That is, if you can get them to talk. They are suspicious of outsiders who ask questions for no good reason. "What do you want to know for?" they ask, suspecting government inquiries, or worse.

But when their fears were allayed, they talked quite freely. A foreman in an office told the tale, assisted by several of his associates who put in extra details. Like this: "It was on a Saturday, about 3:25 P.M., and the men were just pulling out to go home. Then we heard a terrible crash. We ran out and there was Holden No. 2—that's a big gas tank, used to stand over there by the river—with the tail of an airplane sticking out of it. I got a strong whiff of gas, and I knew that gas was mixing with the air and was mighty combustible. There were a couple of locomotives switching cars and blowing hot sparks into the air. It was dangerous as hell. One spark in that gas and it could blow up the whole city.

"I sized the thing up and decided that if there were any people in that tank they were all dead. If they weren't killed in the crash then they were either drowned or gassed to death. Drowned? Of course. All those tanks are sealed with a section of water. The smell of gas made me sure the plane had pierced the water section and made a hole in the main gas tank.

"By that time everybody was running around giving orders and the crowds were coming over all the bridges. First the emergency men closed all the valves that controlled the gas flow, got the locomotives out of the yards and called for ladders and divers. The fire department put up its apparatus, and as it became dark rigged up floodlights. An electrical storm started and it was certainly a weird sight to see the lightning light up the faces of the crowds. They pulled the plane out with derricks and found the bodies of a man and two women. Their heads were horribly smashed, but there were some funny things about them. The pilot had worn hip boots. One was completely off. And each girl had lost one stocking. One girl had one shoe gone; the other had lost both shoes. How do you account for that? We found out that the pilot had taken his fiancée and her sister for a flight, but nobody ever learned what made them crash."

The North Branch has seen other tragedies, not accidental. The most gruesome in crime annals occurred in an old factory building still in use, not far from the river in this neighborhood. Under its roof, more than forty years ago, a middle-aged, taciturn man named Adolf Luetgert ran a sausage factory. He lived with his wife in a cottage across the street. There were reports of quarrels, of threats by the husband, and then, on May 1, 1897, the wife disappeared. When friends made inquiries Luetgert replied that she had gone on a trip. Finally he reported her disappearance to Captain Herman Schuettler of the Sheffield Avenue police station.

What had become of her? The gruesome report went around that he had killed her and cut her up in the sausage factory. An examination of the premises yielded the theory that he had cut up his wife's body in the vats and let the pieces run off into the burdened, abused, contaminated North Branch. The consumption of sausages declined throughout the city. The police found a few clues. On the night of May 1st Luetgert had ordered the night watchman to fire the furnaces, although no work was being done. He had bought a barrel of corrosive chemical, not needed in the factory. A careful examination of a sausage vat yielded some blond hair, pieces of bone, part of an artificial tooth, some organic matter in slime and finally—Mrs. Luetgert's two rings.

On this meager evidence the state's attorney, Charles S. Deneen, later governor and senator, constructed the case that convicted Luetgert. But the best the state could get was a life term for the prisoner. He went to prison at Joliet and died there in 1908, without confessing. While many have forgotten the location of his factory, Howard Vincent O'Brien recalls that as a boy he would walk past the building quaking when he thought of the crime committed there.

In this section of the North Branch Chicago industry began. Here iron manufacturing started on a large scale with the operations of the Chicago Rolling Mills in 1857. In this area the Clybourns had a packing plant and the first steam sawmill.

After passing a variety of bascule and swing bridges, in a wilderness of warehouses, lumber piles, factories, grain elevators and railroad yards, we come to the last bridge for pedestrians, which spans the North Branch at Kinzie Street, named for the old trader. This is the site of the first foot bridge of 1832, a crude affair of logs shaped with the ax, resting on piles. Though the old street appropriately runs over Kinzie land and close to the lots where the members of the ubiquitous Kinzie clan built their homes, it has become a stepchild of a street, tangled up with the Milwaukee and the North Western railroad lines and having a hard time keeping its identity as it runs west.

For here the railroad is paramount. The last bridge to span the North Branch is a small railroad bridge, about three hundred feet above the Forks. Today it is but a minor accessory in the day's work of the great Chicago & North Western, which now runs its numer-

"THE FORKS," 1833. FROM AN OLD PRINT

ous tracks along the west side of the river into a huge terminal station on West Madison Street. But thirty years ago this two-track bridge carried all the trains of that line, both the limiteds and the little yellow commuters' locals of the North Shore, into the attractive red-brick depot that fronted on Wells Street. And it is worth remembering that this was the route surveyed for the first railroad to enter Chicago.

South of Kinzie the North Branch flows down to the Forks, the place where the three arms of the river come together to form the Y that Chicago often uses on its shields. On the east bank lies a barren, cindery area where rank weeds and cottonwoods grow. Farther east, on the site of the old Wells Street station of the C. & N.W. rises the huge office building known as the Merchandise Mart, twenty-two stories high and one block square. It is owned by Marshall Field & Company and houses the studios of the National Broadcasting Company as well.

In pioneer days the land jutted out into the river at the junction of the North Branch and the Chicago, forming Wolf Point. It was called thus because Elijah Wentworth had a tavern there, with the sign of a wolf on a pole in front of it. The Wolf was an Indian chief known to the settlers. On one of his trips to Chicago General Winfield Scott stayed here.

Samuel Miller put up a log house here, stocked it with rum and gin and called it a tavern; in 1826 he had married Elizabeth Kinzie, daughter of John Kinzie by his first wife, the Virginia captive, and as justice of the peace Kinzie had performed the ceremony. Sam Miller and Archibald Clybourn obtained the right to operate a ferry at the Forks and started it June 2, 1829; they carried passengers to each bank of both branches. They had a regular tariff: a passenger paid 6¼ cents; a man and a horse, 12½ cents; a horse and wagon, 25 cents; a carriage with horses or oxen, 37½ cents. Hogs, sheep and goats were ferried at 3 cents each.

The original point of land, and the spot where the sign of the wolf stood, today exists only in old drawings of pioneer Chicago. It was dredged away years ago to make a basin where vessels could maneuver when turning from one branch into another. But the land that remains, the site of early houses and taverns, is once more as vacant as it was when the pioneers drove their logs into the ground and raised their rooftrees. Surrounded on all sides by the huge structures of a metropolis, it might well become the site for a reconstruction of the original cabins from which the city has grown.

PART EIGHT

Bridges and Boats

I

The Old Clark Street Bridge

WHEN a city grows so large that its people can walk about the streets all day without meeting a familiar face, then certain inanimate objects become points of contact between them. Thus the Gothic pinnacle of the Water Tower is a community possession; an acquaintance with Marshall Field & Company will serve to introduce strangers in far places and often, when the wind is wrong, the stock yards become a shared experience. Shop windows, clocks and bridges acquire a specific meaning. In the days that have just vanished over the hill, the old Clark Street bridge was one of them.

The old Clark Street bridge is the bridge of legend. Gone since 1927, when a practical city hailed the removal of an eyesore, it lives in the memories of men who paced its shaky walks as a symbol of a Chicago too hurried, too occupied, too wasteful of abounding energy to build for beauty.

Its lattice of steel girders shut out the sky. Its bridge house, stuck halfway between ceiling and floor, looked like a tool shed. Its two ends, held fast to the central pivot, a turntable with a series of iron wheels, gave way when heavy trolley cars thumped down upon the rails. Its rust fell on the shoulders of pedestrians when huge trucks shook the floor.

But on moonlight nights, when its black frame had lost its sharpness, when men with time on their hands lounged in the shadows on the docks or stood by its railing to watch the amber lamps wobbling in the river's current, it fed the thoughts of poets and the world-weary.

Today a great new bridge spans the river at Clark Street. Walk west along the sunlit Wacker Drive from Michigan Avenue, and you will hardly distinguish the Clark Street bridge from the other wide thoroughfares of steel and stone that span the main river. Like them it shares the decorative effects of Wacker Drive. The steel beams that support its leaves are below it and no unsightly girders obscure the sky. The bridge houses, where the engineers manipulate the levers that make the two leaves rise on their trunnions, stand at each end, faced with graven stone.

Wacker Drive, which leads up to it, is wide and double-decked; below, on a level with the river, move the trucks that do Chicago's hauling. Above there is a spacious prospect under the open sky. Gone are the clumsy stairs that led to the narrow docks and the old brick commission houses of South Water Street, which had walls askew and crumbling chimneys, and windows opening on rooms packed to the ceiling with bags of potatoes and crates of melons.

Once the Clark Street bridge was the bridge of life and death. At its southwest end were enacted Chicago's greatest catastrophies. Here the Christmas ship, the *Rouse Simmons,* tied up year after year with its load of fragrant spruce and pine from the Michigan woods. Here, too, the *Eastland* lay, the day it keeled over on its side and wiped out the lives of 812 passengers. Martin Jeffers, the bridgetender, saw it happen before his eyes. He and others had warned the captain that the boat was listing, and finally saw it go. He helped save sixteen who had leaped from the decks that day.

The old bridge, too, was the last hold that many had on earth. Here came the forlorn, the unemployed, the desperately ill. They would stand by the rail of the bridge and brood over the dark waters. Then they would climb the rail and jump off. Frank Ward, who has been on the alert for those ready to leave the world, has saved the lives of ten of the world-weary.

For years Patrolman Charles R. Conlon was stationed at the old Clark Street bridge. He was typical of many members of the Force—exuding Irish geniality and efficiency, and unafraid. His service had been long and honorable, and in 1920 he was slated for retirement with a pension. A few weeks before that happy event came around he walked into a drug store in Randolph Street to make a purchase and stumbled on four bandits holding up the store. He pulled his gun and shot it out with them, killing one and was himself killed in the battle.

When the old South Water commission houses still stood, Ed Hester conducted his popular fish camp in a South Water Street basement not far from the bridge. When word got around that Ed's fish were something special, the men with fine palates found their way to the camp and ate happily at the plain wooden tables covered with white oilcloth. For Ed was a fisherman himself; he sent his own boats out into the lake to get a fresh catch, and kept a tank of live fish in his restaurant. If he liked you, he amused himself with his little game: he gave you Pilots' License No. 23 in his Pilots and Landlubbers Amalgamated Union. Ed Hester passed with the old houses of South Water Street, just after he had moved to a new Clark Street location, and appropriately, died on a fishing trip at Sturgeon Bay.

More than one hundred and ten years have passed since the early settlers toiled and struggled to build the first wagon bridge across the Chicago. They located this bridge at the Forks, from the West Side to the point where Lake and South Water Streets came together.

Details of this bridge have come down to us and show what a hard task it was. The builders took four logs and fastened them together into what they called a bent, then sank one end into the river, leaving it about three feet above the water. Two of these bents were sunk in the middle of the stream, thirty feet apart. Presumably a whole series of bents was used. Round logs were then thrown to these bents from the bank and small trees, six inches in diameter and ten feet long, were laid transversely for the road, without being clamped down.

It was a primitive affair, and that it shook and rattled under the hoofs of horses and oxen is comprehensible. The animals slipped and stumbled; horses became frantic and jumped into the river to drown. But the four-horse stage got across; its horses were used to uncertain footing and daredevil driving.

By 1834 the settlers attempted a drawbridge. The carpenter who cut the lumber for it, Nelson R. Norton, says it was built from March to June at Dearborn Street. The bridge had a double draw, with an opening of sixty feet; it was sixty feet wide and as long as a city block—three hundred feet. The two leaves of the draw were raised by chains that ran through two wooden frames, one on each bank, which became known as "gallows frames." But it had not been built to withstand the rigorous weather, and in 1839 the high floods carried away part of it. What was left was demolished by the city authorities and a ferry was substituted. A bridge was then proposed for Clark Street, but the settlers refused to support it unless the residents on the north bank subscribed $3,000, which they refused to do. Finally they agreed to a bridge with a floating span for a draw. This and all other bridges went out in the ice jam and flood of March, 1849, when many vessels were destroyed. The first iron pivot bridge was erected at Rush Street with the help of the railroads in 1856. Seven years later it swung open while occupied by a drove of cattle; the animals stampeded to one end, unbalanced it and sent it into the river.

Charles Cleaver tells an odd story about the original bridge across the North Branch at Chicago Avenue. He says that it had no draw and hence was an obstruction to river traffic and a violation of the laws governing a navigable stream. He notified the city authorities to remove it and they did so in two days.

The present bridges are too new to carry many legends; too formal to become endeared to people. Yet even these bridges are beginning to know tragedy. Sit-

THE CHRISTMA

E SHIP

ting in the Tavern, overlooking the river, Charles Collins, conductor of the "Line-o'-Type or Two" column of the *Tribune,* told me of an incident involving the Michigan Avenue bridge. It stands in clear view of the *Tribune*'s city room. One day a member of the city staff looked out of the window and saw a man climb on the rail of the bridge and prepare to jump. He yelled an alarm and dashed out. The man had jumped.

"There was a news story right in our front yard," said Collins, "but it never appeared in print. There were simply too many items to publish that day."

2

The Christmas Tree Ship

CHRISTMAS in Chicago, fifty years ago, was a happy, home festival in a city not yet too rich, too pretentious, to be neighborly. There was usually snow at Christmas; it lay in large heaps in the gutters and was packed solid on the streets. When snow fell it was heavy with moisture; it blocked trains and held up streetcars. The average citizen shoveled his own sidewalks clean and looked after his own fires. A few blocks beyond the Loop, where the gray wooden cottages with their scrollwork porches stretched for miles, householders would be out early in the mornings wielding their shovels, amid shouts to their neighbors, for in those days families lived long enough in one locality to become known to one another.

In the houses on the near North Side, where brick buildings abounded, the windows had little wooden blinds inside through which came the yellow rays of light from gas jets. The air in the streets outside had the close feeling of a low-ceilinged room and shouts rebounded from wall to wall. In that air bells on sleighs jingled in time a long way off and hoofbeats made a dull patter on the packed snow. As the sleigh passed under the light of the gas lamp at the corner you could see the prancing horse, the curved dashboard, the gleam of the nickeled bars across the front, the flash of the runners. The driver would be wearing a wide fur collar and a fur cap; the woman beside him would be tucked under fur robes and look very comfortable in a brown fur neckpiece and toque.

Inside, the house was warm and a bit stuffy with dry air. The carpets had a firm surface and gay curlicues of vine leaves all over them. The hall might be dark; its walls were covered with embossed paper, stained to the color of leather, and the gaslight flickered behind a globe of pink glass ornamented with a trailing vine. You walked quickly past the parlor, which had a mantelpiece of black slate and a mirror over the fireplace and heavy chairs and settees with curved walnut legs, to the back room where all the family gathered. Here the walls were hung with photographs of young and old and there were music racks and bookshelves. If the house was heated by a furnace, the hot air flooded up through a register in the floor, but more likely a big-bellied stove, consuming anthracite coal, gleamed red through mica windows in a corner. And in the bay stood the Christmas tree.

Most likely the father of the family had picked it out and carried it home. Men and women carried their own bundles in those days. Perhaps he walked down to the Clark Street bridge, a week or two before Christmas, to see if the Schuenemanns had come down from Wisconsin with a load of spruce trees. Invariably the two big, brawny lads would be there with a fishing schooner loaded with trees that they themselves had cut in the Michigan woods. They were fine, well-shaped trees and cost so little—for 75 cents you bought a fullsized tree; for $1 you had your choice of the best. Even saplings provided bright decorations for a city where people were making money, but not too much money, and where the average citizen was always fearful of hard times.

As long ago as 1887 the two Schuenemanns, Herman and August, had sailed down in a schooner from Manistique, Michigan, with a load of spruce and tied up beside the dock behind the old red-brick commission houses at the Clark Street bridge. There Chicago found them and bought their stock, and called Herman captain and remembered to look for him the following year. When snow fell on Chicago's streets in December days the father of the family would say, "Guess I'll have to go down to the Clark Street bridge to see if the captain is in and get us a tree."

Fifty years ago the work of providing trees for Christmas was not yet the mass-production business it has become in recent times. No dealer contracted for thousands of trees as a speculation and destroyed great numbers if he had guessed wrong on the demand. No man cut down whole hillsides to satisfy the whims of people who followed a custom but didn't know how to pray. There were plenty of trees for all. The Schuenemanns went into the woods behind Manistique and Thompson, Michigan, where young trees grew on land that had been cut over to make the lumber that went into midwestern houses a generation before. They chose the trees carefully, including some tall ones for which they had orders from churches and hotels. Sometimes they had to work in the snow and when the trees reached Chicago there was still snow on the branches. The brothers thought they had done well when they made a modest profit on a trip that occupied about six weeks of the wintry season, when it was hard to haul other cargoes.

The work was not easy, neither the cutting nor the sailing, for they always came when Lake Michigan kicked up a lot of rough sea. In 1898 August had just set sail with a load of trees when a storm arose and he and his ship were lost. Thereupon Herman determined to carry on alone. In 1899 he was back at the Clark Street dock with his boat, the *Rouse Simmons,* loaded with Christmas trees. He was a jovial man, with a very ruddy complexion and laughing wrinkles around his blue eyes, and everybody liked him.

For eleven years Herman arrived with his cargo and many people depended on him for a tree year after year. Then came the hard season of 1912, with storms and heavy seas on Lake Michigan. Late in November Herman cut his trees in the woods behind Manistique and started for Chicago in the *Rouse Simmons,* with a crew of seventeen men. There were head winds and heavy seas from the start and soon the schooner was struggling in a raging snowstorm. What took place on board we can only guess. The *Rouse Simmons* sailed into the silence that covers all the fine ships that have fallen victim to the gales of Lake Michigan, which have taken the lives of so many, from the days of La Salle's *Griffon* until now.

Long before Chicago missed the *Rouse Simmons* at

its dock reports began to come of the ship's distress. A schooner resembling it was said to have been sighted off Kewaunee, Wisconsin, flying distress signals. The steamer *George W. Orr* reported to the revenue cutter *Tuscarora* that she had seen the *Rouse Simmons* three miles offshore, but the captain later admitted that he might have been mistaken. But on December 5, 1912, fishermen off Two Rivers Point, seven miles north of Manitowoc, Wisconsin, found the tops of spruce trees entangled in their nets. Trees had been roped together on the deck of the *Rouse Simmons,* and how could they get into the lake at that point if not off a ship?

On December 13th a watcher on the beach at Sheboygan, Wisconsin, reported that he had picked up a bottle containing a message that came from the captain. It had been written on a page of the ship's log and read:

Friday—Everybody goodbye. I guess we are all through. Sea washed over our deckload Thursday. During the night the small boat was washed over. Leaking bad. Ingvald and Steve fell overboard Thursday. God help us.

Herman Schuenemann

The men referred to were believed to have been Steve E. Nelson, mate, and Ingvald Nylons, seaman. But if there was such a message, it never reached the captain's wife, who was eagerly waiting for scraps of news in her Manistique home. She was a valiant little woman, with a great deal of stamina. When she realized that her three little girls, Elsie and the twins, Pearl and Hazel, were now dependent wholly on her efforts, she resolved to take up her husband's task.

There was no Christmas ship at the Clark Street dock in 1912. But when 1913 came, Chicago residents who looked over the railings of the bridge beheld another schooner, loaded with trees, as in the days when Captain Herman held forth there. On board was the plucky little wife of the captain. She had gone into the woods with the woodcutters and supervised the felling of the trees. With her, too, were her girls, as well as women to weave wreaths and garlands. Chicago was to become well acquainted with the Schuenemanns. They were to come season after season for twenty-two years after the *Rouse Simmons* went down.

For years Chicago friends would ask the captain's wife whether there had been any definite report on the *Rouse Simmons,* and she could only shake her head sorrowfully. Yet the sea, which guards its secrets well, reluctantly gave up tangible evidence fourteen years after the disaster. On April 23, 1924, the wallet of Captain Schuenemann was found at Two Rivers Point, where the spruce trees had been tangled in the fishermen's nets. It still had the original rubber band around it and the cards and clippings inside seemed to be made of plaster. Some of the clippings related to earlier voyages of the Christmas tree ship. Three years after this find a bottle with a note signed by Charles Nelson was picked up. It read:

> These lines were written at 10:30 P.M. Schooner R. S. ready to go down about 20 miles southeast Two Rivers Point between fifteen or twenty miles off shore. All hands lashed to one line. Goodbye.

Eventually the family made its last voyage to the Chicago market with Christmas trees. The mother had grown gray; the girls were handsome young women. Forty-seven years had elapsed since Herman, as an 18-year-old lad, had steered his first cargo into the Chicago. The ship had become an institution.

Its fame grew. Today when the winds blow hard on the lake and the heavy surf pounds the frozen shore line watchers in the lighthouses recall the *Rouse Simmons*. Long ago it inspired a ballad. When word of its loss reached Chicago newspapers Vincent Starrett, bibliophile and author of many books of fiction and belles-lettres, was a reporter on the *Daily News*. His editor was Henry Justin Smith. "It would make a fine ballad," said Starrett. "Why don't you write it?" replied Smith. So Starrett composed "The Ballad of the Christmas Ship," a poem of many, many quatrains, and Smith found room for it among the crowded columns of the day's news. It may never challenge the efforts of youthful orators as often as "The Wreck of the Hesperus," but the legend is just as moving and the intentions of the poet were as good as Longfellow's.

3

The *Eastland* Turns on Its Side

By 1900 the Chicago River had seen a lighthouse collapse, one fort burn and another fall into ruin, its bridges carried out by floods, and hundreds of fine sailing ships reduced to ashes in the fire that destroyed the city. Now in the twentieth century, it was to experience the greatest loss of life that had ever taken place on its waters—the death of 812 young men, women and children, even babes in arms, when the excursion steamer *Eastland* rolled over on its side at the Clark Street bridge on the morning of Saturday, July 24, 1915.

They were drowned, most of them, in the waters—pinned down between decks with no chance of escape, all dying within a few minutes—all except those caught in pockets between decks and found too late. I have heard men who saw the tragedy describe it in awed tones as if it were beyond belief. One was Macausland, the librarian of the Chicago *Daily News*. He was on board an elevated train coming across the Chicago River at 7:30 that morning. Looking casually out the window, he saw the river and the steamship come into sight;

he saw the masts and funnel of the gray vessel, moored
less than seven hundred feet away, list and keep on listing till it hit the water. Then his train passed between
the brick walls of Wells Street and shut out his view.
The train stopped at a station immediately afterward;
shocked and agitated, he hurried to a telephone and
shouted the news to the city desk.

That is the way all witnesses described it. The harbormaster, who stood close by, the assistant harbormaster, the government inspector, told the same incredible story. The harbormaster told how the vessel listed
first to starboard, that is, toward the dock at the south,
which was built out from the rear walls of the old
brick commission houses of South Water street, less than
fifteen feet away. Then it righted itself, and began
to list to port, until . . . But that is getting ahead of
the story.

The *Eastland* had been chartered for one of those
outings to the sand dunes of Michigan popular with
Chicagoans for generations. The steamship companies
often charged as little as 75 cents and made their money
by carrying heavy loads. After they had landed the
Chicago crowds at St. Joe, they took on a St. Joe crowd
for a "peanut cruise," that is, several hours on the blue
waters in midday, returning in the afternoon to pick
up the Chicago crowd. The Chicago River carried many
big passenger ships in those days—the old whaleback
Christopher Columbus, built for the World's Fair of
1893 and capable of holding four thousand; the *Theodore Roosevelt, City of Benton Harbor, City of South
Haven, City of Racine, City of Petoskey, Puritan,* and
others long familiar to Chicago.

In my first year at the university my roommate and I came downtown on a Sunday morning to take one of these popular trips to Michigan City, Indiana. Maybe they were asking $1 that day; maybe we had forgotten money for meals; at any rate we were short of the requisite funds. So we told our plight to the traffic policeman. "You look like honest boys," he said, reached down in his pocket and handed us the money. "Where can we return it?" I asked. "You'll find me at Jackson and Dearborn all next week," he replied.

The steamer was jammed with people, mostly couples. Pop bottles rolled on the decks. Lovers held hands across the deck chairs. The odor of sizzling hamburgers rose from the refreshment booths. On the main deck the moneyed bloods were gambling at 50 cents a throw, and ropes held back a gaping crowd as barkers spun the roulette wheel and twirled the bird cage. We wandered aimlessly about, commenting on the other passengers, listening to the player pianos, not quite at ease among strangers. It was my one and only excursion on what Chicago calls a "lake boat."

Saturday, July 24, 1915, was designated as the excursion day of the Western Electric Company employees, Hawthorne plant. They had planned to use four ships for 7,000 people, and the *Eastland* was to sail as soon after 7:00 A.M. as the men at the gangplank had clocked off 2,500 passengers. This was a trim steamship of three decks, 1,900 gross tons, with an average draft of 14 feet when loaded. It was very thin forward and, like other lake boats that had used the Chicago River, had a flat keel, for every extra inch of keel meant less for the draft. It had been sailing the lakes for ten years

or more without difficulty but sailors had heard that
it rolled a lot. But as one of the mariners said, "A sailor
don't care how much a boat rolls, so long as she rolls
easy. It's the ship that jerks you off your feet that is a
bad sea boat."

By 7:00 the passengers started to come in droves
and soon the boat was listing badly to starboard, toward
the dock. The inspectors saw an aperture between the
gangplank and the dock; people couldn't get on. The
engineer opened the sea cocks and let in water ballast;
the ship began to right itself. Then it began to list to
port—the north side of the ship. Passengers inside were
startled by a terrific crash—the heavy refrigerator in the
bar, loaded with bottles, went over.

The harbormaster on the Clark Street bridge called
to Captain Pederson on the bridge of the *Eastland* to
right the boat; the captain signaled that he was trim-
ming it. At 7:24 the captain gave the order to stand
by; the boat was ready to pull out and began to turn its
propellers to work the stern out toward midstream,
while a tug stood ready to take the lead. At 7:27 the
list to port became decided; people on board were
frightened; men were seen to throw their suitcases overboard and jump. There were seven hundred to a thousand on the top deck; some began to jump into the
river.

The captain yelled, "Get off the boat the best way
you can!" The boat was slowly listing, continued to list,
25 to 30 degrees, then went slowly over and settled
in the water, with about half the starboard side showing
above the waters of the river, which became black with

panic-stricken passengers threshing around and calling for help.

What happened after that has been told by those who went through it, and those who watched and helped from dock and bridge. Men threw ropes, life belts, planks into the stream, pulled out survivors. It was all life was worth for a swimmer to jump in; he was seized by crazed men and women and had to drag himself free. Some passengers worked their way out through portholes. The assistant harbormaster raced for telephones, called the city hall for ambulances and pulmotors, and ran blocks to locate acetylene torches. Patrol wagons and ambulances began to arrive with clanging bells; the police drew their lines for a block around the accident.

The tugboat made a bridge to the *Eastland*, on the hull of which huddled passengers who had climbed out. Police and workers began carrying bodies from the water to the dock and doctors, shedding their coats, began giving them first aid. Across the river was the large building of Reid, Murdoch & Company, vacant of employees because they, too, were having a picnic elsewhere; the company opened its basement and first floor to the Red Cross.

It was a gray, drizzly morning. The employees, not knowing who had escaped, stood about in bewildered, subdued groups. Those on the boat were led across the tug to the dock and saw the drowned lying in rows. The police commandeered the 2nd Regiment Armory, at Washington and Curtiss streets, for a morgue, wrapped all the bodies in blankets and took them there. Each body was given a number and guarded by the police. At midnight the armory was opened to the long lines of distracted relatives. What happened there duplicated the scenes of grief that had taken place at the burning of the Iroquois Theatre a little over eleven years before.

All day and all night the doctors and engineers worked beside the *Eastland*. Searchlights and torches threw a glare over the scene as they cut holes in the steel plates to liberate imprisoned men. They pulled out passengers who had held on for dear life in dark, damp holes. They found injured and dead. Twenty-two families had been wiped out. Parents had died and left their children orphans; fathers and brothers had perished.

The mayor's committee, the Red Cross and the protective society of the Western Electric employees handled $562,370.39 in benefits; insurance to families reached $267,160. There were the usual investigations— by the United States Department of Commerce, by the coroner's jury and the state's attorney, but no one knew what had caused the *Eastland* to turn over. Some mariners thought the management of the water ballast had been faulty, but that listing was not in itself dangerous, even though the *Eastland* had been known to list before. Others testified that the *Eastland* did not use its water ballast sufficiently. Still others declared that the ship must have rested on the bottom of the river. There had been no sudden rush to port by the passengers, who jammed the decks but seemed well distributed.

When all the missing had been accounted for and mention of the ship was an occasion for grief and mourning, the *Eastland* was still valuable as a hulk of

steel. It was righted and towed away. In time a ship
that bore no resemblance to the original excursion boat
moored beside the Illinois Naval Reserve Armory in
the harbor basin, south of the mouth of the Chicago. It
was the old *Eastland,* with decks changed and name and
occupation gone. There it lies today, serving as a naval
training ship, and it is called *Wilmette.*

4

The Tug *Clifford* Defies the Great Fire

IN October, 1871, the Chicago faced a great test
and failed. It failed twice to stop the progress of the
fire that destroyed the city; first, when the flames swept
across the two hundred feet of water from the West
Division at Van Buren Street into the metropolitan
district; second, when the flames ignited the bridges that
led to the North Division and burned the district as far
as Lincoln Park. The hopes of thousands who gazed
calmly at the huge fire from the other side of the river
were blasted on the night of October 8th when the
flames "vaulted" the river, as one historian puts it,
and ignited the gasworks south of Adams Street.

Maybe Mrs. O'Leary's cow did not kick over the
lamp in the barn on De Koven Street; it is too late now
to establish the truth. Certain it is that the fire started
in the dry, wooden shacks of the O'Leary district and,
whipped by a high southwesterly, spread fanwise to the
northeast. On the night before a row of factory buildings and lumber piles between Van Buren, Jackson,
Clinton and Canal Streets had burned out, even igniting

the coal-loading docks on the water's edge. Now another fire had started in the same neighborhood. Soon the high wind carried showers of sparks to the old frame buildings that stood around the gasworks and routed the denizens of the saloons and dives of Conley's Patch.

Most of the bridges spanning the Chicago had little iron in them. To many they were the only roads to safety. Soon they were jammed with crowds deserting the center of the city for the North and Northwest sides. Drawings of the hurrying mob rushing across the Randolph and Lake bridges portray the demoralization caused by the fire. Cabs and wagons were pressed into service to move goods; their drivers charged first $10, then $50; some of them demanded more money en route, and when it was not forthcoming, dumped the goods on the street, where they were trodden underfoot. A bank cashier paid $1,000 to a driver to carry a heavy box safely to a railroad depot on the West Side; the box contained $600,000.

The tunnels under the river were jammed; one ran under Washington Street, two and a half feet below the river bed; another, recently completed, ran under the river at La Salle Street. This led to the North Division, now North Side, where the citizens watched the fire from their roofs, confident that they would remain privileged spectators. At about three in the morning they saw the cupola of the courthouse fall amid the flames and then discovered to their dismay that the Water Works, at their backs, had been ignited by flying embers. Soon the wooden bridges that crossed the main river were ablaze. Ships with masts and shrouds aflame added to the fuel; the red embers hurtled over the

North Division; the water supply gave out and soon the whole district was endangered.

Watching anxiously from his roof, and working with men to throw water on the embers as they fell, was Isaac N. Arnold, owner of a fine house located in the block bounded by Rush, Erie, Huron and Pine Streets. In that house Abraham Lincoln had been entertained, and among its treasures were many letters and documents dealing with the first campaigns of the Republican party. Arnold was an author, with a fine library. Surprised by the turn of the fire into the North Division, Arnold had no means of saving his treasures; they went up in flames.

Hastily sizing up the situation, Arnold determined to see the fire out from the shores of Lake Michigan. Gathering family and neighbors, he led his party to the end of the pier that ran to the lighthouse, where they found shelter. In the course of this rush through crowded streets Mrs. Arnold and one child became detached from the party. Thus Arnold arrived at the lighthouse torn with anxiety and unable to rest inside its walls.

A propeller barge lying near by caught fire and endangered the pier; the occupants of the lighthouse rushed out to limit the danger and happily saw it sink before it could damage the pier. A short time later the tug *Clifford* came steaming up to the pier. It had escaped through the fire from the river; its paint was blistered but its hull was undamaged. Arnold had an idea. If the *Clifford* had passed through the fire it could do so again. He proposed that the captain take his party aboard, steam downstream (the Chicago had been reversed in July, 1871) to the Forks and up the North Branch, where they could land in safety and Arnold could begin looking for his wife and child. The captain was hesitant, for the bridges at Rush, State, Clark and Wells streets had burned and dropped into the river and the channel contained their charred beams as well as the wrecks of the burned ships. But Arnold was a rich man, and, properly persuaded, the captain agreed to make the strangest steamboat run in the history of the Chicago.

The captain of the *Clifford* got up a good head of steam, attached the hose to its pumps and prepared to spray water over the deck as the boat proceeded through the red-hot area. Women and children were put into the pilothouse and the windows were clamped down. The men covered themselves with wet sheets and lay flat inside the bulwarks. A boy lost his hat, whereupon a man wet a handkerchief and placed it on his head.

The tug thrust its snub nose into the river, and with the forthright insolence of all tugs started its voyage. It met no impediment at Rush Street, but at State the debris of the bridge made the passage difficult and the tug had to slow up. Then the pumps gave out. But the tug kept on, and when it passed Wells Street and turned into the North Branch the passengers shouted, "We are through!" For the Northwest Side had remained unscathed. In the open lots near Lincoln Park huddled the homeless and the lost. Cyrus Hall McCormick and the bums of the road rubbed elbows, and Isaac Arnold, making his way from one group to another, found his wife and child at Newberry Place, where the Mahlon Ogden residence stood forth as the only house of that locality spared by the fire.

In the century of Chicago's history, the Great Fire, which leveled the city of three hundred thousand, is regarded as one of its pivotal events. On the southeast pylon of the Michigan Avenue bridge symbolical figures by the sculptor Henry Hering commemorate the fire under the word "Regeneration." The legend reads:

The great Chicago fire in October, 1871, devastated the city. From its ashes the people of Chicago caused a new and greater city to rise, imbued with the indomitable spirit and energy by which they have ever been guided.

From one point of view a great disaster befell literature. For the ashes of the city were hardly cool when the poets of the nation fell to. Everywhere they grasped their pens and pictured the fiery fiend leaping from roof to roof, the devouring element destroying a city. Whittier's verses with the cry, "The city of the West is dead!" are best known and least objectionable.

The most elaborate celebration of the fire came from Will M. Carleton, long popular for his homely sentimental verse, who wrote "The Burning of Chicago" for—*Our Fireside Friend*. It is impossible to repeat here the opulence of his language in his many verses. He described Chicago in more ways than any boastful man had ever dreamed before. To him it was the famous and wonderful city, the church-guarded city, the templed and altar-decked city, the turbulent, vice-laden city, the rich and voluptuous city, the treasure-strewn, fire-beaten city . . . And of course every poet predicted that it would "rise from its ashes." Even to this day the phoenix is its favorite bird, and sits in symbolical glory on the great seal of the University of Chicago.

5

Biggest of the Bascules

THERE is a bridge that spans the Chicago at a spot that the early explorers would have considered far out to sea—the great Outer Drive bridge that was erected only a few years ago. It is exceptional for its size, its cost, its location and its association with an event that will have its place in American history.

For this is the bridge that was formally dedicated by President Roosevelt on October 5, 1937. Here he made his speech advocating a policy of quarantine against aggressor nations, a message that came at a time when it was far out of line with American foreign policy and caused sharp criticism from his opponents, who considered it a breach of neutral conduct. Subsequent events have made that policy a necessity for American defense.

Today the shore line of Chicago has been pushed so far into the lake that this bridge is almost half a mile beyond the point where the Chicago had its mouth in pioneer times. Now it spans the artificially contrived "source" of the Chicago.

You see it as part of the wide roadway that runs

along Chicago's front yard. Every moment motorcars move rapidly across it. We gain an idea of the recurrent shock to which it is subject when we learn that it was

BIGGEST OF THE BASCULES

planned to carry eighty-five thousand vehicles a day. But more than that—the bridge will carry all the cars that come from either direction on its two roadways, which have four traffic lanes to each roadway. Engineers have calculated carefully the weight of a continuous stream of motorcars over the bridge.

Whirling along the outer drive in the clean air of a summer day, the man in the motorcar coming from the south enters the approach to the bridge at Monroe Street, about eight blocks away. He is riding under the open dome of the sky, with a magnificent, unobstructed panorama on both sides. To the right is the inner harbor protected by breakwaters. At Monroe Street are headquarters of the Chicago Yacht Club; at Washington Street, the Columbia Yacht Club. Hundreds of trim white sloops, yawls, a cruising schooner or two and many motorboats ride at anchor in the harbor. Out beyond the breakwater is the open lake, dark green as bottle glass, always restless, often flecked with whitecaps. Here yachts heel under the driving wind, and far out to the horizon, the low, black hulk of an ore boat, its funnel set far aft, leaves a string of black smudge on the sky.

Just beyond the Columbia Yacht Club the motorist passes the armory of the Naval Reserve. A training ship, the *Wilmette,* usually lies at the pier north of the building. Here the last green patches of Grant Park taper off and the high viaduct of Field Drive crosses the innumerable railroad tracks of the freight yards used by the Illinois Central and New York Central lines. While these yards occupy land reclaimed from river and lake, they have grown from the first tracks that the Illinois Central Railroad built on piers along the margin of the shore line to Randolph Street ninety years ago. Now the site of those piers, washed originally by the waves of the lake, is no longer visible from the outer drive; Grant Park has grown up beyond them and the tracks lie in a depressed area crossed by the Balbo Drive and numerous bridges leading from the streets of the Loop. But the railroad yards are not streamlined. They appear just as they did for half a century—filled with freight cars being shunted back and forth over innumerable switches to the appropriate freight depots, some of which are ancient limestone buildings dating back many years. One lone elevator still stands at the bank of the river in this area where once there were half a dozen. When the Illinois Central bought land here for its yards in 1855, it also bought the ruined Fort Dearborn, and pulled down all except one blockhouse.

The approach turns east into Wacker Drive, and the motorist is on the south plaza of the bridge before he is aware of it. Wacker Drive runs on a viaduct, and there are docks below it. At the entrance to the bridge stand the two bridge houses that control the machinery for lifting the span.

Here is the great bridge itself. Its steel is resplendent with aluminum paint. This is a double-deck bascule bridge, the largest of its kind, but the lower roadway, reserved for trucks, is not visible to the motorist. The bridge is 331 feet across, about the length of a city block, and when its two leaves go up to let ships enter the Chicago it opens a channel 220 feet wide below it. Small boats move beneath it in safety for its lower deck is 22 feet above the surface of the water.

The motorist may be impressed but in no mood for figures; yet today's engineering feats are worth more than the cursory glance that the cross-country traveler bestows on the works of both nature and man. If he should be "held up" by a ship passing through, he would be repaid for the delay by the spectacle of the two leaves rising slowly to a height of 132 feet as the four 110-horsepower motors shift the counterbalance, which is established by huge boxes of concrete. He may guess at the weight of the bridge; obviously it is no small figure. For besides steel the bridge has a surface of concrete. This was poured into units at Clearing, carefully adjusted for vibration to increase density, and then shipped to the bridge site. Here the separate units were lifted into the steel frame and welded into place.

It was a great undertaking, the dream of Charles H. Wacker, chairman of the Chicago Plan Commission, and it was begun as far back as 1926, when the mayor was Anton J. Cermak, the Bohemian lad from the West Side who was to die from bullets intended for the president of the United States. The various park commissions had a hard time financing it, but when the Chicago Park Commission came into existence in 1935 as a consolidation of all the park commissions with which Chicago was blessed, the success of the project was in sight. With its drives the bridge cost $11,000,000; the Chicago Park District raised 70 per cent of this by bond issues; the Public Works Administration, controlled by the secretary of the interior, Harold L. Ickes, long a Chicagoan, provided 30 per cent.

Beyond the bridge on the lakeside, and separating the river from the outer basin of Chicago harbor, are the great locks and gates that control the passing of vessels and the intake of water from the lake. The navigation lock, which has been in operation since September, 1938, is 80 feet wide, 600 feet long, 24 feet deep; it has long guide walls. Here pass over 20,000 vessels a year, but well over half are small craft, tugs, yachts and barges, while the number of vessels of over 500 tons is usually less than 3,000. Today even ships of war, built in the many shipyards of the Great Lakes, enter the Chicago for passage down the Mississippi to the Gulf.

But the whole Controlling Works, as it is called, concerns itself with much more than navigation. Here is the place where the flow of water from the lake into the Chicago is regulated; four sluice gates, ten feet square, set in the basin walls on each side of the stream, regulate the withdrawal of water, and on the landward side of each of the eight sluice gates are tide gates that automatically close when the river threatens to rise higher than the lake. This phenomenon occurs often during the periods of heavy rains in spring and fall, and then the Chicago exhibits the remarkable feat of rising higher than its source.

This, then, is the realization of a dream. A century ago early settlers and ship captains cursed the sand bars that blocked the Chicago River and made lighterage necessary. The bars were dredged out, the channel deepened and widened, and the river was forced to run in the straight line that nature abhors. This bridge and its locks mark man's final conquest of the river barrier.

PART NINE

Trails of the Des Plaines and the Kankakee

I

Picnic Grounds for the Millions

Wᴇsᴛ of Chicago, through the wooded suburbs, winds the Des Plaines River, which now, in common with the Chicago, helps to carry the waters of the
Sanitary District Canal into the Illinois. Far more beautiful than any part of the Chicago, it has become the
possession of the people through the timely institution
of the Forest Preserve of Cook County, which admin-
isters 33,000 acres, along the Chicago and the Des
Plaines, for the recreation of the millions who live here.

In these historic haunts of the Indian, crossed by
roads used by the first emigrant wagons and stagecoaches, wild flowers, trees and wild animals thrive as
they did before the white man came. The white man
comes today in huge numbers, but so vast is the extent
of the Forest Preserve and so well channeled are his
movements that the forests and fields receive no injury
from his holiday romps. Careful planning has its part
in this enterprise. Take, for instance, the matter of picnic groups, which must be provided with permanent
fireplaces, indestructible tables and suitable refuse boxes.
By encouraging with facilities the moderate-sized groups

of around fifty, and sending large organizations to private groves, the Forest Preserve Commission has increased the usefulness of the parks while protecting them.

One day the poet Sandburg walked among the trees of these public grounds and left his impressions in a poem well suited to the free, outdoor air of the West. "And then one Sunday afternoon," he wrote, "I wandered out along the Des Plaines River. And I saw a crowd of Hungarians under the trees with their women and children and a keg of beer and an accordion."

For in these vast meadows, woods, hills and valleys, there is room for a great diversity of recreation and outdoor life. Fishermen try their skill in casting pools and fish in running streams; hikers follow innumerable paths through the woods and riders find bridle paths everywhere. Boy Scouts with their leaders, bicyclists, mushroom experts and humble hunters for dandelion roots and greens indicate that all the fun out of doors is not in gazing from the windows of a motorcar speeding over sun-baked concrete roads.

Here grow bur oak, white oak, cottonwood, poplar, shagbark hickory, black locust, ash, basswood and maple; here, in many varieties, is the hawthorn bush, bright with its red berries in the fall, while briers, wild grape and elders grow profusely. Constantly the officials are at work restoring natural beauty and providing for the needs of human visitors. In many cases the old, natural usages are continued. Several of the ancient fords, which served both Indians and settlers, are still in use.

I remember crossing one of the famous fords of the

Des Plaines in a motorcar several years ago. On the farther bank a number of men beckoned me on and then stood grinning as I began the drive through the swiftly-flowing waters. Mistakenly I put on speed, thereby throwing up a fan of water that was beautiful to see. But in midstream my motor stopped and there I sat, marooned at high tide. With a shout of laughter several men ran out into the stream and pushed the car up the bank. "You have to go slow when you cross that ford," said one good-naturedly, "else you get water in your carburetor." I feared a long trip to a garage and a bill for repairs, but the leader laughed. "Just let her dry out a bit," he said. "You're not the first one; a dozen got stuck here." He and his friends took nothing for their help; apparently pushing cars over the ford was a holiday lark to them.

The visitor who drives, rides or goes on fishing trips through the parks of the Forest Preserve of Cook County gets an impression of their luxuriant foliage and vast extent, but only gradually recognizes the care with which roads have been developed, natural sites preserved, marshes and ponds cleared of stagnant pools, and the original wild life protected. From the Skokie south the North Branch touches some of the Forest Preserve lands adjacent or close to the city; the others are along the Des Plaines and in the Calumet and Sag district farther south.

You have only to come upon some of the friendly signboards that replace the old-fashioned admonitory police orders to recognize a systematic attempt to make everyone feel responsible for the beauty of the Forest Preserve. These signs blend into the landscape. In a wooded area a rustic sign points the way to natural beauty. "I am an old country lane," it reads. "Now I have been officially vacated and closed (I never liked automobiles anyway). I invite you to walk as folks have walked for generations and be friendly with my trees, my flowers and my wild creatures."

To create friendships with trees, flowers and wild creatures—everything works to achieve this result. With hunting and trapping eliminated and fishing restricted to rivers and creeks, the camera enthusiast is encouraged. The wild life native to this region when the whites first penetrated these woods comes back to its old haunts. The migrating herons, egrets and shore birds stop in the pools; the woodcock, upland plover, quail, wood duck, bittern, prairie chicken and ruffled grouse thrive once more. Crops are planted to provide these birds with their usual fare. But artificial breeding and the introduction of exotic birds is considered out of place.

The man who keeps books for the Forest Preserve deals in astronomical figures. His records indicate the huge extent of the playgrounds needed for millions who no longer find the city streets adequate for outings. From one point of view the Forest Preserve is a great pioneer work in recreation; from another it is evidence of displacement. The pioneer had the fields at his back door; the modern man must travel miles for natural beauty and relaxation.

Thus the man with the books puts down that he has over 33,000 acres to provide for; that 4,450,000 people are able to make simultaneous use of them; that for one year the number of individuals seen in the

woods reached 15,000,000; that 567 acres were refor-
ested and nearly 1,000,000 trees and shrubs planted in
1940 . . . We learn of benches cast in concrete by the
thousand; of outdoor fireplaces built to standard size
by the hundred, and the number of shovels used, wagons
filled and unloaded, tires renewed, would convince even
the most skeptical that inanimate objects increase and
multiply.

2

A Prosaic Tale

ROMANTIC vistas along the banks of a river green with verdure are the delight of the idler, but drainage is the prosaic occupation of the engineer. How to absorb storm waters without causing a flood and how to dispose of the sewage of a metropolis are problems that have to be solved anew by each generation so long as the city expands. Finding both the river and the canal inadequate for this purpose, the state of Illinois in 1889 established the Sanitary District of Chicago, an independent body, to build and control the Chicago Sanitary and Ship Canal, usually called the Drainage Canal.

My college work included courses in political science with Professor Charles E. Merriam, under whose direction I visited the Bridewell, the Drainage Canal and other public institutions. Invariably he would stress the wastefulness in expenditure and tax burdens caused by the multiplicity of governing bodies in Chicago, all getting part of the taxpayer's dollar. Such bodies were the numerous park boards, since merged into one park commission; the Forest Preserve Commission and the

Sanitary District, governed by nine trustees. Professor Merriam declared that these provided many overlapping jobs that could be reduced if the work were centralized in the municipality. There were some advantages attached to the separation, and the efficient operation of the Forest Preserve and the Drainage Canal speak well for this, though it is only in the present generation that far-reaching economies have been made.

The Drainage Canal was a new channel, running parallel with the old canal. It started at Robey Street, now Damen Avenue, and was planned to be 28 miles long, 110 to 202 feet wide, and 24 feet deep. Its dredges tore into the plain; its charges of dynamite blasted great holes in the native limestone. Today the Drainage Canal runs like a livid scar across the prairie, its banks piled high with stone debris on which verdure refuses to grow.

By the end of 1899 the Drainage Canal had cost $75,000,000 and was nearly completed. Only a small ridge of earth near Kedzie Avenue separated the new ditch from the old river. The trustees of the district hovered between relief and apprehension. They had surmounted most of the legal fights, but a possible injunction by St. Louis was still a black cloud on their horizon.

Then came January 1, 1900, with the promise of a new century. The time had come to act. The nine trustees, led by their president, B. A. Eckhart, accompanied by their engineer, Isham Randolph, and a few newspapermen, in the gray dawn of the new year went to the Kedzie location. If any of them had been celebrating the night before they must have been pretty tired by now. But inspired by the importance of the event, they grasped shovels and resolutely began digging away at the wall of earth that separated river and ditch. Soon they saw that this was futile. A big dredge, put on the job, proved that "when it came to throwing earth, it was worth several hundred of the most distinguished trustees." It was tough even for the dredge, so four sticks of dynamite were stuck into the last hard soil. With a flash of fire old timbers and soil flew into the air and the waters from the river rushed into the ditch. "It is open! It is open!" exclaimed President Eckhart. Surveying the waters rushing into the breach, he exclaimed, "It is the Niagara of Chicago!"

The river now began drawing water out of Lake Michigan in a torrent. By eleven o'clock 30,000 cubic feet a minute were flowing through the cut; by nightfall, 90,000. It would take ten days to fill the channel as far as Lockport, twenty-eight miles beyond, where the flow could be regulated. At Wells Street the level of the river dropped six inches. Tugboat pilots observed that the Chicago had a perceptible current "upriver." In the meantime the old Illinois and Michigan Canal did not yield any of its prerogatives. Its pumps at Bridgeport were still taking water out of the Chicago and pouring it into the old canal at 50,000 cubic feet per minute. But its days were numbered.

The coup of the trustees made a national sensation. The New York *Tribune* admonished Chicago for its desperate haste and called it not altogether creditable. St. Louis citizens were furious. Momentarily they expected a huge flood of sewage to pollute their river water. Congressman Bartholdt protested to the secretary of war and the attorney general, who told him to go to the courts. The Sanitary District trustees were

jubilant. They had "restored the ancient relations between Lake Michigan and the Mississippi, which were
interrupted by Nature." They did not explain that this
interruption must have occurred half a million years
before, sufficiently long ago for the relations of both to
cool. President Eckhart sent a letter to General Russell
A. Alger, former secretary of war who had authorized
the work, describing how the river had been turned
into the canal "without any public ceremony of any
kind, because St. Louis threatened to enjoin us." With
satisfaction he watched the Chicago reach its full flow
of 300,000 cubic feet of water per minute (that is,
5,000 cubic feet per second) and welcomed the change
from the black, putrid mass of the old days. "The river
is as blue as the sky above us," he wrote. The trustees
voted a bronze medal to General Alger.

But the Drainage Canal did not solve Chicago's
storm and sewage problems. Within a few years Ca-
nadian engineers professed to see the lake waters danger-
ously lowered and a long series of court actions began
to limit the supply of water that Chicago draws from
Lake Michigan. They continue to this day, with Chicago limited to 1,500 cubic feet of water a second, which
has proved inadequate, especially in dry seasons. The
threat of contagion from the polluted waters and the
necessity of keeping the Illinois as free as possible from
sewage has brought about the establishment of extensive
works for the treatment of sewage, provided fertilizer
as a by-product that may prove profitable, and presented the language with such unlovely words as "acti-
vated sludge." The ramifications of sewage problems are
so wide that they occupy the energies of numerous engineers and fill many volumes.

After the Drainage Canal came the new Illinois Waterway project, the 327-mile trade barge route from Lake Michigan to the Mississippi, another development of the dream of Jolliet and La Salle for a water route to the Gulf of Mexico. The waterway was officially opened on February 27, 1933, and as the celebrants moved down the Chicago from the lake they passed a messenger from the antipodes—Admiral Byrd's ship, moored west of the Michigan Avenue bridge. On June 23rd there was another ceremony at the bridge with the secretary of war, George H. Dern, present, and the mayors of New Orleans and Chicago felicitating each other. The mayor of New Orleans emptied a bottle of salt water from the gulf into the Chicago, thereby re-calling how Governor De Witt Clinton of New York joined the waters of Lake Erie and the Hudson more than one hundred years before at the opening of the Erie Canal. The pioneers were not forgotten. Indian canoes mingled with modern gasoline motor cruisers; La Salle, Tonty, Marquette and Jolliet were impersonated, as the dream which the Chicago had called into reality was remembered.

Today Chicago watches with interest the development of the St. Lawrence Seaway project, long the football of politics, which is expected to open the port to heavy Atlantic tonnage from Europe. This is also expected to increase shipbuilding on the Great Lakes. The advantages of building ships of war in the interior are many, if waterways to the sea are available. The federal government recognized this before the war in giving contracts for submarines to shipbuilding yards on the lakes.

3

Lockport and the Des Plaines

THERE is a high wire fence at Lockport, thirty-six miles beyond the gates of the Chicago at Lake Michigan, and you can't approach closely without being hailed and asked your business. For Lockport has locks that are necessary to keep the Illinois Waterway in condition for traffic, and in these days of war the government authorities cannot run the risk of damage by sabotage.

There are two locks at Lockport and though the state built the major lock, the War Department now runs it. Day after day towboats and barges carrying heavy freight—numbering 8,000 to 10,000 craft a year—call upon the government to open its great gates. There is a drop of 40 feet here, and the gates are 20 feet high at one end and 60 feet high at the other. The lock is 110 feet wide and 600 feet long, and it takes 15 minutes to lower the water. A lock for smaller craft is operated by the Chicago Sanitary District and accommodates over 500 boats a year. Here are the locks that help regulate the amount of water drawn from Lake

Michigan. This is also the place where electric power is generated.

Just before Lemont is reached the Calumet Sag Channel, coming from the east, empties its waters into the main channel. The Calumet draws its waters from the Little Calumet, which is part of the extensive waterways system at the foot of Lake Michigan. Its flow is controlled by a lock at Blue Island. It moves through a picturesque valley carved by the glaciers, in addition to which the spades, dredges and dynamite blasts of man have provided it with a channel 20 feet deep, with a bottom width of 60 feet through the Niagara limestone section. At Lockport this greatly augmented waterway flows into the Des Plaines and proceeds toward Joliet and the Illinois.

The Calumet Sag Channel comes from the industrial district that has grown up at the base of Lake Michigan, in Illinois and Indiana. The development of steel mills and allied manufactories in this district has given Calumet harbor a greater tonnage than Chicago harbor. Thus, in a normal year, Chicago harbor receives nearly 2,000,000 tons and sends eastward 1,000,000 tons; but Calumet harbor receives over 5,000,000 tons and expedites eastward nearly 3,000,000 tons. This alone does not account for the traffic jam at the south end of the lake, for it does not include the adjoining harbors in Indiana—Indiana Harbor, which receives 3,000,000 tons for the same period. Freight loadings for the present years of intense activity in the steel mills will be considerably increased, for iron ore creates this huge tonnage, and the low, black ore ships have been multiplying on the Chicago horizon. Once drawn up beside the docks of the steel mills, they are emptied by scoops that run on chain belts and get under way without many hours in port.

So many changes have been made in the channels of the Little Calumet and Great Calumet rivers that the Indians who once roamed these sunken lands would never recognize them. Even Calumet Lake has been tinkered with, and now acts as a sort of pool for overflow, emptying waters into the lake when it is low and absorbing some of the waters of the lake when it is high. Yet with all the slips and channels built to accommodate factories, the Calumet and its tributaries perform the most amazing evolutions through the prairie, as if trying to serve everyone at once—provide water for docks, furnish volume for the Sag Channel, irrigate golf clubs and woods and wind in and out among the cabbage and turnip fields of the Dutch and Polish garden truck farmers. The names given to woods, preserves and golf clubs in this region commemorate Chicago's characters; the Grand Calumet flows through Burnham Woods, while the Little Calumet flows through Beaubien Preserve and Whistler Preserve, and winds in and out among the old stamping grounds of an Indian tribe in Kickapoo Grove. Close at hand the Pipe o' Peace Country Club calls to mind that the white man has found a quiet oasis where the Indian once stalked the pioneers.

Beyond Lockport the waters have but a few miles to go before they reach Joliet and Brandon Road lock and dam. There is a fall of 44 feet in the four and a half miles in the Des Plaines between Lockport and Joliet. Here the dam is 1,350 feet long and there are 21 gates, each 60 feet long; in stormy weather as much as 35,000 cubic feet of water per second have poured over the dam. When the state wanted to convert this power into electrical energy it had to fight Samuel Insull and his associates.

The old hunters and explorers used this route and often mentioned a famous landmark, Mount Joliet, a hill, sixty feet high, that rose above the plain at this point. When Harriet Martineau visited the Kinzies in the thirties, she was eager to see the wild prairie and drove out in a stage. In her book she recalled the wild primrose growing over the prairie and the activity at the ford on the Des Plaines River, where a signboard announced the river as Oplain—a corruption of Aux Plaines. She climbed Mount Juliet and praised the "soft beauty" of the view. The town of Juliet, laid out in 1834, became the town of Joliet in 1845. The city of Joliet, with over forty thousand inhabitants, has grown up on the prairie that Harriet Martineau saw, but none of its residents can climb to the top of the famous hill. Finding no reference to it in modern guidebooks I inquired of the authorities. C. J. Kellem, manager of the Joliet Association of Commerce, supplied its epitaph:

Mount Joliet was composed of a high-grade gravel which was quarried and sold over the years.

About seven miles beyond this point the Du Page River flows into the Des Plaines. A large highway bridge, 350 feet long, crosses the river just above the confluence and gives a view of the surrounding country. There is something that evokes the musing of the philosopher in the spectacle of the little town of Channahon, with its few houses standing like sleepy old men above the tree-lined towpath and crumbling locks of the old Illinois and Michigan Canal. Indeed, Edgar Lee Masters has brooded over this evidence of misused enterprise, recalling that once this was a lively, noisy hamlet on a road where "countless wage-slaves dug a hundred miles of waterway." In his poem about Channahon, which means the meeting of the waters, Masters tells us that "an ancient house up-stream looks out with window eyes over the dead canal." Channahon survives to become a picnic ground, for the state is developing roadside parks along the old towpaths. Not far away are the remains of ancient mounds, some of them covering skeletons buried a thousand years ago, indicating that this region was a favorite haunt of the red man ages before the white man came to riot wastefully with nature's bounty.

We have but a few miles farther to go to reach the place where the Kankakee River joins the Des Plaines. From this point on it is called the Illinois and the history and modern significance to commerce of that waterway has been fully described by James Gray in *The Illinois*. But the Kankakee comes into the Chicago orbit, partly because Indians, trappers, explorers and settlers used this route as an alternative when the Des Plaines was raging in flood and the Chicago covering a wide area with its overflow. Also because, in more recent decades, the Kankakee has drawn poets and artists from the Chicago region to its wooded banks.

When the roving bands of Miami and Shawnee Indians penetrated the Illinois country or wandered back to their villages along the Wabash and the Ohio, they used the route of the Kankakee. When they went to the trading post at the mouth of the St. Joseph they came this way. The Kickapoos were at home here. The channel was full of dead timber and underbrush and the place was pockmarked with treacherous bogs, but that made it the resort of wild animals and gave good hunting. When the white men came, they, too, took advantage of the excellent game and fish and trappers made their homes in isolated cabins that lasted down to our day.

4

Fabled Marshes of the Kankakee

THERE is something musical and satisfying about the word "Kankakee." As nearly as the whites could apprehend the sounds the Indians uttered, it was Kyankeaku, or Beautiful Land. Later the settlers transcribed it as Theakiki and Judge Storrow, one of the early travelers, demonstrated how it turned into the present word when he wrote it Kienkiki. Judging by the description Marquette gives of his final trip back to Michigan, it was this route that he followed in 1675 when, weak from illness, he left the Indian village of Kaskaskia, where he had preached about the glories of the Immaculate Virgin for the last time. La Salle came this way with his men from the St. Joseph in the hard journey of 1679 that led to the building of the ill-fated Fort Crèvecœur. Tonty of the Iron Hand marched this way from the east. Early in the 19th century Hubbard, the trader, was stopped by the ice in the Kankakee.

Earl H. Reed was one of the Chicago men I knew who wrote about the Kankakee. An architect, he enjoyed making delicate etchings of the Kankakee wilds and the stunted oaks on the sand dunes below Lake

283

Michigan. On his vacations he visited the Kankakee, became acquainted with the picturesque French-American hamlets, and gloried in the bird life and rank vegetation of the roving river. He enjoyed sitting on the porch of a country store on a drowsy afternoon discussing rain and politics with old farmers and complacent storekeepers. But though he wrote about quaint characters on the Kankakee he often betrayed the same melancholy note with which Edgar Lee Masters views the ruin of human enterprise in this region. Reed saw the coming destruction of this haven of wild life, and appropriately named his book *Tales of a Vanishing River*.

Reed told me that the landowners had a theory that the Kankakee wandered over the most fertile soil of the state, made so by the deposits of manure from the great flights of birds that had stopped on the Kankakee for countless centuries. If they drained the bayous and channeled the river they could reclaim this land for rich farms. After long agitation they got funds and dredges began uprooting the brush and digging deep channels to carry the water to a central channel. Woodcutters followed and cut the trees and farmers turned the black loam with their plows and planted their corn and wheat. It was all that was needed, he said, to complete the ruin of the bird sanctuary, already invaded by hunters with quick-firing guns.

In the backwaters of the Kankakee Reed had found the horns of deer and elk and traces of the buffalo; the inhabitants talked about woodchuck, raccoon and foxes; wildcats roved the timberlands and the prolific muskrat swam among the reeds. Here, indeed, was a river of legend, the waterway known to man and beast, fre-

quented by all the wild life of the prairie and hence the
favorite ground of hunter and trapper, Indian and
white. Sluggish and meandering, like all rivers in a land
with only a little declination, the Kankakee was even
more boggy, marshy and overgrown with brush and
trees than the old Mud Lake area of the early Chicago.
Its vegetation was luxuriant—oaks, maples, willows,
ash and sycamores grew in its bayous and on its islands:
woodbine and poison ivy spread their flaming autumnal
colors over the trees, and all forms of prairie grasses and
rushes were to be found there. Migratory ducks, geese
and heron stopped on their flights north and south.
Overhead the passenger pigeon darkened the skies and
bore down the branches. Partridges, wild turkeys, mal-
lards and canvasbacks refreshed themselves in these
waters. Crows, permanent residents, added to the noise.
Reed saw this wild life go. The dredges tackled not only
undergrowth but routed old trappers and destroyed
their cabins. The push of population was depriving
America of another oasis. Mournfully Reed recorded
his sorrow: "The Vanishing River moves on through a
twilight of ignorance and error." Almost too late the
people recognized their loss. The Kankakee State Game
Preserve was formed and twenty-three hundred acres
were donated by farmers of Indiana. Part of the land
has been restored for the use of wild life.

In Chicago there lives today an alert, energetic man
named Wallace Bruce Amsbary, a poet, a lover of folk-
lore and a lecturer on literature. A number of years ago,
when the White Paper Club was still young, and Emerson Hough, Frank Morris, Dr. Lee Alexander Stone,
Frank Reilly, Keith Preston, William Gerard Chapman

and other bookmen used to meet at the University Club, I heard Amsbary throw his powerful zest into the recitation of ballads, from "McAndrew's Hymn," which was sired by Kipling, to the "Captain of the Marguerite," which belongs to *The Ballads of Bourbonnais*, which he wrote himself.

Bourbonnais is a dreamy village in the Kankakee country, and like St. Anne and a few other hamlets was settled by French Canadians and still retains its characteristic atmosphere. The shrine of St. Anne, visited annually by many, dates from 1852. The French Canadians liked the backwoodsy air of the Kankakee lands. When the Illinois Central Railroad mapped its route through their town, it met with an unexpectedly hostile reception. While other towns pulled wires to get the railroad, Bourbonnais fought the project so doggedly that the Illinois Central took its tracks to the city of Kankakee. True, Kankakee is but three miles away, but Bourbonnais was satisfied.

As a boy Amsbary visited the Kankakee country and became acquainted with the homely ways of the people. In later years he was talking with James Whitcomb Riley when the latter said, "There's a lot of poetical truck layin' round and goin' to waste." The quaintness of this Hoosier remark impressed him and he began turning over in his mind the treasure trove of the Kankakee. One night Charles Eugene Banks invited him to a party in his studio in Chicago; like the rest of the guests Amsbary was expected to entertain by producing an original verse. He recalled the lore of the Kankakee and after several hours of wrestling, produced the first of his ballads of the French Canadians: "De

Cirque at Ol' Sainte Anne." It caught on. In New York Mrs. Cathern Hunt, wife of Richard Hunt, the architect, asked Amsbary to contribute to a program at the parish house of Grace Church and he recited the poem. Mrs. Hunt was pleased with it and communicated with Richard Watson Gilder of the *Century Magazine,* who wrote Amsbary that if he would consent to a slight change in one of the lines he would accept it.

"I was out on a Chautauqua lecture tour," said Amsbary, "and by a curious coincidence I received Gilder's check for $20 the very week I was speaking in Kankakee. He asked for more ballads for a feature on American humor that he was planning. I had had no idea of writing more ballads, but his suggestion made me aware of the soft patois and the interesting ways of the people I met. Each day I was taken to the Chautauqua grounds on a little steamer named *Marguerite.* The skipper was a cocky and self-important, but good-natured fellow named Captain Gougar, and he had a little French-Canadian deck hand who hauled taut the stern sheets, took tickets and ran errands. I used to greet the captain with a salute and 'Well, how's the captain of the *Marguerite* that sails the Kankakee?' The phrase stuck in my mind and became the basis for the ballad about the captain. It appeared in the *Century* in May, 1902, and my book, *The Ballads of Bourbonnais,* was published in 1904."

That's a long time ago, and recalls the period when poets were writing dialect; when Joel Chandler Harris was amusing his readers with legends about Br'er Rabbit; when James Whitcomb Riley was describing barefoot days in Indiana and the old swimming hole had not yet been filled up to smooth the grounds of a golf club. And when Carl Sandburg, having carried a gun to Puerto Rico and back, was wondering where he could get a field hand's job.

PART TEN

Tall Towers and Opera Houses

I

Architects in Babel

IN the spring of 1887 a young man who was to leave his mark on human habitations arrived at the Wells Street station with a portfolio of mechanical drawings. From the farmlands of Wisconsin he came to get a job in the big town. It was dark and drizzling and the arc lights sputtered. He followed the crowd to the Wells Street bridge over the Chicago, and there he beheld "the mysterious dark of the river with dim masts, hulks, and funnels hung with lights half-smothered in gloom—reflected in the black beneath." Years later, when he was a national figure, he wrote his autobiography and thus recalled his first introduction to Chicago:

"Suddenly the clanging of a bell. The crowd began to run. I wondered why: found myself alone and realized why in time to get off, but stayed on as the bridge swung out with me into the channel and a tug, puffing clouds of steam, came pushing along below, pulling at an enormous grain boat, towing it slowly along through the gap. Stood there studying the river sights in the drizzling rain, until the bridge followed after and closed to open the street again. Later, I never crossed the river without being charmed by somber beauty."

The youth was Frank Lloyd Wright, not quite eighteen. He was viewing the buildings of a metropolis for the first time, and already judging their fitness and architectural value and turning aside from some in disgust, while measuring others with admiring eyes. Sensitive to the "grinding and piling up of blind forces" he apprehended the dynamic energy of the city, the turmoil of its streets, the wealth and ruthlessness expressed in the uneven heights of its buildings, which had just begun to thrust their roofs up toward the sky.

For Frank Lloyd Wright had arrived in Chicago at a turning point in its history. The river, which had been flowing past houses that looked more or less like brick cubes, was about to reflect soaring masses and cloud-piercing pinnacles. The successful men who called themselves captains of industry, who had rolled up big fortunes with the expansion of trade, were ready to express their ambitions and accomplishments in stone. And a corps of architects, most of them young, eager to break with tradition and try the unusual, bent over drawing boards, ready to give America an object that symbolized the sudden rise to wealth of a highly individualized society—the skyscraper.

As Wright walked the streets looking for a place to hang his hat, he encountered the beginnings of what architects the world over were to call "Chicago construction." Wright could study the plain brick walls of the Montauk Building, built five years before by Daniel H. Burnham and John Wellborn Root. On the outside it was free from the pillars and curlicues of earlier decades. Inside it had important innovations. Its cast-iron columns were protected against fire and for the first time a structure rested on a floating foundation—a raft of steel and concrete. He could also observe the Home Insurance Building, four years old, the first to use skeleton construction—supporting walls, floors, partitions and roof on the cast-iron skeleton, and, in the opinion of architects today, the first to be entitled to be called a modern skyscraper. This was the design of Major William LeBaron Jenney, who, in the words of Thomas Tallmadge, "stumbled upon it" while seeking the greatest possible window space. There was also the Tacoma of Holabird & Roche, just being built, the second skyscraper, which used rivets instead of bolts, had cast-iron columns and steel girders and hung its façade on the steel. A way had been found to build into the sky, for no longer would the weight of the walls have to rest wholly on a wide base of masonry.

In 1889, two years after his arrival, Wright was to see the erection of the last of the great buildings of solid masonry—the Monadnock, which rears its seventeen stories of brick like a plain pylon at Jackson and Dearborn, with the base walls seven feet thick. Though modern in its appearance, the Monadnock was in truth the last of an era, for it did not use the steel frame. Ironically, Boston investors were responsible for this conservatism, for they did not trust the new Chicago method. It is said that while Root designed the building, Burnham ordered its plain façade and thus created an effect thoroughly in the modern manner. On an opposite corner Burnham & Root erected the Great Northern

Hotel on different principles—a steel frame carrying the brick exterior. The Great Northern was a sensation during the World's Fair of 1893; still in excellent condition, it fell a victim to the new Chicago subway a few years ago, because its owners did not feel justified in expending a fortune for new foundations, demanded by subway construction.

To the young dreamer, the city was cruel, "murderously actual." The billboards, the trucks, the noisy cable cars, gripping the cable that ran beneath the street and plunging over the hard rails; the torrent of smoke that blinded the eyes and filled the throat—these were enough to inspire terror in an artist. "The gray, soiled river with its mist of steam and smoke, was the only beauty," concluded Wright, and then added: "That smelled to heaven."

Wright found a job with an architect at $8 a week, and a short time later learned that Louis Sullivan, of Adler & Sullivan, wanted a man to work on drawings for the new Auditorium, and landed that, at $25. He thus acquired a drawing board in the office of two of America's greatest architects, and they had hired a young man who was to go farther than both of them, who was to build houses that fitted the long vistas of the open prairie, originate construction that withstood an earthquake, and plant his modern ideas in fertile minds throughout the world. For Wright studied houses in terms of environment, material and the needs of the people who were to use them, just as Louis Sullivan reiterated his faith that form follows function, that it interprets the life of the people not in a set style, but in flexible adjustment to the community in which it is to be used.

The growing importance of Chicago as a business center, the clamor for well-lighted offices that could be easily reached, the expansion of headquarters of many railroads and industries, accelerated the demand for new buildings of great size. The river had a part in this conspiracy to pile the chief buildings in a small area, for it had helped concentrate business on the land south and east of the main branch. The routes of commerce, coming chiefly from the west and southwest, dictated the approach of the principal railroads; the river determined the site of the terminal warehouses. Thus the river combined with commerce to map the outlines of the city, upsetting the choice of the pioneers of the Kinzie era, who had built on the North Side.

The Chicago fire of 1871 brought opportunities to rebuild the city along original lines, but the West longed for the flamboyant styles of European capitals. Potter Palmer, who had pioneered in dry goods, built himself a castle of dark, rugged stone that seemed intended to repel land attacks. The Court House and the Palmer House, considered marvels of design, presented a riot of cornices, pillars and dormers, ideal for pigeon roosts. Frank Lloyd Wright thought the Palmer House looked "like an ugly old, old man whose wrinkles were all in the wrong place owing to a misspent life." Yet it was less than sixteen years old.

Many of the buildings destroyed in the fire were rebuilt by John M. van Osdel, Chicago's first architect, who was brought from New York in 1836 by William B. Ogden. When he saw the fire headed toward his office he gathered his blueprints and buried them in a pit in his yard. After the fire he rebuilt over a mile and a half of frontage, and it was said that many of his new buildings looked exactly like their predecessors.

Pioneer Chicago started with log cabins and turned to clapboards when the sawmills began operating, importing shingles and sash from better equipped mills on the Great Lakes. But the substantial building material was brick and limestone, the latter cut in quarries up the south branch of the river. Soon Lake Street was lined with nondescript buildings of red brick, two to four stories high. The Lake House, on the north bank, was Chicago's first substantial hotel and its cupola overlooked the roofs for several decades. But the Tremont became the best-known hotel of early Chicago.

Old-timers could shoot ducks on the Chicago from the porch of the first Tremont House, which stood at the northwest corner of Lake and Dearborn streets. It burned in 1839, and then Ira Couch took hold and built the new Tremont on the southeast corner of Lake and Dearborn. When this burned down in 1849, Couch built the new brick hotel, 160 by 180 feet in size, five stories high, which was to be associated with many famous events and personalities before its destruction in the great fire of 1871.

In this hotel Patti gave her first Chicago concert at the age of eight; from its balcony Lincoln and Douglas addressed noisy political meetings, and here Douglas died. Ira Couch achieved a certain posthumous fame by sleeping in a tomb so well built that it could not be removed from the graveyard that preceded Lincoln Park, and there it stands today. But by the time of the

Lincoln convention, when the Tremont was the head-quarters of the Republican National Committee and the Lincoln managers, the owner was a man with another name destined to become famous in Chicago hotel history—John B. Drake, later manager of the famous Grand Pacific. After the great fire the Tremont was rebuilt as a large, modern hotel, but so swift was the growth of the West that it was outmoded within twenty-five years. Then it became an office building and the Medill School of Journalism of Northwestern University was lodged there before it moved to Wieboldt Hall. Until a few years ago its original lobby pavement of large black and white tiles and its walnut staircases were intact. It was razed during the depression and today its fame lives solely in the sign of the Tremont Auto Park Garage, where you can park your motor car for "25 cents a morning, 6 A.M. to noon."

The most interesting episode associated with the Tremont and other Chicago buildings of the 1850's was the gigantic street-level raising decreed by the authorities to pull Chicago out of its mud. In the first twenty years of Chicago's corporate history not only wagons but pedestrians were mired in the very heart of town. The warning sign "No Bottom Here" was encountered often. Charles Cleaver saw a stagecoach stuck in the mud in front of the Sherman House; not far away two women sank into the mire and were extricated with heroic efforts. The first public loan made by the trustees of the town was for $60 and was used to drain a mud hole in Clark Street, south of Washington. In the late fifties Chicago began raising its streets. The property owners either had to raise their buildings or live in basements. The major work of raising the buildings three to four feet was accomplished by a young engineer named George M. Pullman, who used thousands of jack-screws. It cost $45,000 to pull the Tremont up four feet. When new cellars were dug the excavated earth was thrown into the streets; and as buildings were raised at different times Chicago presented an extroardinary appearance, with sidewalks leading from one level to another by steps, and streets uneven from the filling operations.

W. W. Boyington was one of the best-known architects of the pre-fire era and survived it to build a number of the new railroad stations and the Board of Trade. One of his most distinguished buildings was the Crosby Opera House of 1865, for which he adapted an Italianate style. Less successful was his Board of Trade, which so offended the sensibilities of young Frank Lloyd Wright that he refused to ask Boyington for a job. The original had a tower 225 feet high, which began to sink and had to be removed. But Boyington ought to be remembered for one of Chicago's most graceful relics of the pre-fire age—the tower of the old Water Works, on North Michigan Avenue. This delicate Gothic pillar, now mellowed in golden limestone, had a simple utilitarian function—it contained a standpipe, 138 feet high, which absorbed the throbs of the pumps as they sent water into Chicago's mains. It achieved the dubious distinction of being denounced as an imitation by Oscar Wilde, in the course of a lecture in Chicago in 1882. He called it "a castellated monstrosity with pepper boxes stuck all over it," and said, "I am amazed that any people could so abuse Gothic art, and make a structure look, not like a water tower, but like the tower of a medieval castle." This was the argument of the future—that one age shall not copy the styles of another, and was to be urged by Sullivan and Wright. But Chicagoans loved the Water Tower, and today it is a reminiscence of another American period, and quite distinct from its Gothic originals.

Of the men who began changing the face of Chicago in the 1890's Wright's employers, Adler and Sullivan, were to leave their mark on the city for more than fifty years. Dankmar Adler was born in Germany and served as artilleryman with Sherman; it was said that he "designed" the bridges Sherman hastily improvised on his march to the sea. The great fire was a windfall to him; his firm drew the plans for over one hundred new buildings. Eventually Adler and Sullivan faced their greatest opportunity, the erection of the mightiest building of the Midwest, the Auditorium. It was a symbol of Chicago's aspiration to cultural greatness, just as actually it was proof that the generation of McCormick, Field, Leiter, Peck, Crane, Swift, Palmer, Armour, Deering and Pullman had reached maturity and power.

2

How to Give Away an Opera House

THE Opera House that W. W. Boyington designed for Uranus H. Crosby, the distiller, was an elaborate edifice, but it did not last more than six years. Yet in two years it was known all over the country. It was the subject of a most scandalous lottery, when, on January 22, 1867, it was offered to the public at $5 a chance. If speculation was in Chicago's blood, this brought it to fever heat.

Uranus H. Crosby built the Opera House on the north side of Washington Street, about midway between State and Dearborn, in 1865. Crosby had made a fortune as a distiller and was said to have put about $600,000 into the structure. It betrayed, in its classic lines, the aspiration to culture and artistic eminence of the owner and his associates, who turned from trade to cultivate art. It had a formal Italian façade, surmounted by a mansard roof; the main entrance had a high arched opening. It seated twenty-five hundred; its stage was spacious, its proscenium high; there was a huge balcony, and when the hundreds of gas lamps were lighted it provided a fitting setting for the display of gowns of

Chicago's fashionable set. The first floor front was occupied by such music enterprises as W. W. Kimball, Bauer & Company, and Root & Cady. It had an art gallery packed chiefly with examples of the storytelling art of the day. It was one of the show places of pre-fire Chicago, the house where Adelaide Ristori, still tingling from being snowbound in Indiana, spoke the classic lines of Medea and trod the boards as the tragic Mary Stuart.

In January, 1867, Uranus H. Crosby made the classic gesture of theater managers and announced that he was broke. He could finance the house no longer. He proposed to pull out of his hole and bestow a great favor on the community by giving everybody a chance to own the Opera House—a gigantic lottery of 210,000 tickets, at $5 a ticket. To sweeten the proposal he also offered 305 works of art, to be drawn separately, but included in the original price. Tickets would be sold direct or by agents; one-half would be disposed of in New York. The drawings would take place in Chicago; a committee of leading citizens, headed by the president of the Board of Trade and including a former governor, would preside.

The news sped across the country and fed the speculative fever anew. Once more, as in the days when town lots were in demand, Chicago became synonymous with opportunity. A magnificent opera house for $5— what a gamble! Today's hazards of operation are so great that the man who inherits an opera house is likely to feel crushed, asking, in a whisper, "What will it cost me in taxes and upkeep?" But nowhere, in all the detailed chronicles of this event, is there a hint that anyone who held a $5 ticket in 1867, raised this question.

The 305 works of art included in the lottery were not to be despised, though some of them seem suspiciously like those sadly faded paintings now visible in auction rooms. There were included, it is true, the Volk bust of Lincoln, a landscape or two by George Inness, paintings by Vedder and Chavannes, and a portrait of Lincoln by Cogswell. But most of the works bore such titles as "Washington Irving and His Friends," "Scene in the Tyrol," "Selecting the Bridal Dress," "The Sultan's Daughter," "Trailing Arbutus," and the two much-admired companion pieces, "Raspberries" and "Strawberries."

Many people ventured more than one purchase and pools were formed to buy from $100 to $1,500 worth of tickets. The Board of Trade took to the gambling naturally; the Opera Ring identified a group of fashionable people. The Chamber of Commerce made a pool. Others registered under names that read like a roster of winners of the Irish Sweepstakes. Here were entered Dead Broke, Bloody Tub, Kiss Me Quick, General Grant, General Sheridan, Titter No. 1, Pork Packers, Ladies Friend, Bohemian Club, Bottom Dollar. When orders came the management mailed out tubes containing the tickets, which had handsome engravings of the Opera House. But the *Tribune* saw nothing elevating in the scramble and warned the gamblers that there would be over two hundred thousand disappointed losers. It spoke of the implied tragedy of the Opera House—"its sublime conception, the disastrous failure of its proprietor." It warned that this was a sorry business in which men squandered their money, set a bad example to children and poorer neighbors, violated the statute against lotteries and in general demonstrated moral guilt. In other words, the *Tribune* was against it.

The momentous day of the drawing arrived. Early in the morning gaping crowds formed outside the Opera House. At 8:30 o'clock the committee of wealthy bankers and managers headed by the president of the Union National Bank, solemnly sat down to count 210,000 tickets, printed by a bank engraving company and numbered like banknotes. Three times they counted the tickets to avoid duplication; then, each man carrying a box of tickets under his arm, they filed gravely onto the stage. Here an elaborate lunch was served them behind the closed curtains, while the audience was taking its seats in tense apprehension on the other side.

With the house filled with a crowd of candy and peanut eaters, and seats in the orchestra cleared for tables for newspapermen, the scene opened before noon, the gas was turned on, and the two wooden wheels from which tickets were to be drawn were shown. The chairman announced that over 25,000 tickets remained unsold and hence belonged to Crosby. The drawing proceeded and the crowd attended in high spirits. When the painting of "Strawberries" was awarded, the audience called for cream; when "Chickens" was drawn, it yelled "fowl play." Finally ticket No. 58,600 drew Prize No. 1—the Opera House. Silence met the announcement; nobody knew who held the winning number.

Said the chairman, "The committee thinks that Mr. Crosby has not drawn the house and they trust that it has gone to some poor man who will make good use of it."

The drawing was no sooner completed when those who had failed to win the house began to ridicule the proceeding with laughter and gay quips. The anonymity of the successful winner gave rise to all sorts of horseplay. Some spread the news that the Opera House had been won by a convict with a year to serve. Others congratulated a well-known hack driver nicknamed "Shanghai." A crowd of two hundred persuaded the bartender for "Bock" Meyer, a German saloonkeeper, to stand treat and drank seven kegs of beer before the owner arrived and threw them out.

Then came word that the lucky ticket was held by Abraham Hagerman Lee of Prairie du Rocher, Illinois, down in the rich farming lands of the American Bottom. For days no one knew anything about him. "The eyes of all America are fixed upon him," said the *Tribune,* "on fortune's cap he is almost the very button." How to reach him? There was no telegraph to his town, but there was the old road from East St. Louis down into Cahokia and past old Fort Chartres to the little town that was a relic of New France. Who was Lee? Was there really such a man, or was he a blind for Crosby himself? The "shipwrecked" losers became sarcastic, witty, bitter at his expense. It was ascertained that there were scarcely fifteen inhabitants in Randolph County; what backwoods farmer had won the Opera House? Speed became necessary. Crosby notified a lawyer in St. Louis, who commissioned a man in Belleville, Illinois, the nearest town with a telegraph office, to ride to Lee with the news. "The magnificent edifice is rushing to him on horseback," said a newspaper.

The first to reach Lee with the news of his great

luck were two horsemen from St. Louis, who, having read the report in their paper, rode out to see him. They found him in his cottage reading to his sick wife. Whether they hoped to bargain with him or not, nothing came of their trip. The next to appear was the man from Belleville. He failed to find Lee unduly agitated. The lucky winner answered his call by appearing in a long-tailed nightshirt. Presumably the Belleville man sent word to Chicago describing Lee. He was not, it seemed, a country bumpkin but a man of experience. He had risen from cabin boy to captain of the packet *Nashville,* and in the Civil War had been captain and later colonel of Illinois troops. Then he had married a Frenchwoman and settled down in Prairie du Rocher.

Lee agreed to come to Chicago, but a baffling secrecy enveloped his movements. When finally spotted on Chicago streets he was in the company of U. H. Crosby and a lawyer. One report said he bore a resemblance to Webster. When questions were asked, Albert Crosby, brother of Uranus, was designated as owner of the Opera House. The whole business looked tricky to the critical losers, who suspected fraud. Neither were they satisfied when it was announced that Lee had resold the Opera House to Crosby for $200,000. The New York *Tribune,* which declared that "this business of lotteries is fast becoming an intolerable nuisance," figured that Crosby had held one chance in seven in his own lottery. The whole transaction smelled of deceit.

While some hard losers threatened to contest, arguing that Crosby could not convey the Opera House, others indulged in hilarious take-offs, especially in "saloons below the street level." The group that called itself Pork Packers, having won a painting called "A Rocky Coast," staged a raffle with five hundred tickets in a pork barrel and used a simulated Indian messenger on a mule to notify the winner.

Lee had a final session with the Crosbys at which toasts were drunk. Then Lee was bundled out of Chicago on the special train that carried Adelaide Ristori and her troupe to her next engagement. The Chicago public was mystified and angry. The *Tribune* treated the affair with sarcasm. Figuring up what Crosby had taken in, and what he had paid in commissions, the *Tribune* announced that, even if he paid Lee $200,000 to get his theater back, he had cleared $650,000. Did Lee act for Crosby? It would seem so. Maybe the atmosphere became too frigid for Crosby, for he turned the Opera House over to his brother Albert and moved east. Four years later it vanished in the great fire and was never rebuilt.

On January 24, 1867, when all Chicago was debating and criticizing the Opera House lottery, a calm, scholarly man from the East spoke in Unity Hall. It was Ralph Waldo Emerson, reading his essay on "Napoleon, The Man of the World." Compared with the Opera House crowd his audience was a mere handful; what he said was not even reported. But in his lecture he spoke truths that are valid today: "Every experiment by multitudes or individuals, that has a sensual and selfish aim, will fail. Only that good profits which we can taste with all doors open, and which serves all men." It was a message that might well have been engraved on the tickets for the big lottery.

3

The Auditorium: Its Rise and Fall

ONE blustering night in 1941 I walked down the broad, wind-swept pavement of Michigan Avenue to Congress Street, to bid good-bye to an old friend who had been condemned to death. It was the huge Auditorium, standing like a mighty fortress that had been lost by treachery. The windows were dark. The halls that had been the lobby of a famous hotel were empty. The long bar of golden oak against which had leaned the sons of the best families, was free of bottles and glasses. No amber lamps glowed above the doors once used by presidents, singers and a music-loving public, which came to hear the finest artists of two generations, from Patti to Caruso, from Paderewski to Heifetz.

The Auditorium had fallen on evil days; in an era when huge sums had been lavished on expositions, parks and drives, when millions had been expended on motor cars, when immense booty had been extorted by gangsters, the Auditorium had become sick for lack of nutrition. "The passion to sell," its architect, Louis Sullivan had written, "is the impelling power in American life." The Auditorium had been robbed of its ability to sell anything.

It was built before my time, but in my college days I adopted it. From the first time that I sat in its peanut gallery, to see, for fifty cents, one of those huge benefit programs that included all the stars of the current stage, to the time when I heard Galli-Curci, Mary Garden, Schumann-Heink and Bori inside its walls, it had been to me a symbol of cultural aspiration. Now it was equally a symbol of commercial decay. It was condemned because men had invented new rooms, new wall decorations. The house was still as solid as ever; it stood foursquare against the winds of heaven; it enclosed the finest hall for opera in the country. But Chicago rushed ever to embrace the new, undermined its fundamental strength by destructive taxes, built the city up and tore the city down. America had not yet learned that constant replacement of usable goods is a sin against the Lord's bounty. The Auditorium, shouldered out by the Civic Opera House, left behind by modern hotel and office buildings, was doomed after fifty years of use. Only the war stayed the wreckers' hands, when it was found useful as a center of recreation for service men, and bowling alleys were built on the floor of its famous hall.

Its building, in 1887-1890, made many hearts beat faster. It rose because one man, Ferdinand W. Peck, demanded a hall commensurate with Chicago's wealth. The settlement on the Chicago, which had come into culture through its schools, its churches, its institutes of art and music, demanded a focus for expression. The old Interstate Exposition Building on the lake front was inadequate. Peck now summoned bankers and architects. And the architects were Dankmar Adler, master of acoustics, and Louis H. Sullivan, master of design, and in their office a young rebel and pathfinder, Frank Lloyd Wright, presided over the drawing boards.

The Auditorium is not a skyscraper—its walls do not hang on a steel frame. Neither does it rest on steel pillars that reach down to bedrock. It has for a foundation a raft of concrete and stone that grows wider toward the bottom. The huge tower, weighing 30,000,000 tons, has its own "floating raft" of steel and concrete, 67 by 100 feet wide, to counteract the treacherous shifts of the sandy loam in Chicago's subsoil. Since it weighed more than the adjoining walls it posed a problem; to keep the settlement uniform, the architects piled on pig iron in proportionate amounts, and as the tower rose, removed the iron.

Its design grew under the hands of Sullivan and Adler. It was influenced by the plain, massive stone walls of the Marshall Field Wholesale Building, the work of that eastern genius, H. H. Richardson. I had passed that Wells Street building often, wondering at its stupendous walls, which, despite their impressive appearance, were hardly necessary to enclose open, well-lighted floors filled with displays of dry goods. Richardson's building should have been a civic monument, but it passed from the earth when its usefulness as an office ended in the 1930's; today a parking lot on its site better serves the tax collector.

The plaster was still wet, the doors were not yet on their hinges, when the Republican National Convention of 1888 met inside the unfinished Auditorium and nominated Benjamin Harrison for the presidency. Its formal opening came December 9, 1889, and gave

Chicago an hour of grandeur and a fitting prelude to the ceremonies of the Columbian World's Fair and Exposition. Indeed, the Auditorium helped convince Congress that Chicago, instead of New York, should have the funds to celebrate the four hundredth anniversary of the landing of Columbus.

More than fifteen thousand people stood shoulder to shoulder in the great hall for the opening ceremonies. President Harrison came from Washington with Mrs. McKee and spoke of "this witching and magnificent scene." Harriet Monroe wrote an ode which Frederick Gleason set to music; it began:

> Hail to thee, Chicago! On thy brow
> America, thy mother, lays a crown . . .

The crowd was enraptured by Patti, who sang with her usual charm, and a commercially minded commentator estimated that when she trilled, each vibration cost 30 cents. It was appropriate that this fine voice should be the first to be heard here. The hall was decorated in ivory and gold and had on its walls an allegorical painting by Charles Holoway, bearing the legend familiar to all who ever sat in that famous room: "The utterance of life is a song, the symphony of nature."

Such an event was not without its characteristic oratory. This tornado of words was unleashed by John S. Runnells, who was moved to superlatives. "What words can be said that befit this occasion?" he asked. "There is an eloquence in the spectacle before me which speech cannot rival, nor tongue surpass. I speak in a hall grander than any which could resound to a human voice anywhere in the civilized world. . . . If Demosthenes could come back to earth and, standing upon this rostrum, plead again for the honor he had won, who could measure his eloquence under such an inspiration? . . . As the walls of Babylon were hung with fragrant gardens, so these walls are adorned with the spirit which far outshines their cold colors or their figures and shall be immortal when they have faded."

He also referred to the Acropolis, the pyramids, St. Paul's of London, Marathon, the Agora, Pericles, Trafalgar, the Arch of Triumph, Louis XIV, Washington, Lincoln, the rock of Horeb, Ajax, Kean, Garrick and Drury Lane.

When the program ended and the first families called for their carriages, they faced what we call a traffic jam. There was "chaos for an hour" as the drivers tried to maneuver their rigs into favorable positions in front of the entrances of the Auditorium. Carriage numbers, apparently, were not in use. The reporter who observed the muddle commented: "Big as Chicago is, it is not big enough to grapple with the conundrum presented when 1,200 rigs appear at one hall on a single night and all expect to be assigned to one place, and that directly in front of the main entrance."

Chicago was still a decade or two away from the reign of the automobile. The making of horseless carriages had only a brief life in Chicago and coincided with the infancy of the motion picture, when Essanay made westerns on the far Northwest Side. When these two great industries of the twentieth century came to full flower they had passed Chicago by.

4

Columbus Sails the Chicago

O<small>N</small> the evening of October 21, 1892, the lamps were blazing in the Potter Palmer mansion on the North Side. Its mistress, Bertha Honoré Palmer, acknowledged first lady of Chicago society, was preparing to issue forth in state to open a ball. It was not her first or last ball, but it would probably outshine all that came before and after. As president of the Board of Lady Managers of the World's Columbian Fair and Exposition, Mrs. Palmer would join the heads of the government, the ministers of foreign nations and the opulent, gem-bedecked representatives of Chicago's wealth, to honor a persistent and badgered Genoese named Christopher Columbus who, four hundred years before, had stumbled on the western continent.

That Mrs. Palmer would be gaily caparisoned was without question. That she would call forth "Ah!" and "Oh!" from innumerable feminine throats was obvious. It was a period when the female body was considered a suitable prop to hold a generous assortment of woven and knitted dry goods and minerals quarried from the earth. The hair was worn full and high. Shoulders were left bare and plump bosoms were so desirable that those who had none contrived, by the use of whalebone and much discomfort, to appear well favored. Society women would appear with V necks, covered with iridescent faille, with elbow sleeves, long and full court trains, dripping pointe duchesse lace and embroideries, waving ostrich-plume fans and sparkling with diamonds. The acme of the dressmaker's art—the word "couturier" was not yet in general use—was worn by Mrs. Potter Palmer and thus described:

"A French conception in tilleul and golden yellow, built of soft plain satin and velvet. The high puffed sleeves of golden velvet and shaped like a calla lily. A loose puff of the velvet bordered the long train, and from this soft finish vandikes richly embroidered in crystal and gold and dazzingly jeweled, tapered gracefully towards the waist. The décolleté corsage also elaborately ornamented by the exquisite and brilliant bullion embroidery. The jewels worn with this costume were diamonds and pearls, including a necklace composed of ropes of magnificent pearls and a diamond tiara."

This brilliant company gathered in the Auditorium, where the decorations suggested the pomp of an international event. Everywhere the initials of the king and queen of Spain were visible. The room was hung with wild smilax, held by rosettes of red and white ribbon. Behind a bank of palms and ferns an energetic young conductor, John Philip Sousa, led the United States Marine Band in the brilliant "Washington Post March." The president of the United States, Benjamin Harrison, was absent, because of "a personal affliction," but the vice-president, Levi P. Morton, did the honors.

While a select company danced in honor of Columbus at the Auditorium, fireworks had the democratic masses goggle-eyed. The Chicago authorities shot off $25,000 worth of fireworks in Lincoln, Washington and Garfield parks. A Niagara Falls in fire, 600 feet long and 60 feet high, surpassed all expectations. The caravels of Columbus blazed. Five thousand rockets rose into the air—some said simultaneously. In the words of the North Side Germans, who numbered many thousands, it was colossal.

The inaugural ball was not the beginning, but the culmination of festivities that concentrated national attention on Chicago. They began with an elaborate parade. Parades were important in the nineties, and this one precipitated an acrimonious controversy. Should the parade pass up one street and not another? The argument was settled peremptorily by the head of the United States Army, General Nelson A. Miles. He announced that it was "not gotten up for the benefit of the public but by the President to honor the representatives of foreign nations."

The event brought Chief Justice Fuller and the members of the Supreme Court in a special train. The diplomatic representatives of foreign nations had another train to themselves. There were so many celebrities about that people stumbled over them at every street corner. Present were Rutherford B. Hayes, former president; Cardinal Gibbons, Archbishop Ireland, Lyman Gage, Whitelaw Reid, John Sherman, Governor McKinley of Ohio, Robert T. Lincoln, the minister at the Court of St. James's; Augustus Saint-Gaudens, Charles H. Schwab, Richard Watson Gilder and Richard Harding Davis. Eugene Field had written a drinking song for the occasion. It went: "Clink, clink, clink, merrily let us drink," and all of Field's friends loved it.

When the dedicatory exercises of the World's Fair were held on the afternoon of Friday, October 21st, Cardinal Gibbons appeared in his red robes and shared the religious exercises with Bishop Fowler. Henry Watterson and Chauncey Depew then raised their voices, depicting Columbus as a sort of spotless candidate for office. Mrs. Potter Palmer spoke of the high place woman had held in the discovery of America, saying it required an Isabella, which nobody could deny. Then the "Dedication Ode" was read by Sarah C. Le Moyne. It had been written by a young woman named Harriet Monroe, who now appeared, frail, pale and graceful, to accept a wreath amid the plaudits of the vast crowd.

In the meantime informal activities went on everywhere. The crowds sang new words to the old army tune of "Marching Through Georgia":

> Hurrah! Hurrah! The button has been pressed,
> Hurrah! Hurrah! Chicago'll do the rest,
> She's modest, she's retiring, but she'll do her level best,
> While we are honoring Columbus.

Others honored Columbus in characteristic ways. John B. Drake, the hotelier, presented a drinking fountain, which had a compartment that could hold three tons of ice and thus keep the water cool. The Columbus store, at State and Monroe streets, advertised a "Landing Sale."

In October, 1892, cities, villages and crossroads hamlets paraded in honor of Columbus. Brass bands blared the march music of Sousa. School children, waving the banners of Spain and the United States, marched the streets·followed by floats depicting the three caravels. All over the West children wrote essays on Columbus, struggling with the curlicues of Spencerian penmanship, for exhibition at the World's Fair.

Politics was muddled and business was in the trough of a depression. The settlement on the Chicago had its elevators bulging with grain, and trains thundered across its bridges as in better years, but the banks were shaky and industry was borrowing to meet deficits. Benjamin Harrison had been renominated for the presidency and defeated by Grover Cleveland. The *Tribune* sized up Representative William J. Bryan of Nebraska as a man "glib of tongue, an active, spry, shifty debater," but concluded, "Bryan's sun is setting."

The discovery of America by Columbus was far outdistanced by the discovery of Columbus by America. He became the greatest man in history, and the clergy gave him qualities not granted to George Washington. Priests, ministers and rabbis vied to exalt the great admiral. M. M. Mangasarian, who regularly addressed a large liberal audience, extolled the discovery as a purely Catholic enterprise. The Reverend Dr. Stern praised the supernatural in a sermon on "Was the discovery of America accidental or divine?" The Reverend Charles L. Morgan declared the name of the continent should be changed. The Reverend Mr. Butler asked the supreme honor for Columbus; he must be canonized and join the company of the saints.

Nearly fifty years later an Italian cartoonist, resentful of the foreign policies of the United States, pictured a compatriot standing before a statue of "Columbus Discovering America" and asking, "Why did he do it?"

The World's Fair of 1893 was more than an exposition—it was a cultural stimulant of the first order. It was far more influential than the Century of Progress Exposition of 1933-1934, because it was a new phenomenon, in a land where only businessmen and the wealthy traveled far by trains; where there were no good roads, no automobiles, no motion pictures, no radios.

From Chicago millions of western visitors—teachers of public schools, merchants, farmers—went home with eyes opened to new goals in community efforts. Sculpture, painting, music, choral singing, public forums, gained a tremendous impetus. Recognition of women's activities accelerated the movement for woman's rights. The parliament of religions gave new meaning to tolerance at the close of a century that had begun with bigotry. Visitors became familiar with ships of the United States Navy, the Corliss engine and the Pullman parlor car and stood spellbound before the Liberty Bell.

When the public beheld the buildings with their Graeco-Roman lines, their fluted columns, all blazing white, in a plaster material not hitherto used—they called it staff—it gasped. To the public the White City was a dream of beauty. But architects quarreled over it. The newspapers said that the buildings "withstood the greatest critical and uncritical bombardment of modern times."

To Louis H. Sullivan, master architect of the Auditorium, and Frank Lloyd Wright, his young associate, the architecture of the World's Fair was a national calamity. They saw its popularity speeding the romantic borrowing from European palaces, and setting back the flowering of a native style. They blamed Daniel H. Burnham, chief of construction, for conceding too much to eastern conservatives on the board. When the board turned over to Sullivan the planning of the Transportation Building, he departed from the Roman lines to design his brilliant "train shed," which, with its golden door, proved one of the triumphs of the fair. The door was a large square portal containing receding arches, brilliantly ornamented and covered with gold leaf. Sullivan had developed the principle in the Auditorium and the Garrick Theater, where similar arches may still be seen. They antedated the proscenium of the Radio City Music Hall by forty years. But Sullivan had no praise for the rest of the fair. To him it had "spurious beauty" and popularized "the bogus antique."

All summer long, and well into the comfortable, midwestern fall, millions paraded up and down the Midway Plaisance. They gaped at the Eskimos, shuddered at the crater of Kilauea, marveled at the dress of spun glass and lifted huge steins of beer in Old Vienna. Rarely were they tempted to look over the high board fence to discover what stonemasons were building in the grass-ridden, marshy land just north of the Ferris wheel.

There, unobstrusively, rose gray, limestone buildings that would outlive the fair and bring honor and culture to Chicago. They sheltered a new school that called itself a university. Three men had set it in motion by easing $4,000,000 painlessly out of the pockets of John D. Rockefeller and wheedling a bit more out of a group of Chicago Baptists, who expected the school to teach immersion. The men were Thomas W. Goodspeed, Frederick T. Gates and a 34-year-old professor of Hebrew from Yale, William Rainey Harper, a little man with fat cheeks and snappy black eyes, who had accepted the presidency after many prayers and hesitations.

Two buildings were up, 600 students were attending classes and 120 experts were teaching, among them eight who had been college presidents. The land had been given by Marshall Field, whose name was therefore applied to the athletic field as a good pun. Despite his financial help, his name on the field in time yielded to that of Amos Alonzo Stagg, who had led the teams to football glory. The president was everywhere, tirelessly inaugurating new methods of teaching. His ideas were so grandiose that the university ran up a shocking deficit from the first day, thus embarrassing its founder, who had called it "the best investment I ever made in my life."

The university, no less than the fair, was to affect the architecture of the future. Borrowing heavily from the halls and pinnacles of Cambridge and Oxford, its architects gave currency to the general use of Collegiate Gothic. Here, on the marshlands, flowered the most extraordinary renascence of Old World themes, adapted to modern heating, plumbing and classroom needs.

The Ferris wheel is rust, the jangling tunes of the Streets of Cairo persist as an amusing memory. The

Midway is now a broad boulevard, lined with elms, link-ing Jackson and Washington parks. But the university body still sings, somewhat tunelessly:

> The City White hath fled the earth
> But where the azure waters lie,
> A nobler city hath its birth,
> The City Gray that ne'er shall die.
> For decades and for centuries
> Its battlemented towers shall rise,
> Beneath the hope-filled western skies,
> 'Tis our dear alma mater.

Deeds and Words

I

Background of the News

ONE evening in December, 1898, the City Council met in its chamber in the City Hall. Great issues were at stake and the gallery was packed with spectators. As the aldermen entered to take their seats a hempen rope was lowered from the gallery. At the end of the rope dangled a noose.

This was an outrageous object to fling in the face of a deliberative body, but, as the democratic experiment was conducted in Chicago, it was a form of popular expression, in keeping with the traditions of the frontier. It was a warning, by decent citizens, to the "boodle aldermen," who were thought ready to sell their votes for money to Charles T. Yerkes, who was trying to get a 50-year streetcar franchise over the opposition of the mayor, Carter H. Harrison, and civic organizations.

The mayor had been fighting the streetcar "steal" in public meetings for weeks. He was a practical politician, and the reform element didn't like him, but in this fight he was blocking the crooked men. He knew that if it came to an immediate showdown he would be outvoted by "the old gray wolf pack." He had behind him only an "honest minority." Honesty was often in the minority in the fight to save the streets and utility rights for that vague, irresponsible mass, the People. He depended on his knowledge of political tricks to defeat the rascals. Before the opposition knew what he was about, he had maneuvered the franchise bill from the Committee on Streets and Alleys, which he didn't control, into the hands of the Committee on the City Hall, which he did. And there it was smothered. From that time on the machinations of Yerkes began to fail.

Yerkes had tried, in Chicago and in the State Assembly of Illinois, to get what he wanted by favors and bribes. He had the temerity, when the notorious Allen bill was being pushed through the State Assembly, to sit at the head of the stairs leading to the two legislative chambers in Springfield and interview his creatures as they came to vote. One of the newly elected representatives from Chicago was said to have received $20,000 for his "virgin vote." He decided that he had entered a paying profession. The mother of another told Mayor Harrison, "When Billie came home from Springfield, he took his roll out of his pants pocket; it was big enough to choke a horse—and, Mr. Mayor, it was all those yellow-backed boys, too!"

Chicago had a close shave from domination by "Baron" Yerkes, who went on to greener pastures. One of these was London, where he started the Underground. He lives in Chicago traditions as the crooked magnate Chicago licked. But not all causes were so well defended. Other men had Yerkes's idea that public officials were venal. Some of them were justified; others overreached themselves, were exposed and sent to ignominy by an aroused public opinion. But that public opinion was not always on tap. It had to be electrified by newspapers, clean-politics organizations, the school-teachers and the clergy. When Harrison was fighting his battle against Yerkes school children were instructed to ask classmates who were sons and daughters of suspected aldermen, "Is your father a boodler?" It was an early form of the war of nerves.

When elections came to Chicago every faction fought for advantages. A generation after citizens had dangled a noose in front of the aldermen in their own council chamber, William Hale Thompson was campaigning against his former associate and later rival, Dr. Robertson. At public meetings he would produce a rat trap with a live rat in it, and calling it "Doc" would berate it for its supposed treachery. It marked a high spot in political abuse. Historians who had declared the frontier was gone revised their conclusion to except Chicago.

Politics was always a tough battle for privileges, waged with bitterness, claims of virtue and charges of dishonesty. Many of the political regulars were picturesque characters. Mayor Fred A. Busse used to retire nightly from the City Hall to a North Clark Street saloon and with his feet on the brass rail swap yarns with his political cronies. "Bobbie" Burke, a Democratic pillar, had the rotundity of a fair-sized beer barrel, a full-moon face, twinkling eyes and a laughing mouth, said Harrison. Alderman Jimmie Quinn was known as Hot Stove Jimmie because he used to say of others,

"He'd steal a red-hot stove." The inseparable aldermen from the First Ward, John Coughlin and Michael Kenna, were a curious pair. Coughlin was known as Bathhouse John, or "The Bath"; Kenna was called Hinky Dink all his days. Between them they ruled an empire of flop- and bawdyhouses. Coughlin composed poetry and recited "Dear Midnight of Love." Kenna ran a large saloon called the Workingmen's Exchange where the flotsam and jetsam of the town exchanged its nickels for enormous schooners of beer. In those days politicians drew on flophouses and saloons when they needed extra voters, at fifty cents a vote. Hinky Dink was a master at controlling this riffraff. Chicago gave the vote not only to the living but to the dead and the unborn. In the ruthless, undemocratic election of 1896, when Mark Hanna saved the Union from free silver, sixty thousand "phantoms" were voted against William J. Bryan in Chicago alone.

Many times have the wires from Chicago carried news of political upheavals that rocked the nation. It was on the banks of the Chicago that an aroused constituency defeated the attempts of the Republican stalwarts to run Grant for a third term; it was here that a convention of Democrats presented the third-term nomination to Franklin D. Roosevelt with fulsome eulogies. Here the Progressive hope rose and fell as the psalm-singing delegates from the Middle West nominated Theodore Roosevelt in a campaign that was to split the Republican party and elect Woodrow Wilson to the presidency. But none of these battles approached the frenzy of that day in 1896 when William Jennings Bryan closed the debate on the free silver resolution

with his ringing challenge: "Having behind us the producing masses of this nation and the world, supported
by the commercial interests, the laboring interests and
the toilers everywhere, we will answer their demand for
a gold standard by saying to them: You shall not press
down upon the brow of labor this crown of thorns, you
shall not crucify mankind upon a cross of gold."

He came to Chicago that summer from Nebraska,
a tall man of thirty-six, with wavy black hair not too
well trimmed, a strong nose, and a straight mouth
clamped shut by a powerful jaw. He wore the conventional stiffly starched turn-down collar with a black
string tie loosely knotted under it; he had on a black
alpaca coat with rumpled sleeves and baggy trousers.
He took a narrow 75-cent room in the Windsor-Clifton
on Wabash and Monroe. Bryan had served in Congress,
then tried for the Senate and failed; now he was
desperately holding on to his credentials as a delegate,
against the opposition of Cleveland's secretary of agri-
culture, J. Sterling Morton, who came from Nebraska.
Asked what candidate he meant to support, Bryan replied mildly, "Perhaps I may become the candidate;
stranger things have happened."

A few days later his oratory rocked the walls of the
old Coliseum on 63rd Street, near Stony Island Avenue,
which Buffalo Bill had used after the World's Fair,
and he won the nomination in a spontaneous burst of
confidence. But the very issue that raised him as a national leader—free silver—terrified the banks and industries of the nation and led to his defeat.

For years the city had echoed with political scan-
dals, but the "purchasable human cattle" who sat in the

City Council were but petty offshoots of that gigantic struggle for wealth that went on all over the Chicago area. Men gambled for high stakes; some won them honestly; others crushed their competitors with cut-throat methods, fattened on special advantages.

After the great fire of 1871, the homelike, intimate character of "the garden city" was at an end. Rebuilding at a terrific rate, the city responded to the national demands for processed meats and manufactured goods with huge shipments. It became a vast workshop, with factories standing end to end along the countless miles of railroad tracks. By day the sky was obscured by the gray-black blanket of soot and smoke from countless factory chimneys; by night the sky was red from the flames of roaring furnaces.

Always new labor poured into the city—from the immigrant ships of Europe, from the farms of the Middle West. Labor was a commodity bought and sold in the market place. Thousands of brawny, muscular men milled around the employment offices of Canal and West Madison Streets, manned the factories or shipped out as farm hands. Trains thundered endlessly over the steel bridges of the Chicago into the central area; cattle arrived daily by the thousand at the Union Stock Yards. Elevators on the river's bank bulged with grain; here ships loaded and sailed for eastern ports. It was a tough, crude, lusty city, with work to do, where it paid to be able to swing a hammer or drive a four-horse team. It was a city of contrasts, where the culture-loving citizens, emerging from a Beethoven symphony concert conducted by Theodore Thomas, would brush elbows with gamblers attired in fancy vests and pearl-gray derbies, sporting huge sparklers in their shirt fronts, the profits of their Clark Street gambling houses. And always it expressed itself violently—in its political brawls, in its fierce slugging matches, as competing news dealers established their rights to favorite corners with their fists, and finally, in the incredible period of the 1920's, when lawless thugs roamed about with sawed-off shotguns, "hi-jackers" robbed one another's trucks of illegal liquor and rival gangs ambushed their victims in the city's streets.

2

The Days of Personal Journalism

As the city lived, so the newspapers recorded its daily history. Their writers were the first to tell the story of this grinding struggle for wealth and power, page by page. No wonder, for they were up to their necks in it. Their editors fought political battles on personal terms, using every verbal weapon, from polished appeals to scurrilous denunciations. Their reporters tramped the streets. They were present when General Sheridan and his troops, fresh from Indian battles, pumped lead into the Halstead Street crowd during the railroad strike of 1877. They covered the shooting at the labor demonstrators on Black Rock Road in 1886, which led to the Haymarket protest meeting. They recorded the long, bitter struggle against cuts in wages at Pullman and the fight that Eugene V. Debs and the American Railway Union lost to the troops of General Nelson A. Miles when Attorney General Olney crushed the railroad strike of 1894 over the protest of Governor John P. Altgeld.

Chicago newspapers never have been complacent. They started as belligerent organs of opinion and fought for their views. The Chicago *Democrat* began to express its opinions soon after John Calhoun landed a hand press from a boat in November, 1833. It appeared as a daily in 1845 and was Long John Wentworth's personal organ when the *Tribune* took it over in 1861. Money it never made. It was one of a long procession of ailing, unprofitable newspapers that tried to subsist on circulation income before advertising revenue became a lifesaving factor.

Of the nineteenth century editors Wilbur F. Storey made so much noise that his reputation for eccentricity survives to this day. He bought the Chicago *Times* in 1861 for $23,000 from Cyrus H. McCormick, who also had political irons in the fire. For over twenty years Storey amused, alarmed, shocked and angered the people of Chicago. Just as the *Tribune* became the powerful supporter of Abraham Lincoln, so Storey became his most bitter critic in the name of states' rights. He blasted General John C. Frémont for freeing the slaves in Missouri and turned his guns on Lincoln when emancipation was proposed and enacted. His defense of Vallandigham led people to call his paper "Old Storey's Copperhead Times." He was Old Storey at forty-five, when he wore a patriarchal beard that was white, except when he dyed it black. When the great fire burned him out he felt he was ruined for life. "I am now an old man," he lamented—at fifty-three. But the chance for another fight made him forget self-pity and he rebuilt his newspaper and lived long enough to tantalize the town and finally go mad.

Historians still recount how Lydia Thompson, the star of the British Blondes, tried to horsewhip Storey

on the street for calling them "beefy." La Thompson
was fined $100 and costs, and the fine was suspended;
Storey made the most of it. But the biggest battle of
his career came when General Ambrose F. Burnside, the
originator of the parted whiskers, took it on himself
to suppress the *Times* because it had attacked Lincoln
for arresting Vallandigham. With a troop of federal
soldiers from Camp Douglas General Burnside closed
the paper on June 3, 1864.

This was an issue Storey liked. He had written:
"We believe in freedom of speech and the press, un-
checked by anything save responsibility to the law of the
land. Wicked and treasonable as we believe abolitionists
and secessionists to be, they must have their legal rights
everywhere." Burnside's action brought an immediate
protest against the suppression, in which opponents of
Storey joined. Judge David Davis and Isaac N. Arnold,
old friends of Lincoln, denounced it to Lincoln as high-
handed. So thoroughly was the nation devoted to free
speech that people who hated the *Times* helped organize mass meetings to defend it. Storey applied to the
courts for an injunction against the troops. Before any
action could be taken Lincoln rescinded the order. The
Times had lost only part of one edition and one full
day. Storey was disappointed; he had hoped for a greater
triumph.

Years later Franc B. Wilkie, Storey's editor,
tweaked General Burnside's beard. Meeting him in an
Indianapolis hotel and recognizing him by his characteristic whiskers, Wilkie was "seized by a rather malevolent
idea." He approached Burnside and said, "General, I
have been waiting for many years to thank you for a

great service you conferred on some of my friends during the war. . . . It rescued a great institution from a collapse; it is something for which the beneficiaries can never sufficiently thank you. General, I am one of the editors of the Chicago *Times*." The general, "with a pained sort of look," moved swiftly away.

Sometimes the noise on the Chicago led New York editors to consider entering the field. But their efforts were unprofitable until W. R. Hearst founded the Chicago *American* early in the twentieth century and made his headlines heard over the tumult of the Loop. One of the first Easterners to try Chicago was Charles A. Dana. He arrived in 1865 to start the *Republican*, merging it with the first Chicago *Post*. In 1870 John Hay, who had served as editor of the Chicago *Journal*, wrote Whitelaw Reid that the *Republican* was hopelessly waterlogged. Dana sold it to John B. McCullagh. The paper was destroyed in the great fire and never revived.

John Hay had taken employment with Reid on the New York *Tribune* and was sent to Chicago to cover the results of the fire. The Associated Press was the only news association that had a wire out, and after long pleading Hay and his associates got its consent to send one thousand words. The New York *Herald* sent five men, who left for New York in relays and prepared their dispatches on the way.

When J. Young Scammon founded the *Inter-Ocean* in 1872 as an organ of the conservative Republicans, he made an effort to get John Hay to edit it. But Hay preferred to remain with the New York *Tribune*. He wrote Reid a comment on Scammon that may apply to a more recent arrival in the Chicago newspaper field.

"You know who he is—one of the salt," said Hay. "He has made wads of money—more than he will have when his paper is a year older."

Gradually the emphasis on political views was displaced by the growing importance of the news columns. Great mercantile houses could no longer reach the eyes of the metropolis through their street windows; they had to announce their wares in the newspapers. When the wrecking of the *Maine* in 1898 brought to a head the agitation to free Cuba from the grip of Spain, the dashing war correspondent, clad in khaki and tramping with the troops, chartering motor launches and making lavish use of the cables, dramatized the news and awoke both editors and the public to the possibilities of the foreign field. For many years large photographs of the sinking Spanish cruisers demolished by the United States Navy off the coast of Cuba decorated the walls of the Chicago Press Club, where Stanley Waterloo, William Lightfoot Visscher and Opie Read were wont to meet and swap dialect stories.

It was John T. McCutcheon, the beloved cartoonist, whose drawings in the *Tribune* have spread good cheer at the breakfast tables of Chicago for nearly forty years, who witnessed Dewey's victory at Manila in 1898 as correspondent of the Chicago *Record*. Although three correspondents had agreed to file their reports simultaneously, one of them scooped the others by sending a bulletin at urgent rates. It went to the New York *World*, which had gone to press, but was printed in the Chicago *Tribune*, which hired the *World* service and had an hour to spare. When, early in 1904, the Russo-Japanese War broke out Chicago newspapers sent their ablest writers to the Far East, but were pitifully rewarded, because the Japanese excluded them from all important engagements. But Victor F. Lawson built a solid base for the great foreign service of the Chicago *Daily News,* envisioning it partly as a necessity for a newspaper that had among its readers a large proportion of the foreign-born citizens of Chicago. With Charles H. Dennis as his editor, Lawson had at his command, when the Great War of 1914 broke out, a service unequaled by any other American newspaper, with such well-informed correspondents as Edward Price Bell in London, Paul Scott Mowrer in Paris and Raymond Swing in Berlin, and half a dozen others at strategic points. The efficiency of that service is today a national asset.

A legend told for years in the office of the Chicago *Daily News* reveals the opera-star temperament characteristic of early war correspondents, who took their cue from the dashing Richard Harding Davis. At the end of one of the campaigns a correspondent, who had been supplied liberally with money, returned home and made no mention of that bugaboo of reporters, the expense account. Miss Harriet M. Dewey, known to all Chicago newspapermen as the watchdog of the money box for over half a century, didn't insist on an itemized statement, but she thought she ought to have a bit of paper to place among her records, showing that the sum of over $30,000 had been used for the purposes intended. She approached the correspondent and politely suggested a brief memorandum. The correspondent was insulted. Miss Dewey explained that she knew very well that the money had been used for legitimate purposes; her request was merely a matter of routine. The correspondent quit the paper cold. Miss Dewey was apologetic; she hadn't intended to hurt his feelings.

3

From Marquette to Sandburg

WHAT was there to write about in this noisy market place, this roaring boiler factory? Obviously, the struggle of man against nature and against his fellows; his rise to wealth and power. That was a different chronicle from the one that the first writer on the banks of the Chicago put prayerfully on paper in the cold, water-soaked days of 1675. Father Jacques Marquette faithfully entered into his Journal the circumstances of his devotions, his meetings with French and Indians and his keen observation of the vagaries of the river. Louis Jolliet, too, set down the details of his pioneer explorations in this area only to lose them in the rapids near Montreal. Later he dictated a report to his superiors, but it must have omitted much that he had recorded from day to day.

Marquette's Journal is the first milestone in Chicago letters; the second is Juliette Kinzie's *Wau-Bun,* *the "Early Day" in the Northwest.* That dealt not with prayers, but with the toil and troubles of the pioneer. In 1844 Mrs. Kinzie published a brief account of the Fort Dearborn massacre, from the memories of

337

her mother-in-law, Mrs. Eleanor Kinzie. In 1856 she elaborated this into *Wau-Bun*, adding the accounts of her trip west to Fort Winnebago and her arrival at the Chicago by way of Laughton's Ford on the Des Plaines and the old stage road of Ogden Avenue. "Wau-Bun" was an Ojibway word meaning "early day" or "dawn"; it was customary for authors to use Indian words as titles. Juliette Kinzie's book was not written wholly from firsthand observation, but she has preserved a picture of early Chicago and the customs of traders and boatmen who used the river and the portage. Harriet Martineau visited with her in 1836 and wrote of the Chicago colony of which she was the center: "It is a remarkable thing to meet such an assemblage of educated, refined and wealthy persons as may be found here, living in small, inconvenient houses on the edge of a wide prairie."

In the first half of the nineteenth century the life of the West was still judged by Cooper's portraits of the noble savage and a romantic hope tinctured all writing. But Caroline Mathilda Kirkland, in such books as *Western Clearings*, foreshadowed the objective truth of rural life that Hamlin Garland was to explore in the 1890's. When this young author won the support of William Dean Howells he became associated with the realistic aspirations of the East. When he announced that realism, veritism, and Americanism were synonymous with sincerity, he stirred the ire of Mary Hartwell Catherwood, who had peopled the wilderness with noble Indians. "Is looking at the beautiful side of life insincerity?" she demanded "What is sincere or more truthful than love and gratitude?"

Eugene Field, conducting the popular column "Sharps and Flats" in the Chicago *Daily News,* fanned the controversy. His editor, Charles H. Dennis, relates that Field was always an outspoken opponent of the realists, although his praise of Mrs. Catherwood was whimsical. "She believes with us in fairy godmothers," he wrote: "Mr. Garland's heroes sweat and do not wear socks."

The columnists were always more conservative than the reporters, who turned easily to naturalism to express their times. Eugene Field loved sentiment and set great store by the humorous dialect poems of James Whitcomb Riley. But Keith Preston, the brilliant columnist and literary critic of the *Daily News* in the 1920's, was by training a classical scholar with an ear attuned to the Greek and Latin poets. Master of a barbed wit that he expressed in pungent quatrains, he sparkled in the circle that included the calm Sandburg, the bantering Sherwood Anderson, the ebullient Ben Hecht, and the generous Henry Justin Smith, who, as a newspaper editor, gave rope to a score of young writers and, as the author of *Deadlines* and other novels about newspaper life, proved himself perhaps the most sensitive artist of them all. These were the decades when Bert Leston Taylor, (B.L.T.), Burton Rascoe, H. E. Keough, Percy Hammond and Ring Lardner scintillated for the *Tribune*. It was during his Chicago tenure that Lardner began capitalizing his experiences as a sports writer in *You Know Me, Al.*

This blaring, sweating, fevered town attracted all the youths from the small towns who needed a job. In 1887 it drew into its orbit a gangling, 16-year-old

fellow from Warsaw, Indiana, named Theodore Dreiser.
It put him at backbreaking labor and its spirit went into
his bones. He was never to get it out of his mind.

First he washed dishes in a Greek restaurant and
then he had a $5 a week job in the hardware house of
Hibbard, Spencer, Bartlett & Company. It was located
on the banks of the river at State Street and loaded its
freight direct on lake boats. He left for a brief college
experience in Indiana and returned to drive a lumber
wagon. For five months in 1892 he worked on the *Globe*
at $15 a week and picked up odd items about the Demo-
cratic convention that was nominating Cleveland. Brief
as this experience was, it gave him knowledge of the
city's ruthless ways, taught him the hard fight for sur-
vival and left his mind buzzing with pictures of sweatshops, cheap boarding and gambling houses that years
later filled his tenacious memory.

Dreiser did not write *Sister Carrie* until 1900 and
he was in Cleveland when he wrote it, but it was Chicago. He was east, too, when he began his story of his
financial titan, Cowperwood, but it was Yerkes and
the fight for Chicago street railway privileges that fired
his imagination. Dreiser had been deep in the muck of
American life in Chicago and simply didn't have the
patience to accept its illusions of gentility or to reject its
corruption as unsuitable for literary treatment. When
he wrote he recalled the freebooters of the Midwest, the
strident boastfulness, the ruthless gamble for power and
money, of a sprawling frontier town.

All this was intuitive in Dreiser, but by no means
singular. What Dreiser found was ably seconded by a
Harvard-educated Easterner, who appraised the primi-

tive forces in Chicago life with a cold, unromantic eye.
For Robert Herrick—keen, analytical, discriminating—
Chicago was a laboratory. Called to the young University of Chicago by Harper to teach English, he became a leader in the vigorous, realistic school that was
based on the Midwest. What a Dreiser might have ex-
perienced on his arrival in Chicago Herrick described
crisply in the opening pages of *The Memoirs of an
American Citizen.* That circumstantial study of the reverse of the American medal granted for success was in
the van of the social criticism that inspired novels by
Henry B. Fuller, I. K. Friedman, Will Payne, Brand
Whitlock, George Cram Cook, Robert Morss Lovett,
and, to a limited extent, Henry Kitchell Webster and
Samuel Merwin. It was Herrick who tackled the knotty
problem of social responsibility for the Haymarket
bomb of 1886, when the demands of labor for an 8-hour
day were complicated by the revolutionary agitation of
Johann Most and his anarchistic associates. The men who
were hanged for the act of an unidentified bomb-
thrower were scapegoats to society, and thus Herrick
portrayed them. All his years he hit at graft, waste and
lives broken by greed and possessiveness.

Writers who had pitched their tents under other
skies were pulled toward Chicago like satellites to a
planet. Frank Norris, though born in Chicago, had lived
chiefly in the Far West; now he trailed the epic of wheat
to Chicago's elevators and salesrooms; he talked with
Joseph Leiter about his disastrous corner in wheat on the
Chicago Board of Trade and wrote *The Pit.* Upton
Sinclair, energetic crusader for socialism as a remedy
for economic ills, came to the stockyards for the theme

of *The Jungle* in 1905 and precipitated a government investigation. "Chicago must be ours!" was the slogan of his socialist spokesman, but Chicago's masses, eager for the jobs and promotions the bosses could give, held firmly to the two major parties, despite the knowledge that returns were often juggled and elections often won by fraud.

In Wisconsin Edna Ferber, pounding her second-hand typewriter, won a prize of $25 from the *Tribune* and plumped for a story-writing career. Soon she was in Chicago, captivated by the boiling life of the "tough, lusty, unformed city," watching clerks in the stores, truckmen on their wagons, housewives at their shopping. Here she found prototypes for Emma McChesney, the dynamic saleswoman; here she located *So Big,* with its unforgettable picture of the self-reliant Selina, driving to market from the truck farms on the southern sand lots. Chicago's air, Chicago's life, were electrifying to the girl from Appleton: "I walked miles and miles and miles along the Lake, buffeting the winds and finding it exhilarating; I wrote, I read. I prowled Chicago's streets and byways. . . . I found it then, and I find it now, one of the most vital, unformed, fascinating, horrible, brutal, civilized and beautiful cities in the world." Thus confesses Edna Ferber.

Many writers who won national distinction and influenced the writing of their time cut their eyeteeth in the printshops on the Chicago. Those truly native never strayed far from the Middle West. Their stars may have led them to New York and Hollywood, but in spirit they remained sons of the middle empire. The land that shaped their childhood dreams dominated their imaginations in maturity. Little was eastern about Dreiser, as he rolled up an American chronicle in the plain speech of his western towns. In the heart of Old Chelsea, Edgar Lee Masters turns back to the farms and rivers of Illinois, recalls the days of that hard-bitten liberal, John P. Altgeld, and writes with nostalgic sorrow of mid-American lives. Ben Hecht's *Thousand and One Afternoons in New York* are but his *Thousand and One Afternoons in Chicago,* hopefully transplanted. John V. A. Weaver picked up the native idioms of *In American* from the talk in drugstores and streetcars of Chicago. Meyer Levin's Chicagoans quarrel over their bridge in *The Old Bunch* and the workers and police of *Citizens* battle in the sand lots before Chicago's steel mills. And when James T. Farrell, toiling at a desk in New York, rebuilds the imaginative world of Studs Lonigan and Danny O'Neill, it is the congested city of South Side apartment houses that surrounds him.

Poets, novelists, editors, dramatists—they keep coming on. The literary ferment of the town never stops boiling. To name all those busy today on the banks of the Chicago would require many pages. Of the titans of other days who left their mark on our times, there remains Old Carl. They called him that when he was thirty because he was slow of speech, looked long and earnestly at you, took his time. With one Carl Sandburg to guard the native hearth, what matter the Dreisers, the Ades, the Garlands who warmed themselves at other fires? His long, patient reconstruction of Lincoln's life has given America a major biography, touched with genius.

Today Carl Sandburg's shock of wind-blown hair

is white, but his eyes are as patient, kindly and searching as they were over twenty-five years ago when he covered labor for Ned Cochran's Day Book. His yardstick of men has not shrunk; success has not made him hard to find. About the basic value of money and honors he was never fooled. Unswerving is his confidence in the plain people, the fish crier on Maxwell Street, the Dago shovelman, the work gangs, the teamster who loved the noises of his town. Long ago, when he called Chicago the City of Big Shoulders and celebrated its Gargantuan force as hog butcher for the world, toolmaker and stacker of wheat, he was thinking of the people who wrote their lives into the town.

A bog, created near the Des Plaines because the slope from the Valparaiso moraine was too gradual to move much water, became responsible for the evolution of the sluggish channel now called the Chicago. Swollen with freshets from the ice in spring, it receded to a shallow canal in summer, moving uncertainly among sand bars. But it determined the site of the port that transshipped the goods of the interior. The schooners of the Great Lakes abetted its trading career. The railroads expanded it manifold. Markets and industries drew hordes of human beings to its site. Like the cowpath that finally commanded the traffic of a continent, the Chicago inspired the metropolis. The shortest of all strategic rivers, it unlocked the continent.

The trading post that du Sable sold for a fortune and John Kinzie developed by hook and crook became a huge, sprawling, unkempt camp. Even today it shows the incongruities of a frontier town on a vast scale.

From the modern office buildings of the Loop to the cheerless wooden houses on the outskirts, Chicago exhibits the extremes of opulence and poverty, of luxurious living and arduous toil. Airplanes come in on a beam through the gray smudge of coal smoke. Endless barracks of brick house the workers of the city, with never a tree to mitigate the uniformity. Yet at intervals tree-lined parkways stretch for miles into the distance. On the outskirts of Washington Park Negro children play around Lorado Taft's statue to Time. At the University of Chicago, white-coated interns study hospital routine. The railroad that once lined the lake shore now runs inland, for the water has been pushed back by man-made parks and drives. Huge towers of glass and brick give dwellers of thousands of modern apartments access to the fresh winds that blow in from the lake.

The newspapers still bear witness to the turbulent character of civic life and to the intensity of political partisanship. The reports of election fights and the bloody battles of gangland are evidence of misplaced energy, no less than of explosive vitality. But the baton that beats time for the Chicago Symphony Orchestra is the true measure of cultural progress. Year by year new thousands throng the expanding galleries of the Art Institute and wear to tatters the books in the Public Library. And answering the need of the nation, great throngs of the city's sons drill to defend their birthright with arms. Once more bugles blow on the banks of the Chicago, and night and day the Coast Guard Reserve patrols the shores of Lake Michigan and sends its speedy boats up the river to keep the channel clear of obstruction for the increased traffic in foodstuffs and materials essential to war industries. This chronicle began with the explorers and traders who raised their cabins on the banks of the Chicago and thus founded a settlement. It closes with word of the vast torrent of human energy that now flows through the city's streets, the people who, in the words of Sandburg, "put the city up, tear the city down, put it up again."

APPENDIX

Sources

THE number of books and documents dealing with the settlement on the Chicago is incredibly large; many were consulted in the writing of this book, and it would serve no useful purpose to enumerate them here. Especially helpful were the collections of the Chicago Historical Society, the Chicago Public Library, the Newberry Library of Chicago and the New York Public Library.

Also valuable were the publications of the Illinois State Historical Society, the reports of the Illinois and Michigan Canal, the Mississippi Valley Historical Society, the Supreme Court of the United States and of other courts dealing with water litigation, and the files of Chicago newspapers, *Mid-America,* the *Prairie Farmer, Hunt's Merchants Magazine,* the *Dial,* and of commercial organizations.

For information placed at my disposal I wish to thank the Department of Public Works of the City of Chicago, Mr. Oscar E. Hewitt, commissioner; the Board of Forest Preserve Commissioners of Cook County; the Illinois Waterways Division of the Department of Public Works; the Illinois and Michigan Canal Commission; the Chicago Sanitary District; the Chicago Park District and the Chicago Regional Port Commission.

I am especially indebted to the writings of Dr. Milo Milton Quaife, editor of the Burton Historical Collection of the Public Library of Detroit; his tireless research over many years revealed important documents affecting the careers of Point du Sable, John Whistler, John Kinzie and other pioneers; no one can write about Chicago without acknowledging the importance of his original work. Also valuable was *A History of Chicago,* by Bessie Louise Pierce, of which the first two volumes were available; this work is especially useful for its analysis of social and cultural forces. For suggestions and courtesies I wish to thank Miss Adele Rathbun, librarian of the Chicago Historical Society, Wallace Bruce Amsbary, Oliver R. Barrett, Charles Collins, William H. Dunn, John Drury, Lloyd Lewis, Hermon Dunlap Smith. For permission to quote from Charles Edholm's poem I am grateful to Miss Minna Mathison, editor of *The Chicago Anthology.*

SUPPLEMENTARY READING

ADDAMS, JANE, *Forty Years at Hull House.* New York: The Macmillan Company, 1935.

ADE, GEORGE, *Stories of the Streets and of the Town.* Illustrated by John T. McCutcheon, *et al.* Chicago: The Caxton Club, 1941.

ALVORD, CLARENCE, *Centennial History of Illinois.* Springfield: Illinois Centennial Commission, 1922.

AMERICAN GUIDE SERIES, *Illinois.* Chicago: A. C. McClurg & Company, 1939.

ANDERSON, SHERWOOD, *Memoirs.* New York: Harcourt, Brace & Co., 1942.

ANDREAS, A. T., *History of Chicago. History of Cook County, Ill.* Chicago: A. T. Andreas, 1884-1886.

ASBURY, HERBERT, *Gem of the Prairie*. New York: Alfred A. Knopf, 1940.

BARNARD, HARRY, *Eagle Forgotten: The Life of John Peter Altgeld*. Indianapolis: The Bobbs Merrill Company, 1938.

CLARK, HERMA NAOMI, *The Elegant Eighties. When Chicago Was Young*. Chicago: A. C. McClurg & Company, 1941.

COLBERT, ELIAS, and CHAMBERLAIN, EVERETT, *Chicago and the Great Conflagration*. Chicago: J. S. Goodman & Company, 1872.

CURREY, JOSIAH SEYMOUR, *Chicago: Its History and Its Builders*. Springfield, Ill.: S. J. Clarke Publishing Co., 1912.

DAVID, HENRY, *The History of the Haymarket Affair*. New York: Farrar & Rinehart, 1936.

DENNIS, CHARLES H., *Victor Lawson: His Time and His Work*. Chicago: The University of Chicago Press, 1935. *Eugene Field's Creative Years*. New York: Doubleday, Doran & Company, 1924.

DRURY, JOHN, *Old Chicago Houses*. Chicago: The University of Chicago Press, 1941.

ELLIS, ELMER, *Mr. Dooley's America: A Life of Finley Peter Dunne*. New York: Alfred A. Knopf, 1941.

FERGUS HISTORICAL SERIES. Chicago: Fergus Publishing Co., 1876-1914.

FISKE, HORACE SPENCER, *Poems on Chicago and Illinois*. Boston: Stratford Publishing Company, 1927.

FLINT, HENRY M. *The Railroads of the United States*. Philadelphia: J. E. Potter & Company, 1868.

GARLAND, HAMLIN, *A Son of the Middle Border*. New York: The Macmillan Company, 1917.

GILBERT, PAUL, and BRYSON, CHARLES LEE. *Chicago and Its Makers*. Chicago: The Mendelssohn Company, 1929.

GOODSPEED, THOMAS W., *A History of the University of Chicago*. Chicago: The University of Chicago Press, 1916.

GRESHAM, MATILDA, *Life of Walter Q. Gresham*. Chicago: Rand, McNally & Company, 1919.

HALSTEAD, MURAT, *Caucuses of 1860*. Cincinnati: Follett, Foster & Company, 1860.

HARRISON, CARTER H., *Stormy Years*. Indianapolis: The Bobbs Merrill Company, 1935.

HECHT, BEN, *Thousand and One Afternoons in Chicago*. Chicago: Covici-McGee, 1922.

HUSBAND, JOSEPH, *The Story of the Pullman Car*. Chicago: A. C. McClurg & Company, 1917.

HUTCHINSON, W. T., *Cyrus Hall McCormick*. New York: D. Appleton-Century Company, 1930.

JOUTEL, HENRI, *Journal of La Salle's Last Voyage*. Albany, N. Y.: Jos. McDonough, 1906.

KENTON, EDNA, *The Jesuit Relations and Allied Documents*. New York: A. and C. Boni, 1922.

KINZIE, JULIETTE, *Wau-Bun*. Preface by Milo Milton Quaife. Chicago: The Lakeside Press, 1933.

KIRKLAND, JOSEPH, *The Story of Chicago*. Chicago: Dibble Publishing Company, 1892.

KNIGHT, ROBERT, and ZEUCH, LUCIUS H., *The Location of the Chicago Portage of the Seventeenth Century*. Chicago: The University of Chicago Press, 1920.

LEWIS, LLOYD, and SMITH, HENRY JUSTIN, *Chicago: The History of Its Reputation*. New York: Harcourt, Brace & Company, 1929.

LINN, JAMES WEBER, *Jane Addams*. New York: D. Appleton-Century Company, 1935. *James Keeley, Newspaperman*. Indianapolis: The Bobbs Merrill Company, 1937.

MARQUETTE, JACQUES, Recit des Voyages et des Découvertes du R. Père Jacques Marquette. Albany, N. Y.: Weed, Parsons & Company, 1855.

MASON, EDWARD GAY, *Chapters from Illinois History*. Chicago: Herbert O. Stone & Company, 1901.

MASTERS, EDGAR LEE, *Illinois Poems*. Prairie City, Ill.: James A. Decker, 1941.

McILVAINE, CAROLINE M., *Reminiscences of Chicago During the Civil War. Chicago in the Forties and Fifties. Chicago During the Great Fire*. Chicago: Chicago Historical Society, 1913-1915.

MONROE, HARRIET, *John Wellborn Root*. Boston: Houghton, Mifflin Company, 1896.

MORRISON, HUGH, *Louis Sullivan, Prophet of Modern Architecture.*
New York: W. W. Norton & Company, 1935.

NEVINS, ALLAN, *John D. Rockefeller* (Vol. 2: The Rise of a
University). New York: Chas. Scribner's Sons, 1940.

PIERCE, BESSIE LOUISE, *A History of Chicago.* Volumes 1 and 2.
New York: Alfred A. Knopf, 1940. *As Others See Us.* Chicago: The University of Chicago Press, 1935.

PRUSSING, ERNEST W., *Chicago's First Great Law Suit.* Madison,
Wis.: State Historical Society of Wisconsin, 1915.

PUTNAM, JAMES W., *The Illinois and Michigan Canal.* Chicago:
The University of Chicago Press, 1918.

QUAIFE, MILO MILTON, *Chicago and the Old Northwest.* Chicago:
The University of Chicago Press, 1913. *The Development of
Chicago, 1674-1914.* Chicago: The Caxton Club, 1916. *Pic-
tures of Chicago 100 Years Ago.* Chicago: The Lakeside Press,
1918. *Chicago's Highways Old and New.* Chicago: D. F.
Keller & Company, 1923. *Checagou, 1673-1835.* Chicago:
University of Chicago Press, 1933.

SANDBURG, CARL, *Chicago Poems.* New York: Henry Holt & Com-
pany, 1916. *Smoke and Steel.* New York: Harcourt, Brace &
Company, 1920. *Abraham Lincoln: The Prairie Years.* New
York: Harcourt, Brace & Company, 1924.

SCHOOLCRAFT, HENRY R., *Travels in the Central Portions of the
Mississippi Valley.* New York: Collus & Hannay, 1825.

SMITH, HENRY JUSTIN, *Chicago, a Portrait.* New York: D. Appleton-Century Company, 1931.

STARR, JOHN W., *Lincoln and the Railroads.* New York: Dodd,
Mead & Company, 1927.

SULLIVAN, LOUIS, *The Autobiography of an Idea.* New York: Press
of the American Institute of Architects, 1924.

TALLMADGE, THOMAS E., *The Story of Architecture in America.*
New York: W. W. Norton & Company, 1927. *Architecture
in Old Chicago.* Chicago: The University of Chicago Press,
1941.

THWAITES, REUBEN G., *The Jesuit Relations and Allied Documents.* Cleveland, O.: The Burrows Company, 1896-1901.

WAKEFIELD, SHERMAN D., *How Lincoln Became President.* New
York: Wilson-Erickson, Inc., 1936.

WERNER, M. R., *Julius Rosenwald*. New York: Harper & Brothers, 1939.

WILKIE, FRANC B., *Personal Reminiscences of 35 Years of Journalism*. Chicago: F. J. Schulte & Company, 1891.

WILSON, HOWARD E., *Mary McDowell, Neighbor*. Chicago: University of Chicago Press, 1928.

WRIGHT, FRANK LLOYD, *An Autobiography*. New York: Longmans, Green & Company, 1932.

YELLEN, SAMUEL, *American Labor Struggles*. New York: Harcourt, Brace & Company, 1936.

Index

THIS IS THE CHICAGO AND THIS SPOT IS A